PUFFIN BOOKS

Editor: Kaye [illegible]

THE YOU [illegible]

Romantic Ja [illegible] t kind of man was [illegible] rancis and Annabe [illegible] ark in the North R [illegible]

Seumas M [illegible] was a Jacobite – how could he dare admit it when they might betray him? – but Francis and Annabel, who were loyal themselves (in spite of their father and family), were easily convinced that the dashing stranger shared their secret hopes.

So began a long period of anxious and dangerous deception, concealing the fugitive in the Dower House and smuggling food to him by night, till they could help him get farther away. And always the wavering and anxious doubts would slip into their minds – was their friend really all he seemed, and were his tales of battles and adventures true?

This exciting story by the author of *Hero Tales from the British Isles* is also a remarkable character study of the Rimpoles and the mysterious protégé, with many sidelights on eighteenth-century life and attitudes thrown in.

For readers of ten and over.

The Young Pretenders

BARBARA LEONIE PICARD

PENGUIN BOOKS

Penguin Books Ltd, Harmondsworth, Middlesex, England
Penguin Books Australia Ltd, Ringwood, Victoria, Australia

—

First published by Edmund Ward (Publishers) Ltd 1966
Published in Puffin Books 1971

—

—

Made and printed in Great Britain
by Richard Clay (The Chaucer Press) Ltd,
Bungay, Suffolk
Set in Linotype Pilgrim

1

WHEN Francis Rimpole overheard, one October morning in 1745, that young Mr Marivel of Hazlett Hall, five miles away, was gone from his home to ride to Edinburgh to join Prince Charles Edward, he became, all in a matter of thirty seconds, an ardent Jacobite. Until that moment, had anyone asked him – not that any older person would have troubled to ask a fourteen-year-old boy such a thing – whether he was for King George the Second or for the Pretender, he would undoubtedly have answered that, like his father and all at Thorsby, he was a good Whig. But Mr Marivel's wearing of the White Cockade altered all this. William Marivel, whose lands lay alongside those of Sir John Rimpole, was young, elegant, and handsome, the most intrepid rider to hounds in the whole district, and the best marksman in any shooting party. Since inheriting his uncle's North Riding estate and coming to live at Hazlett Hall two years before, he had been Francis's idol; and though, in all that time, he had not spoken to Francis above three times, on each of those three occasions he had said exactly the right thing; and said it, moreover, without the slightest trace of that condescension which a boy of fourteen might expect from a young man ten years his senior. Thus it was quite understandable that, on learning his hero was a Jacobite, Francis should immediately fancy himself one, also.

From then on, Francis followed the progress of the Jacobite army with pride and enthusiasm – yet feeling sadly the lack of anyone at home with whom he might have shared that enthusiasm and discussed the progress. He tentatively tried to find an ally and sounded everyone in turn, from his father to the least important of the servants; but the squire, distressed by the latest news and foreseeing the possibility of another civil war, and concerned by the comparative proximity of Yorkshire to Scotland, dealt shortly with his son's cautious overtures and said roundly that he would tolerate no Jacobite nonsense from anyone in his house. Francis's mother, on the other hand, did not even take him seriously. She raised her charming eyebrows, laughed delightedly, and exclaimed to no one in particular, 'What quaint notions children sometimes have, to be sure!' a carefully chosen insult which – had anything been able to do so – might well have quenched Francis's loyalty. His sister's governess, Miss Amelia Proudfoot, who had taught him, also, in earlier years, was shocked speechless; and when she did recover her voice, could only exclaim, 'Thank heaven that Annabel is not in the room! I only beg of you, Francis, if you must hold such treasonable views, that you will never utter them in your sister's presence.' Even the servants gave no support. From Keighley the butler and Mrs Keighley the housekeeper, down to Ben the youngest stable lad, the reaction was either, 'Eh, now, Master Francis, whatever would Squire say if he could hear you?' or, 'But, think on, Master Francis, you surely cannot want a murdering papist for our King?' He mentioned his sympathies to the vicar, to whose home beside the church in the village he went every day for lessons. Dr Mortlake was not shocked; but he spent a full half-hour explaining tediously to Francis exactly why it was preferable that England should be ruled by the House of Hanover rather than by the House of Stuart, and then another ten minutes on tracing, in detail, the descent of King George the Second from King James the First and Sixth, and then making Francis repeat this family tree until he had it by heart.

In the end Francis gave up his vain efforts to find a fellow Jacobite. There was only one person in Thorsby Hall whom he had not approached, and that was his sister Annabel – and that not because of Miss Proudfoot's injunction, but because she was only eleven and a girl.

However, after the fall of Carlisle in November, while the rest of the household was sunk in apprehensive gloom, Francis could no longer contain himself. He had to have someone with whom he could share the glorious news that Prince Charles Edward had had his first success on English soil. A mere girl or not, a baby of eleven or not, he had to have an ally. And being only a girl she would be easily shown the error of Whiggery. If by some mischance she proved stubborn, then he could, without much difficulty, browbeat and bully her into agreeing with him, he was certain. He went in search of his sister.

Finding her alone in the schoolroom, he said challengingly and aggressively and without preamble, 'The Jacobite army has taken Carlisle.'

She stared at him. 'Carlisle?'

'Yes.'

For a moment she continued to stare, while he marshalled his arguments – which were remarkably few and vague – in favour of the Stuart cause, and prepared a crushing retort to her inevitable shocked reception of his news. Then she jumped from her chair, dropping her needlework, and clasped her hands together while a look of incredulous joy spread over her face. 'He has taken Carlisle! How wonderful!' She picked up her skirts and began to dance a triumph-dance around the schoolroom table, singing to the tune of the new National Anthem which had been printed in the *Gentleman's Magazine* for October and which Miss Proudfoot had been teaching her, 'God bless King James the Third! God bless King James the Third!'

It was now Francis's turn to stare, not only at her unladylike behaviour, but at having the wind so completely taken out of his sails.

At last, being inclined to plumpness, she stopped, out of breath and panting; and seeing his look of astonishment and mistaking it for disapproval, her smiles died and she stood herself in front of him, looked up at him defiantly – she was a good foot shorter, since he was tall for his age and still rather thin, due to several years of childish ill health which he had now outgrown, but which had delayed his going to Eton – and said, 'Of course, you will be like all the others and for King George. You will say that I am only a silly girl and know no better. But I do not care. You can say what you wish: I'm for the Prince and King James.'

Francis was still so dumbfounded that all he could manage was, 'So am I.'

Her plump face dimpled into smiles. 'Oh, Francis, how wonderful! Just the two of us against the world!' This was not strictly true, but it sounded very fine, even to the more level headed Francis; and he began to experience a slight, surprising, and unexpected respect for his sister.

'But, Bella, how long have you been a Jacobite?' he asked.

'Ever since the beginning, of course,' she replied, astonished that he should doubt her loyalty to be anything but long-standing. 'From the moment that Miss Proudfoot told me the Prince had landed. Oh, Francis, is he not brave? To come with only seven friends to win a kingdom for his father!' Her eyes sparkled and her cheeks glowed as she visualized the handsome young Prince, stepping out from a little cockleshell boat which tossed on a stormy sea, on to the wild and inhospitable shores of Scotland with his seven companions – such a magical, evocative, and legendary number, seven! – to regain his father's lost crown. For Bella was exceedingly romantic, and the arrival of Prince Charles Edward in Scotland seemed to her to surpass even the very best of fairy tales, and she had day-dreamed about him and prayed for his success ever since she had learnt of his arrival in August, clasping her secret to herself so successfully that not even Miss Proudfoot had guessed it.

At the extraordinary news that his despised little sister had been a Jacobite for two months longer than he had, Francis's new found respect for her rose enormously; but not for anything would he have admitted to her that his loyalty was younger than hers.

'Oh, how wonderful!' she was repeating. 'Now there are two of us to talk about it. It is the biggest secret anyone could possibly have.'

The circumstances of their common devotion to the Prince's cause resulted in a degree of friendship between Francis and Bella which had been unknown before. This state of affairs, when noticed by their parents, who knew nothing of its origin, was thoroughly approved, Sir John saying, 'Francis needs young company, even if it is only his sister's. He has been too much alone and too much with grown-ups for a boy of his age, and is in danger of becoming a self-complacent little coxcomb – a plaguey coxcomb, and not yet fifteen!' adding, 'However, all that will be remedied when he goes to Eton after Christmas, I do not doubt. Meanwhile, he might do worse than spend some of his time with Bella. It will do him no harm.' While Lady Rimpole said, 'I am glad to see Francis being attentive to Annabel. It is right that a boy should take a kindly and courteous interest in his sister.'

And indeed, Francis certainly seemed to be taking a kindly interest in Bella. They met at least once a day to discuss in whispers the latest news of the Prince and his army, following with enthusiasm his progress southwards. Together they rejoiced over the taking of Manchester; and, early in December, the word of his arrival in Derby threw them into transports of joy – although they did wish with all their hearts that he had chosen a more easterly route which would have taken him past Thorsby. And then together they deplored his retreat from Derby two days later, pursued by the Duke of Cumberland. Bella, who had in imagination already seen the Prince in residence at St James's, was particularly disappointed; but Francis, more hopeful, assured her that it was only a temporary setback, a cautious withdrawal to avoid a pitched battle with Cumberland and to await French help. But, all the same, in a household where everyone else was rejoicing and once again breathing freely in relief and beginning to think that Christmas that year would, after all, be a time of gaiety and mirth, they went about with heavy hearts and long faces, and not even the preparations for the Christmas festivities – the making ready of the gifts of warm clothing, hams, preserves, and tea, which were each year sent out from the Hall to all Sir John's tenants, the extra ale in the brewery and all the feverish activities in the kitchen, where quantities of pies and cakes were being baked, and the green boughs being cut down in the park and carried into the house for decoration – not even these things, usually so full of promise and thrilling anticipation, could cheer them.

But, in spite of their anxieties, and mainly because there was no bad news from Scotland, where both the Prince's and the English armies seemed to be biding their time, Francis and Bella managed to enjoy Christmas almost as much as usual; and they certainly did justice to their share of the Christmas beef, the boar's head, the turkey, the manger-shaped mince-pies containing chopped beef and mutton and tongue, the Yorkshire Christmas-pie – three feet across – whose rich crust covered a whole turkey, several brace of partridge, numerous pigeon and woodcock and a hare, as well as over eight pounds of butter, and the huge Twelfth Night cake with which the festivities closed. Indeed Miss Proudfoot had to admonish Bella several times for eating more than a gentlewoman should, and for not remembering how easily she became fat. Lady Rimpole added her well-meant warning to this. 'Yes, Annabel dear, you will be sorry in a few years' time, when you want to look your best for balls and routs, and you see yourself in your mirror, fat and plain.'

But Sir John laughingly stood up for his daughter. 'You eat as much as you like, Bella. What does it matter if you do get as fat as a Michaelmas goose? You are young yet, after all. When the time comes for you to look your best for your beaux, you'll be as slim and pretty as your mother was, I'd lay any odds.'

Needless to say, on this occasion, at any rate, Bella paid attention to her father, and not to her mother or Miss Proudfoot.

News of the victory at Falkirk on January the seventeenth cheered Francis and Bella. After that there was nothing reported that was decisive either way until the spring, when, after March had been brought to a close by Easter, with its traditional Yorkshire tansy puddings, on a day in April the bells of Thorsby church rang out in joy and thankfulness for the disaster at Culloden. Francis was utterly cast down by this complete destruction of Jacobite hopes and Bella wept bitterly for her defeated Prince. From then on they waited daily for news of Mr Marivel, about whom none of his former neighbours and friends seemed to have heard anything, and of the fugitive Prince, hunted up and down Scotland, upon whose head there was the immense reward of thirty thousand pounds; and with every day that passed without news of his capture, they became more hopeful that he might, in the end, evade his enemies and escape to the Continent.

2

THE handsome new front of Thorsby Hall, which had been built in the reign of Queen Anne as an enlargement and improvement of the old Tudor manor which had stood in that spot for two centuries, faced south. To its left lay a walled, formal garden; to its right, also behind a wall, were the stables and outbuildings which served it; and behind it lay the walled kitchen garden and orchard. Directly in front of the pillared portico of the house, after a broad terrace, its balustrade topped with ornamental urns, a short drive, flanked by beeches, led down to the front gates and the road. On the three other sides, the house and its gardens and outbuildings were surrounded by Thorsby Park, about seven hundred acres in extent and entirely enclosed by an eight-foot stone wall. To the north and north-east of the park, sloping ever upwards to the hills, stretched Thorsby Moor, vast and lonely; bleak and barren in winter time, but, in its own way, beautiful when the heather was in bloom.

Outside the huge wrought-iron front gates of the Hall, the road ran straight from east to west, following the wall of the park; and, about three quarters of a mile on, leaving the road to find its way southwards to the little market town of Thirsk, a lane broke away northwards, keeping alongside the west wall of the park for a mile or so, before bending westwards towards the village of Thorsby with its alehouse, its church and vicarage, and its scattering of cottages.

Every morning, for five mornings a week, while Bella had lessons with Miss Proudfoot, Francis went to the vicarage to study with the vicar, Dr Jonathan Mortlake. From the front gates of the Hall to the vicarage it was more than two miles by the road; but from the stable yard a path ran below the length of the orchard wall and then, where the orchard ended, turned to run roughly north-east across the park for about half a mile, coming out into the lane by the west gate of the park a little way below the spot where it bent westwards towards the village. Francis, sometimes on foot, but more often riding, always took this path when he went to the vicarage, leaving the house after breakfast, at about nine, and coming back in good time for two o'clock dinner.

For the past few weeks, since the weather had improved with the coming of the later, northern spring, Bella had always walked across the park to meet him, so that she might be the first to hear if there were any news of the Prince from the village; and Francis had grown to expect to find her waiting for him at the west gate. Sometimes he would dismount and return to the Hall on foot with her, and sometimes he would take her up behind him on his grey pony; but, either way, it gave them a short time alone together when they could be absolutely sure of being neither interrupted nor overheard, and they could talk treason to their hearts' content.

One day at the very end of May, Bella, wearing her slightly stouter outdoor shoes and her scarlet, hooded cloak, set out across the park as usual soon after midday. It was a fine afternoon and she was glad to have escaped from the stuffy schoolroom and Miss Proudfoot and her dull globes. For it had been a geography lesson that morning, and Bella much preferred history which was all about interesting and inspiring people like the Black Prince, King Richard the First, and Joan of Arc. It was pleasantly warm walking, and after only a minute or two, Bella took off her cloak, folded it neatly as Old Nurse would have wished, and carried it over her arm. A wood pigeon was cooing from one of the trees, and far overhead the larks sang.

Spring was by now on its way out, and summer was coming to Thorsby, touching the moor beyond the wall of the park with green, and darkening the freshness of the young foliage of the larches in the copse. Rigby, the head-gardener at the Hall, was watching closely and with pride the progress of his vegetables – peas, beans, and lettuces – and the swelling fruit on the fruit bushes. Mrs Keighley, the housekeeper, had long since finished her spring-cleaning of the Hall. All dust which had lain unnoticed in corners throughout the dull winter days had now been swept or polished from floors and furniture; all soot caused by the need to cheer long winter hours with fires and candlelight had been washed or brushed from walls and curtains; brass and silver shone once more without the tedious need for daily rubbing. The Hall was now as spick and span as half a score of under-servants could ever make it. In her enthusiasm, busy Mrs Keighley had even found time, a week or two before, to march her little regiment, armed with pails and scrubbing-brushes, beeswax, brooms, and dusters, across the park to the – at present empty – Dower House, near the west gate of the park, where Sir John's widowed stepmother had lived until her death, just over a year before, and set it to work there.

Not only spring, with its flowers and its bird-song, but also the warm weather which attended it, had cheered everyone, Bella thought as she walked on the bright grass, dotted with daisies and buttercups. Miss Proudfoot's thin, lengthy nose had long since lost the permanent pink tip which winter gave to it. Even Mahomet, Lady Rimpole's little Negro page, who had spent all the shivering days of winter coughing pitifully, looking like nothing so much as a little skeleton covered with stretched, dark skin, its skull thatched with woolly hair, was by now growing plumper, and his black face beneath its huge, plumed turban had lost its greyish tinge. Temporarily, he was coughing less, and his broad, white smile was once again in evidence. He was really Mahomet the Fifth, Lady Rimpole having had no fewer than five black pages of this name since her marriage. His predecessors had all been kindly treated and their duties had been light, but none had lasted longer than three years. As each one in turn had fallen a victim to the cruel northern winter and been laid in Thorsby churchyard, she had replaced him, on her next visit to London, with another pretty little slave, born under the hot sun of Africa. She had now, however, made up her mind that Mahomet the Fifth should be the last of them, declaring that it was too provoking to be always losing one's page when he had just become thoroughly used to one's ways, and having to start all over again with another; and she had given it as her firm intention, when the present Mahomet died, to make do without a page, and to buy, instead, those other fashionable pets, a marmoset and a green parrot.

Before long Bella had reached the west gate of the park, which was closed but not locked. It was one of the duties of Bradford, the gamekeeper, to unlock this gate the first thing every morning, for the convenience of anyone wishing to take the shortest way between Thorsby Hall and the village. He locked the gate against poachers at dusk every evening and took the key home with him to his cottage on the outskirts of the village; but at the moment it was in the lock on the inside of the gate, where he always left it during the day. Bella was strictly forbidden to go outside the park unaccompanied by a grown-up, so she stuck her head through the bars of the gate as far as she could and looked up the lane to see if Francis were in sight. He was not, so she pulled her head in again, disarranging, as she did so, the little lace-frilled cap she wore. She set her cap straight and pushed up a lock of dark brown hair that had fallen down onto her shoulder, thinking regretfully as she did so – and not for the first time – of Francis's much fairer hair, which she would have liked for herself. Dark hair was so uninteresting, and Francis's light brown hair, though it could not, however much one used one's imagination, be called golden, was a far prettier colour, she considered. Then, because she knew she was quite alone, she pulled up her stockings which had begun to slip down during her walk through the park. They were one of the nicest of her everyday pairs of stockings, being green, ornamented with red silk clocks: though, of course, they could not vie with any one of her dozen pairs of fashionable white stockings, which were only worn for best.

To the right of the gate, close to the wall, there was a young sycamore tree, already well-leaved, and, just beyond it, the trunk of an old tree which had been blown down in one of the winter's storms. The branches had been lopped from it and it had been laid at the foot of the wall to await removal. As she often did if she arrived before Francis, Bella sat down on this tree trunk, first carefully laying her folded cloak on the bark to spare her dress, so that Old Nurse would not scold at her. She sat staring across the park and thinking how pleasant it looked in the sunshine, beneath the blue sky. The grass, just here, where the cows had not eaten it, was growing tall, with buttercups and sorrel in it; the leaves on the trees were still delicate and pale; and here and there, towards the wall, under the trees, there yet remained patches of fading bluebells. Her mind drifted from the pleasant, peaceful scene before her to the desperate, hunted Prince – as it all too often did these days. She wondered where he was at that moment, and how close his enemies were to him; and she was very soon lost in a day-dream in which she, the daughter of a loyal Scottish laird, was daring untold dangers to help her Prince.

She was roused by the sound of feet running along the lane on the other side of the wall. It could not be Francis, she knew, because he had taken his pony with him that morning; and besides, she had never known Francis to run back from the vicarage, it was not the kind of thing he did, being rather staid for his years. She heard the footsteps stop outside the gate and leant forward slightly so that she could look through the foliage of the little sycamore. From where she sat she could not see much; but she caught a glimpse of a face peering through the bars. Then whoever it was tried the gate, found it unfastened, glanced back over his shoulder, opened the gate a little way and slipped quickly through, closing the gate very gently and silently behind him. Then, finding the key in the lock, he turned it and removed it. Keeping close to the wall, so that he was now hidden from Bella by the sycamore tree, he came rapidly towards her until he was close enough for her to hear his panting breath. Then he was past the little tree and face to face with her. He recoiled with a dismayed gasp; and Bella, a little nervous, but more indignant than afraid, stood up, and they stared at one another.

He saw a rather plump little girl with a round, pleasant face and pretty, dark eyes, a small cap perched on the top of her piled-up hair, wearing a low-cut white silk dress patterned all over with large blue and pink roses and green leaves, looking at him with unfriendly suspicion; and Bella saw a young man with a lean, insolently handsome face and very dark blue eyes. He was in need of a shave and wigless. His own dark hair, which badly required repowdering, was tied back with a sorry-looking black ribbon; the silver braiding at the cuffs and down the front of his crumpled blue coat, and its silver buttons as well, were tarnished; and Bella had time to notice the large, three-cornered tear in one coat sleeve and the elaborate blue-and-white flowering on his grey waistcoat, before there was the sound of more footsteps along the lane, and voices, coming closer.

Bella opened her mouth to say with dignity, 'This is a private park and you are trespassing. Please unlock the gate and go away.' But she never got even the first word out because the young man flung himself at her and clapped a hand over her mouth, putting his other arm around her and pulling her to him. She struggled frantically and tried to bite the hand over her mouth.

'If you make a sound, it's choking the life out of you I'll be,' he said in a low voice.

She struck at him with her fists, kicked his ankles and tried to scratch at his eyes. Beyond the wall, the voices and the footsteps came nearer. The man twisted her round and held her with her back to him, one arm pressing her close and his other hand over her mouth. He pulled her with him to the wall and stood flat against it, with her in front of him, both of them hidden from the gate by the leaves of the sycamore tree. The footsteps stopped at the gate. He bent his head and hissed in her ear, 'Keep still and you'll not be getting hurt.'

Terrified, Bella kept still. She could feel the man's chest heaving behind her as he tried to pant noiselessly, and two of his silver buttons were pressing painfully into the back of her neck.

A voice from the gate said, 'Do you reckon he went in here, like?'

She heard them rattle at the gate, trying to open it.

Another voice said, 'It's locked.'

The first voice suggested, 'Happen he climbed over.'

With scorn, the second voice exclaimed, 'Don't be daft! How could he? It's ten foot if it's an inch.'

There was silence then, while they peered through the bars; and in the silence Bella could hear the wild hammering of her captor's heart. He was, had she known it, as terrified as she was – and with far more cause.

After what seemed to her like a lifetime of terror, the second voice said impatiently, 'Come on. While you bide here, admiring someone's estate, he's getting away from us.'

The first voice said regretfully, 'Happen you're right, and he could not have got over.' Then, more briskly, 'Make sharp, now. Let's go.'

'Make sharp, is it? Whom are you telling to make sharp? It's you who's been wittering about, doing nowt, not me.'

The footsteps ran off down the lane and there was silence. The man continued to hold Bella tightly for a minute or more, then he said, 'If I take my hand away, you'll not start screaming your head off?'

Dumbly, Bella tried to shake her head. His grip on her relaxed, and slowly and warily he took his hand from her mouth. She did not scream. The moment for that was past. Nor did she even try to run away – but only because her legs felt too weak to carry her more than two paces.

'Good girl.'

He released her entirely. She took one tottering step away from him and then turned round to face any further possible danger. She found that he was smiling at her.

'It was a bad moment – was it not? – for the both of us, I'm thinking. And it's sorry I am if I scared you. But, sure, a kind young lady like yourself would not be wanting to see a man taken by his enemies, would she now?' He moved away from her and raised one hand to his cocked hat in a swift gesture of farewell. 'It's leaving you fast, and this very instant, I'll be.' He took the key from the pocket where he had put it, went to the gate, opened it cautiously and looked up and down the lane, slipped through the gate and was gone.

Bella's legs managed to carry her to the tree trunk, and she sat down heavily on it. She had never been so frightened in all her life. She was feeling sick from shock, and now began to tremble uncontrollably.

She had stopped trembling, but was still feeling shaken and weak when she heard Francis's pony trotting down the lane. It was a moment or two before she could bring herself to rise, however; and Francis, for whom she always opened the gate when he was mounted, shouted out impatiently, 'Bella! Bella! Are you not here yet?'

She stood up and found to her surprise that she did not immediately fall down. She walked towards the gate and reached it safely. She opened it for Francis and he rode through. While she closed the gate, he dismounted.

'I'm late. Old Mortlake was in a reminiscent mood this morning. Lord! How I hate Latin!' He looped Sultan's reins over his arm and started off along the path, leaving Bella to follow. After a few yards he was aware that she was not with him. He stopped and turned round. 'Oh, hurry up, Bella! I have several things I want to do before dinner and old Haughtyhoof will fuss if I am late.'

She caught up with him and he said accusingly, 'You are very quiet. What's the matter with you?' He glanced at her and remarked, unperturbed, 'Heavens, Bella! You look as green as a pea. What is it?' Then, at a sudden thought, he stopped dead, looking down at her anxiously. 'Bella! There's not been any news, has there, about Him?'

She shook her head vigorously. 'No! No!'

'What's the matter, then?'

She told him; and by the time she had finished, he was frowning. 'How abominable!' he exclaimed. 'Did he hurt you?'

'No. It gave me a fright, though.'

'I should think it did! I wish I had come along in time to catch him, the scoundrel. He must have been a poacher.'

'In the middle of the day?'

'Well.... Perhaps not. But I do not see what else he could have been. Unless he was trying to make away with something belonging to the two men who were chasing him.'

'Did you see any strangers in the village?' Bella asked.

'None at all. But, don't forget, I was in the vicarage almost all the time, so I could have missed a score of strangers. Anyway, I'll tell father of it, and he will order Bradford to keep a watch out. But come on now.'

They set off again in silence; and after a moment or two,

Bella said, 'If you tell father, he will forbid me to walk in the park alone, and I shall never be able to go and meet you again unless Miss Proudfoot comes too.'

'That's true. We certainly don't want Haughtyhoof with us.' He considered this, and then said, 'Oh well, it's a pity, but I must tell father. We cannot have you being attacked by poachers.'

'Francis, I do not think he was a poacher. He was a stranger.'

'To you, maybe. But then you've not seen everyone who lives near Thorsby, have you?'

'No . . .' After a few seconds she said with conviction, 'But I am sure that he came from a long way off. He . . . he was . . . different. He had a strange manner of speaking, not like a Yorkshireman.'

'Do you mean he spoke like a gentleman?'

'No, not that. But it was a way of speaking that I had never heard before.' She paused and then said slowly, 'It sounded rather pleasant when he said that he was sorry he had frightened me. A singing sort of a voice.' She thought hard for a moment and then declared firmly, 'He was not a poacher, Francis.'

'Whatever he was, I shall have to tell father. Perhaps he will be able to discover something about him. As he's a Justice of the Peace, they will bring the man to him if he steals anything and is caught, so we shall find out then.'

They went on. Halfway across the park Bella suddenly stood and said in an odd voice, 'Francis?'

'Oh, what is it now, Bella?' He stopped a few paces on and looked back at her impatiently.

'Francis, do not tell father. The man spoke in such a . . . a different fashion, and he said that I'd not want to see him "taken by his enemies". Would a poacher or anyone like that call the people he was robbing "his enemies"? Francis, suppose he was a Jacobite – a Highlander: that would account for the way he spoke – and we told father about him and he was caught and hanged or imprisoned because of us.'

Francis was shaken. This explanation had not occurred to him, but now it seemed almost possible. Yet because it had been Bella who had made the suggestion, he was bound to ridicule and oppose it. 'What would a Highlander be doing all the way down here? Don't be silly, Bella.'

'He might have found his way home cut off after the battle and run in the only direction he could. Or perhaps the soldiers had destroyed his home and driven away his wife and children and he had nowhere else to go. Or perhaps he's someone important and there's a price on his head and he thought it a clever notion to flee to England instead of back to the Highlands where they would be sure to look for him. There are any number of reasons why he might be in Yorkshire.'

Once Bella's romantic imagination had warmed to the task of providing reasons, she could have gone on for an hour without repeating herself; but Francis, who had been thinking the matter over while she had been eagerly making suggestions, said slowly, 'I suppose it is possible.' He thought a moment longer. 'The men who were after him, could they have been redcoats?'

'I never saw them, but they could have been soldiers. They were Yorkshiremen, but I did not recognize their voices. And now that I come to think about it, Francis, they were most certainly strangers. I remember hearing one of them say something about "somebody's estate" – meaning the park – and anyone who was not a stranger would have said "Squire's" not "somebodys".'

A minute or two after Francis had made up his mind. 'Right, let's say nothing to anyone. But be careful when you are in the park alone, Bella, in case he was a poacher, after all.'

The rest of the way back to the Hall, both their minds were running on fugitive Highlanders pursued by soldiers.

3

THE next day was Saturday and Francis did not go to the vicarage for lessons because Dr Mortlake always wrote his sermons on Saturdays, ready for Sunday. Since his sermons were very long and always liberally embellished with texts, they took him a full day to prepare.

On this particular Saturday, it had been planned that Francis and Bella would go out after breakfast with Miss Proudfoot, to spend the day on the moor, taking with them a basket containing their dinner, rugs to sit on, and all the rest of the paraphernalia which Miss Proudfoot considered necessary for such an expedition. Before dinner they were to walk on the moor, searching for botanical specimens upon which Miss Proudfoot would discourse at length. After their dinner, while Francis wandered around studying natural history, Miss Proudfoot and Bella were to sketch the scenery. Then, after a light snack of whatever remained from dinner, Miss Proudfoot would read to them a chapter from some improving work; that done, they would pack the empty basket with botanical specimens and anything else which Miss Proudfoot thought that they should take with them, and set off for home. They usually did this several times during the summer months, and in spite of the botanizing and the sketching and Miss Proudfoot's enthusiasm for the beauties of nature, they always enjoyed the outing; and they were therefore disappointed when, at breakfast, Miss Proudfoot complained of a headache and feared that she might not be able to take them out. Her headache grew rapidly worse; and by the time they should have been making ready to set off, she announced, between sniffs at her smelling-bottle, that she felt far too unwell to go, and it seemed as though the expedition would have to be abandoned. But when it was discovered that the dinner basket was already packed and waiting for them, and two rugs for them to sit on were neatly folded and lying beside it, and the weather promised to be particularly fine, it was decided that Francis and Bella might go off alone for the day into the park with their picnic, provided that Francis made sure that Bella did not venture out on to the moor.

They were delighted by this unexpected piece of luck, and politely concealing their pleasure at being deprived of her company, said, 'Yes, ma'am,' to all Miss Proudfoot's instructions and admonitions, wished her a speedy recovery from her headache and set off from the side door on the west of the house, which led by the shortest way into the park, Francis carrying the dinner basket and Bella the two rugs. They hurried out before Miss Proudfoot should remember that they had with them neither charcoal nor paper for sketching, nor an improving book, and send one of the servants running after them with the forgotten articles; and they reached the park safely without being called back. There they slackened their pace.

'Where shall we go? Let's get as far away from the house as possible,' Francis said.

'If we go to the very end of the park, we shall be almost on the moor,' said Bella.

Since this was exactly where Francis had intended going, whether Bella wanted it or not, he said, in the way of one granting a favour, 'Very well, then, if that's what you would like,' and they started off.

Heading up the park they made their way in a leisurely fashion towards its northern boundary. After about half a mile, the trees were fewer and the land became progressively less parklike, with coarser grass and an occasional clump of heather. A few hundred yards from the boundary, the ground began to slope upwards very gently towards the wall. Here there was more heather underfoot and a few bushes of broom, now just opening into gold, and an occasional outcrop of rock; as though the moor had crept slowly and insidiously beneath the eight-foot wall, like a sly and irresistible trespasser.

Fifty yards or so from the wall, near the narrow gate which opened on to the moor – and from which a path beyond the wall ran westwards to curve round to meet the lane to the village; and eastwards and then south-eastwards, through land farmed by Sir John's tenants, to meet the road – they put down the basket and the rugs on the shady side of a group of rocks, not sorry to be rid of them, for it was by now very warm. Ordinarily, on such an expedition in Miss Proudfoot's company, they would have been accompanied on their outward journey by one of the under-footmen, to carry these things; but today, in spite of arms that were beginning to ache, they were glad to be entirely on their own.

All the same, Francis gave a sigh of relief as he set the basket down. 'I'm not sorry we have arrived here. That basket has become heavier every yard. It must weigh a ton by now.'

'It contains Miss Proudfoot's dinner as well as ours,' said Bella with satisfaction. 'And it will not be so heavy to carry back.'

'You greedy little pig! I carried it, so I deserve to have Haughtyhoof's share.'

'I carried the rugs –'

'They are much lighter.'

'– so I deserve half her share.'

'Whether you deserve it or not, I know you will have managed to stuff it inside you before I have even finished my own dinner.'

'Never mind, Francis. So long as the basket is empty to carry home, it does not signify who has eaten the food,' said Bella placatingly, quite confident of being able to hold her own in any eating match with her brother.

They spread out one of the rugs and sat down on it to rest for a while. Francis leant back against a rock and shut his eyes, but Bella sat staring thoughtfully before her. After ten minutes she said, 'I wonder where He is now, and what he is doing.'

Francis opened his eyes. 'Embarking for France, I hope.'

After another pause, Bella said, 'Francis, do you think he will get safely away?'

Francis sat upright. 'Of course he will. He must still have many loyal supporters in Scotland,' he said firmly, trying to comfort himself as well as her.

Bella said slowly, 'It's a very big reward . . .'

'Would you betray him for ten times as much?'

'Of course I would not!'

'Then neither will his friends. He will escape safely, you'll see.'

If Bella noticed that her brother needed reassurance on this point as much as she did, she gave no sign of it, but sat thinking in silence, and was soon lost in her current favourite day-dream of escorting the Prince by night through country infested with hunting English soldiers, to the coast of Scotland and a waiting ship, manned by trusty sailors, and of the Prince smiling his thanks to her in the moonlight as she bent low in a sweeping curtsey on the wet sands.

She was brought back to the realities of daylight and Thorsby Park when Francis rose, stretched his arms and said, 'I'm going to see if I can find any birds' nests. Are you coming, Bella? Or can you not bear to leave the dinner basket?'

The unfairness of this brought Bella to her feet instantly. 'Of course I am coming. Do you think there will be any nests?'

'Not as many as on the moor, but we should find a lark's nest, and maybe a plover's.'

'Should we take something home with us for Miss Proudfoot, do you think?' asked Bella as she shook out her skirts. 'Just to show her that we have been thinking of her and studying natural history. Do you suppose she would care for a plover's egg?'

'I fancy she would probably prefer flowers.'

'I know! We could take her some broom. Have you your penknife with you, Francis? There's a fine bush of broom over there.'

'Yes, I have. But do not cut any broom now, silly. It would be dead by the time we went home. Leave it until later. Now, come on, if we are going to look for nests.'

They went first to the gate and peered through the bars at the forbidden moor stretching before them up to the hills. A few partridges were feeding a short way off. Francis found a stone and threw it over the gate to fall near them, and with rapid cackling cries of alarm and a great beating of wings, they rose and flew off. Francis and Bella counted nine of them.

They wandered together about the northern reaches of the park for the next hour or so, and found two plover's nests, scraped hollows among the heather with eggs in them, and one lark's nest. They watched a lizard sunning itself and disturbed a grass snake, which made Bella give a squeal of fright. Francis tried to kill it with a piece of rock, but he was not quick enough, and it escaped him. Bella collected a pheasant's tail-feather and two magpie's wing-feathers for Miss Proudfoot, and Francis stuck them in the gold braiding of his cocked hat for safe keeping.

By midday the sun had become very hot and Bella was beginning to feel both tired and hungry. 'Is it not time for dinner, Francis?' she asked hopefully.

'You little glutton, Bella!' Francis looked up at the sun. 'It is another two hours yet to dinner-time.' But since he, too, was feeling ready to eat, he added generously, 'Though if you want to, we can have our dinner now.'

They made their way back to the group of low rocks where they had been sitting. As they were approaching the spot from the south-east and they had left the basket and the rugs in the shade on the north side of the rocks, it was not until they were about fifty yards off that they could see the spread out rug and the dinner basket on it. But the basket was not as they had left it. It was now wide open and a man, his back towards them, was kneeling beside it, hastily helping himself to its contents, putting food into his mouth with one hand, and with the other heaping more food on to a handkerchief beside him.

'Well, I'll be hanged!' exclaimed Francis indignantly. He hurried forward, shouting out, 'What are you doing? Come away from that basket immediately!'

The man turned round and jumped to his feet all in one rapid movement.

Bella, who had hung behind, ran a few steps after Francis and clutched at his arm. 'It's the man I saw yesterday,' she said urgently.

He stood there waiting for them as they approached, a half-eaten leg of chicken in one hand. He looked even more dishevelled than on the previous afternoon. Then he recognized Bella, grinned at her, swept off his hat with his free hand and made her a low bow. 'So it's meeting again we are, ma'am. A very good day to you.'

'What do you mean by stealing our food? And how dared you attack my sister yesterday?'

'Sure and there's no one could regret it more than I.' He turned again to Bella. 'I beg your pardon, ma'am, and I hope you'll forgive me, but I could not have had you shouting out and telling those murdering brutes where I was, could I now?' He looked down at the basket. 'And as for the food, I've not eaten a bite since the day before yesterday and it's starving I am.'

'The day before yesterday! How terrible!' gasped Bella, truly distressed at the thought.

'That's God's truth, ma'am, that I'm after telling you.' He took a bite from the chicken leg.

'What are you doing here?' demanded Francis.

'Och, it's escaping from my enemies I am. Have they not been after me for days and for miles now?'

'Are you . . . are you a Jacobite?'

The man's eyes narrowed and the wariness which had never left them, in spite of the seeming openness of his manner, changed to a puzzled suspicion as he stared at Francis for a long moment, considering the implications of the question. Then his eyes flickered towards Bella for an instant and he saw that she was watching him expectantly, her lips parted a little, as she waited for his answer. Looking again at Francis, he said slowly, 'That's a strange question to be asking. Why should you be thinking I'm a Jacobite?'

He had not admitted it, they thought. But then, how could he know he could trust them? And he had not denied it, either. They stared back at him, unsure still.

It was Bella who spoke first. 'If it's so long since you have eaten, we shall be glad to share our dinner with you. Shall we not, Francis?' She added reassuringly to the stranger, 'We have an extra portion with us, so we can spare it.'

His suspicions seemed to vanish in an instant and a rapid smile lightened his expression. He made her another bow. 'Now that's very kind of you, ma'am. So long as it is pleasing to the young gentleman?' He looked inquiringly at Francis.

Francis nodded. 'I suppose so,' he said rather doubtfully.

'Help me with the other rug, Francis.'

But it was the stranger who helped her unfold it and spread it on the ground while Francis looked on uncertainly. They sat down, Francis more hesitantly than the other two; and Bella, as hostess, began to distribute food. The stranger ate as though he were indeed famished, which touched Bella's heart, and she secretly determined, with great self-sacrifice, that he should have half her portion as well as the whole of Miss Proudfoot's. For a while the three of them ate in silence, Bella slowly, so that it would not be apparent to the stranger that she was deliberately eating less than her share. Francis was thoughtful, every now and then looking askance at their odd guest, who seemed to be taking no notice of his scrutiny

Their meal was almost over before any one of them spoke again; and then it was Bella who said, 'If there is any food left over, perhaps you would care to take it with you for your ... for your journey?'

The stranger gave her his quick smile. 'Now, that's a truly kind thought, ma'am. It will be most welcome, since I'm likely to be ... journeying ... for a long while yet.'

Bella began to collect left-overs on a napkin; and Francis, suddenly and with great casualness, passed to her his last venison pasty. 'Here, you can have this. I've had plenty. I could not eat a mouthful more.'

Bella knotted the ends of the napkin together and laid it down beside the stranger. He thanked her.

'Have you had enough?' she asked anxiously.

'More than enough, thank you. It's good it is to feel full again.' He stood up and looked all about. 'I can tell you what I would like, though. I'd dearly love to be taking a nap after that fine dinner. It's hardly a wink I slept last night, for fear that those who are after me would be stealing up and I asleep and making it easy for them.'

'Where did you spend last night?' Francis broke in.

The stranger gestured vaguely in the direction of the moor. 'Out yonder somewhere. But I'll feel safe enough having a little rest and you two by me to wake me if anyone comes in sight. Would you be doing that for me?'

'Of course we will,' said Bella warmly.

The stranger promptly lay down in the shade under the

rocks and almost as promptly went to sleep. Bella watched him, thinking how fearful it must be to be hunted by one's enemies; and Francis watched him, still uncertain.

As soon as he was sure that the stranger was really asleep, Francis whispered, 'Bella! Bella!' to gain her attention.

She turned to him and he rose quietly and beckoned to her to get up and go with him. She did so, and they walked a little way off, out of earshot.

'What do you think he is?' demanded Francis, who had not yet made up his own mind and so was reduced to asking his sister's opinion.

Bella's reply was immediate. 'A Scottish Jacobite. I am sure of it. Have you noticed what I said to you yesterday about the way he speaks?'

'He does not sound like a Scotsman,' Francis objected. 'He speaks nothing like Mr Seton the apothecary.'

'That will be because he is a Highlander. Mr Seton comes from Edinburgh, and I expect they speak differently there. I know Mr Seton comes from Edinburgh because he was telling me about it the last time he came to prescribe for father's gout.'

They both kept glancing at the sleeper while they talked in whispers.

'I'm not sure of it,' said Francis. 'Supposing that he is only a poacher or a vagabond, after all?'

'Of course he is a Jacobite, Francis.'

'He never said so when we asked him.'

'Would you expect him to admit it? He could not know that we would not betray him instantly.'

'That's true enough.' But Francis still stared dubiously at the stranger, lying fast asleep – though he was beginning to waver in his doubt.

Bella, impatient with him, glanced away down the park in the direction of the Hall, well out of sight behind the trees in the distance. She gave a sudden gasp. 'Francis! Look!'

He looked where she indicated. About a hundred yards away and heading in their direction, were two figures, accompanied by a dog.

'It's Bradford and Jem,' he said.

'Whatever shall we do, Francis? There's nowhere for him to hide.' She made as if to dash away to wake the stranger, but Francis took hold of her arm.

'Don't be a fool, Bella. Try to keep your head. They cannot see him from where they are now. Go back to him quietly and tell him to hide himself as well as he can by the rocks, and I will go and speak to Bradford when he's a little nearer and head him off.'

Bella, her heart thudding, walked as calmly as she could to where the sleeper lay, oblivious of all danger. As soon as she was out of the sight of Bradford and Jem, behind the shelter of the rocks, she flung herself down beside him and shook his shoulder. 'Wake up! Wake up!' she said in a frantic whisper.

He came awake in an instant and sat up, almost flinging her aside in his nervous haste. 'What is it?'

'There are people approaching. The gamekeeper and his son. My brother is going to prevent them from coming close, but you will have to hide.'

He looked about him wildly and was about to rise, but she thrust him back.

'No, no! Keep down. You are taller than the rocks. They'll see you if you stand. You will have to crouch down, and then, as they come level with us, you must crawl around to the other side of the rocks. I'll tell you when to move.'

He dropped to hands and knees, facing away from the danger, ready for her signal. Her agitation was so sincere that he trusted her good faith unquestioningly. They waited in silence, and then they could hear the others speaking; first Francis calling out over-heartily, 'Good morning.'

'Good day to you, Master Francis.'

'Good day, sir.' That was young Jem.

Francis began a tale about having noticed a pair of stoats in the other direction; and then Bella, standing on tiptoe beside the stranger and peeping over the tops of the rocks, saw the dog, possibly scenting their meal, come loping in their direction. Jem called to it, but it came on towards the dinner basket and Jem ran after it. Discovery could hardly be avoided. Francis called to Jem – something about showing them both where he had seen the stoats – and Jem turned his head for long enough to shout, 'With you in a jiffy, Master Francis. I must catch Bouncer.'

For one moment Bella remained rigid with fear, and then the next moment she had bent and, concealed from Jem and the others by the rocks, had snatched up one of the rugs from the ground. She flung it over the stranger with a hissed, 'Keep still!' and sat down, just as Bouncer reached the spot. A few seconds later, when Jem, also, arrived there, Bella, her skirts spread neatly about her, was sitting on a rug which was apparently laid over a rock, her hands in her lap.

Jem grabbed at Bouncer's collar and ducked his head at Bella. 'Good day, Miss Annabel.' He cuffed Bouncer. 'Dratted old tyke!'

'Good morning, Jem.' Bella hoped her voice did not sound as shaky as it felt. 'What a beautiful day.'

'Aye, it is that, and all.' He grinned at her shyly and dragged Bouncer back to the others.

Meanwhile, Bradford was saying to Francis, 'If I might have a word, like, with you, Master Francis, without Miss Annabel hearing me.' He moved farther away, to Francis's great relief, and dropping his voice, said, 'I've heard in t'village that there's a dangerous criminal lurking in these parts with t'militia after him and all, and happen he might get into t'park. I'd not wish to be scaring Miss Annabel, now, so don't you say owt to her. But you'll be handy-dandy and keep your eyes open, like, won't you, sir, and tell Squire if you see any strangers about?'

'Of course I will,' said Francis. 'I'm glad you told me of it, Bradford, but I doubt if he would dare to come into the park.'

'No more do I, Master Francis. But it's best to be prepared, like. We're on our way to Teal's farm, Jem and I. We'll keep a sharp look out ourselves on t'moor for any strangers.' He touched his cap, and he and Jem and Bouncer went towards the gate, through it and on across the moor.

Francis, his legs feeling weak, returned slowly to Bella. 'All's clear! They have gone, thank heaven!'

'Oh, I am so glad!' She got up and lifted the rug off the stranger. 'I hope I was not too heavy,' she said apologetically. 'But it was all that I could think to do in so short a time.'

Francis was startled into being complimentary. 'Bella, what a capital notion!'

The stranger raised himself from the ground and sat back on his heels, looking at Bella with a broad smile. 'Faith! You're as light as a feather, Miss Bella.' He chuckled. 'And haven't you the quickest wits of anyone between here and London town!'

From sheer relief, Bella started to giggle; and in a minute they were all three laughing uproariously, Bella until the tears ran down her cheeks, Francis leaning against one of the rocks, shaking with mirth, and the stranger sitting on the grass with his head thrown back, as merry as though he had not a care in the world.

When they had finally stopped laughing and Bella was wiping away her tears with Francis's pocket handkerchief, the stranger stood up, looked carefully all about and said, 'Now I'd best be off, I'm thinking, while the coast is still clear.' He smiled at them. 'And my thanks to you both for what you've done for me.' He gestured towards the gate. 'Were I to be going through there, would it be coming to the highway at last I'd be?'

Francis nodded. 'Yes. Keep to the path beside the wall – it goes eastwards – and where the wall turns south you'll see a track going across the moor and then through fields, roughly south-east. It reaches the road about three miles along from our gates, just on the borders of Mr Marivel's land.'

'No village or cottages there?'

'No. Only the lodge to Hazlett Hall, about another mile farther on. The lodge is empty at present, I believe, and there are only the housekeeper and a very few of the servants up at Hazlett Hall.'

For a moment the stranger's eyes gleamed with sharp interest, then he gave a wry smile and a slight sigh which sounded regretful. But if he had been about to speak, he did not; and then Bella broke in meaningly, 'Mr Marivel is a Jacobite, and he went to Scotland to fight for the Prince.'

The stranger looked at her – as she thought, oddly – for a moment. Then he said, 'Did he now?' Before she could say more, he had turned to Francis, 'Will I be reaching any large town in that direction?'

'No.' Francis shook his head. 'Eventually you should reach Scarborough and the coast.'

'It's unfortunate that is. But it cannot be helped.'

'Why is it unfortunate?' queried Bella, surprised. 'Do you wish to go to a town?'

He smiled at her. 'Sure and I do. It's easier for a man to be hiding himself in a town than here where any stranger stands out like a cow in a flock of pigeons. Once I'm well away from here, it's making for a large town I'll be, as fast as my legs can carry me.' He straightened his rumpled cravat, shook out the soiled frills of his shirt cuffs, and brushed down the skirts of his coat and then said briskly, 'Now, if you'd be doing me one last kindness and giving a look through that gate to be sure that there's no one in sight, it's on my way I'll be.'

Francis ran to the gate and looked through while Bella picked up the napkin of food and handed it to the stranger. 'We shall be thinking of you a great deal. I hope you get safely home – and soon.'

He smiled at her with that crinkling at the corners of his eyes which she had already grown to like, as he took the bulging napkin and stowed it away in one of the capacious pockets of his blue coat. 'Faith! It's glad of your kind thoughts I'll be, and I needing them, too.'

From the gate Francis signalled to them, shaking his head to indicate that there was no one in sight and beckoning. They hurried over to him and he held the gate ajar. 'Straight on beside the wall and then south-eastwards along the track to the road.'

'Again, my very grateful thanks to the pair of you.' After a rapid glance in either direction, the stranger slipped through the gate and was off along the path to their right, walking quickly. About thirty yards away, he turned and, taking off his hat, waved it to them.

They watched him out of sight, their two heads through the bars of the gate. Then they withdrew their heads and looked at each other silently for a long moment.

Bella was the first to speak. 'Oh, Francis,' she breathed, 'we have done something for the Cause at last.'

Francis nodded. In a voice as low as hers, he said, 'I hope he gets safely away.'

'We shall never know if he does,' said Bella regretfully.

'No news will be good news. We should no doubt hear of it if they were to catch him anywhere near Thorsby.'

At this thought, Bella clasped her hands together. 'Oh, if only he is not caught!'

They walked back to their basket and the picnic things and sat down beside the rocks. There should have been so much to talk over; but, oddly enough, they were both quiet and strangely reluctant to discuss their adventure. Later, perhaps, when they had heard no word of the fugitive's capture and might imagine him safe – or comparatively safe – in York, or some large town, they might feel more like recalling it; but for the present they were silent.

After a while Bella finished packing the basket. 'We shall have to pretend that we lost one of the napkins, if anyone notices and asks us.'

Francis, staring thoughtfully at a clump of heather a yard or two away, did not reply; but a few moments later he said indignantly and with scorn, 'A dangerous criminal! Bradford said that he had heard there was a dangerous criminal lurking in the district.'

As soon as Bella's own indignation at this description of the stranger had subsided, she tried to be fair. 'Well, I suppose that to father and to everyone else, a Jacobite is a traitor, and a traitor is a criminal, and as he has been bearing arms for King James, then he might perhaps be called dangerous. But it is very foolish!' she added with spirit.

'It is absurd!' said Francis, remembering Mr Marivel on his big bay, taking the becks and the ditches unhesitatingly.

4

ABOUT half an hour later they set off for home, going the longest way round under the east wall of the park and not attempting to hurry. They strolled along, and this time, as the basket was empty, Francis carried one of the rugs as well. They were about two-thirds of the way back, and walking once more on soft, green grass kept short by Sir John's fine herd of dairy cattle, Bella with an armful of broom and two very early sprigs of bell-heather for Miss Proudfoot, and Francis with another pheasant's feather in his hat and a sloughed adder skin in his pocket, when they heard a shot in the distance. It was shortly followed by another, a little closer, and by the sound of voices shouting a good way off. They stopped to listen.

'It's out on the moor,' said Francis. 'Or perhaps in Bly's field.'

Bella crushed the branches of broom to her. Above their gay yellow blossoms her face grew white. 'Francis, do you think they have caught him?'

Francis said nothing. It seemed only too likely that they had.

They stared miserably at the high wall which separated them from the farming lands and the moor beyond, and cut off their sight of whatever was going on outside the park, both of them seeing in their minds their Jacobite taken by his enemies. Then suddenly, about twenty yards farther on, two hands and a head and then a whole body appeared on the top of the wall. The cocked hat fell off as they watched, and the dark hair, which had escaped from its confining ribbon, straggled forward, concealing the face; but the blue coat was easy to recognize.

'Francis, it is he!'

They both began at the same moment to run towards him, still carrying basket, broom, and rugs; their minds too much filled by the desire to help for them to think of dropping their burdens that they might make better speed.

He saw them coming, gave one quick glance of recognition

in their direction, and then, poised on top of the eight-foot wall, looked back over his shoulder towards his pursuers, whose voices were by now considerably closer. He brought both feet over, so that, for a moment, he was sitting on top of the wall, preparing to jump down. There was another shot, he jerked forward, clapped his right hand to his left upper arm, swayed, lost his balance and fell heavily forward, landing in the shallow ditch which ran along the base of the wall.

By the time they reached him blood was already staining his sleeve, and he was trying to get to his feet, supporting himself by the jutting stones of the wall, his face twisted with pain. He sank back. 'It's hopeless it is,' he gasped. 'I cannot even stand. My leg is broken, I think. They have me this time, the devil take them.'

For perhaps ten seconds they stared at him helplessly, and then Francis said, 'Cover him with the rugs, as you did before. I'll lead them away from here.' He dropped basket and rug and ran back the way they had come, keeping close under the wall.

Bella looked at the stranger with concern. 'Do you think you could lie down in the ditch?'

Painfully managing his right leg, he lay down full length in the ditch, face downwards, so that his back was level with the top of its sides. Only pausing half to unfold the rugs, Bella flung them both over him and set basket and bunch of broom on top of them; then, as an afterthought, pulled off her wide-brimmed hat and dropped that also on to the rugs, about where his feet should be. She gave a frantic glance at her handiwork, saw his fallen hat and thrust it under a rug.

'Nothing shows. But lie still. Please lie still.'

The voices were coming very much closer. Bella looked anxiously after Francis. About twenty-five yards away he was clambering up the wall, setting his feet into the little ledges and clefts made by the rough, flat slabs of stone, and hauling himself upwards. As soon as he was able to look over, he saw seven or eight militiamen, carrying their muskets, running clumsily across Farmer Bly's cornfield, crushing down the green spikes as they made for that point of the wall over which the stranger had disappeared from their sight. He shouted to them and they turned their heads. He heaved himself on to the top of the wall and, perched there, waved his arms and shouted again, 'This way. Not down there. This way. He went this way.' He pointed in a roughly north-westerly direction. All but one of the militiamen wavered, slowing down in their chase. 'This way! Over here!' repeated Francis wildly.

Two of them started in his direction, then hesitated. The others stopped and stood still in the corn – all but the one, who continued doggedly in the direction of Bella and the stranger.

'Oh, hurry! You'll lose him,' shouted Francis, precariously gesticulating from the top of the wall.

The corporal who was in the rear of the others, a heavy, lumbering man, yelled at them, 'Make sharp, men, what are you waiting for?' and set off towards Francis. All but that same one of the men followed him, trampling over the young corn like a herd of bullocks. The corporal gave a glance behind him and saw that just one of his men had not obeyed him, but had gone steadily onwards to reach the foot of the wall at the exact spot where the stranger had climbed over, and was even then beginning to haul himself up. The corporal stopped and bellowed at him. 'What do you reckon to be doing, Brown, you naffhead? Come here, at once.'

'But he went this way, corporal,' protested the panting militiaman.

'Come on, you daft gowk, do as you're bid. If we lose him now, think on, it will be you as made a mummacks of it.' The corporal, crimson in the face from the chase and from rage, shook his fist at the young militiaman.

Bella, standing rigid on the one side of the wall, heard the man curse the corporal and, breathing heavily, drop down into the ditch on the other side and run off clumsily. She gave a sigh of relief and then turned to watch the militiamen appear one by one on the wall beside Francis and lower themselves into the park to stand looking in vain in the direction in which Francis continued to wave them on. They seemed put off at seeing no sign at all of their quarry; but since there were a number of scattered trees and two score or more of cows grazing in the direction Francis was indicating, and since the fugitive had had a good start, it seemed just feasible that he should by now be out of sight, hidden, possibly, behind one of the fine oaks planted by Sir John's ancestors.

Several of the men glanced towards Bella, twenty yards or so away, standing guard beside the rugs and the basket, stiff and tense and ready to protect them and what they covered with all her puny strength; and it suddenly occurred to her that they might be wondering at it that she neither showed as much enthusiasm for the pursuit as did her brother, nor came to join him. With all the self-consciousness of guilt, she believed they must regard her behaviour as in the highest degree suspicious, and she felt obliged to do something to render it less so, but without leaving her post. She began to jump up and down, as though excitedly, on the same spot, alternately clasping her hands beneath her chin and pointing towards the cows and calling out, 'He went that way! Oh, please make haste and catch him!'

Her very real agitation made this a surprisingly convincing portrait of an excited and nervous little girl; and several of the men, including the corporal, called reassuringly to her, 'We'll catch him, never you fash yourself, miss,' and, 'He'll not be shut on us this time, the villain!' And it was her performance as much as Francis's efforts which sent them off across the park, running more easily now over the smooth grass.

Francis saw the last of the sweating, grumbling men over the wall before jumping down himself. He hesitated a moment, glancing at Bella; and then, thinking it best to make sure that they did not come back, he waved his hand to her and tried to indicate that though he would go with them, she should remain where she was; and then he set off after the militiamen, eventually catching the corporal up and running beside him, encouraging him to greater speed and assuring him that if they were not very quick, they would lose the fugitive, as he would undoubtedly have made his way towards the west gate and so out into the lane. The corporal was too breathless to answer in more than grunts; but since the park was unknown land to him and his men, he was glad enough of the young gentleman's enthusiasm and assistance.

Bella watched them all to a safe distance and then sat down thankfully on the grass by the ditch. Her legs were trembling and her heart was hammering. Without looking at the rugs and the basket, so as not to draw attention to them, in case anyone could still see her, she asked in a low voice, 'Is all well with you?'

A muffled answer came from the ditch. 'It's wondering about that myself, I am.'

'They have gone,' she said.

One end of the rugs heaved a little; and Bella, catching the movement from the corner of her eye, said quickly, 'No, no! Do not stir yet. Francis has gone with them to mislead them. You had best stay as you are until he comes back to tell us all is safe.'

There was an attempt at a chuckle from beside her. 'Faith! I suppose one might as well die in a ditch as at the end of a rope!'

'How is your arm? And your leg?'

'The one is bleeding finely, I'm thinking. And the other I'd rather not be thinking of at all.'

Bella was distressed. She half turned towards him. 'I wish I could do something to help.'

'Och, it's helping a deal you are already, ma'am, and I'm grateful to you.'

Bella sat in silence for five minutes or so, and then she said, 'How are you now?'

His reply was fainter and more muffled than before. 'No different at all, thank you.

She was perturbed by the weakness of his voice; and after another five minutes she again asked anxiously, 'How are you now? It will not be long before my brother is back, I hope.'

There was no answer. She repeated her question more loudly, but again there was no answer. She turned completely and looked full at the rugs. There was no movement about them at all. They were not even rising and falling gently, as they had been at the very first, with his panting – though that was only to be expected, since he had by now had plenty of time to recover his breath. She spoke once again, more loudly yet; but still there was no answer. She got to her feet, looked about, saw no one and knelt down by the head end of the rugs. 'Can you hear me?' she asked agitatedly.

He gave no reply and made no movement. Suddenly very

afraid, and hesitatingly for fear of what she might find, she pulled back the rugs as far as his shoulders. His head was turned towards her. He lay very still; almost not breathing, it seemed. His face was deathly white and very peaceful; and there was blood on the grass. She shook his shoulder gently and spoke again; but he never stirred. She touched his pale cheek reluctantly. It was cold and damp from the ditch. She looked about her frantically, fighting down a desire to stand up and scream for Francis. Then, knowing that there was nothing she could do, she covered his head again with the rugs and sat down beside him, her hands clasped tightly together, willing Francis to return and say that the militiamen had gone.

It was another twenty minutes before Francis returned. Alternately running and walking for a few yards at a time, he was all but exhausted and longing to sit down and rest; yet the thought of Bella and the stranger waiting fearfully for his return had kept him on his feet and moving. But the last three hundred yards were almost too much for him – after all, it had not been so very long before that he had been a delicate boy, cossetted and fussed over and never allowed to overtax himself.

Bella, sitting facing the wall, watching the inert shape under the rugs, did not hear him until he was almost upon her; and then it was his sobbing breaths that she heard, rather than the sound of his feet on the grass. She started and turned her head, her look of shocked apprehension changing to relief when she saw that it was only her brother. 'Oh, Francis!'

He flung himself down full length beside her, gasping; only raising his head from the grass for a moment to say, 'They've gone . . . out of the . . . west gate . . . to the village. Very lucky . . . Daft Isaac . . . there. Said he'd seen him. They believed . . . it. His head dropped back on to the cool grass again.

Daft Isaac was the half-witted lad from the village, who always tried to please people by giving them the information they wanted, whether he knew anything about the matter in question or not; and who often appeared to strangers to be a good deal less foolish than he really was.

Bella was far too concerned over the fugitive to notice how spent Francis was. 'Oh, Francis! I'm so glad you are back. Francis! I believe he's – I believe he's dead.'

He raised his head. 'Dead?'

Bella nodded. 'He does not move and I think he is not even breathing.'

'Do you mean ... to say that shot ... got him after all?' said Francis incredulously. 'I thought it was ... only his arm.'

The disastrous news lashed him back into action. He pulled himself to his hands and knees, crawled to the ditch and dragged the rugs from the stranger's head. Bella joined him and together they stared down at the still, silent, white face.

'Help me turn him over, Bella, and we'll see if his heart is still beating.'

They flung off the rugs and the basket and the flowers and, heaving and struggling, managed to turn him on his back in the ditch. Their handling was unintentionally clumsy and rough. The dark eyelashes quivered slightly, the ashen lips parted and the stranger groaned.

'He's alive!' exclaimed Bella.

'If there were some water in the ditch, we could throw it over him.' Francis looked impractically about him, almost as though hoping a miraculous spring would gush suddenly forth from the earth.

'We have some feathers. We could burn them under his nose, as Mrs Keighley did when Miss Proudfoot swooned after slipping on a piece of ice on the terrace and hitting her head. Do you remember?'

'Don't be such a goose, Bella. We have no fire or tinder box. How could we burn feathers?'

The blue eyes opened and looked up at them. 'What happened? And where in all the world am I?'

'With friends,' said Bella promptly and reassuringly, answering that which seemed to her the more important of his questions.

He made to pull himself into a sitting position, and gave a gasp of pain as he moved his arm. 'I remember now. The militiamen. And I fell off the wall. Where are they?'

'Down in the village. I sent them in the wrong direction,' said Francis.

The stranger managed a grin. 'It's the clever one you are.' He sat up more cautiously, holding his left arm stiffly. Then he said, 'If you could just be helping me up, it's on my way I'd be before they come back.'

They helped him to his feet willingly; but his attempt to walk was a failure. Sitting on the grass below the wall, he said, 'My ankle's broken or sprained or something of the kind, I'm thinking.'

Between the three of them, they got his boot off, cutting it away with the knife which he provided from his pocket. His right ankle, though badly swollen, seemed unbroken. Bella tied one of the two remaining napkins about it. Then they got his coat off and examined the bullet wound in his arm. Fortunately, it was merely a deep graze on the upper arm, and the bullet had not lodged in the flesh. This was a considerable relief to them all. The bleeding had almost stopped, and Bella tied the last of the napkins around it. After these ministrations, the stranger, still as white as a sheet, half in and half out of the ditch, leant his head back against the wall and closed his eyes. 'It's not far from here I'll be getting, and they after me,' he said.

Bella, kneeling beside him, said ardently, 'We will help you.'

He opened his eyes. 'How will you be doing that?'

'We'll hide you, and then, when your ankle is better, we'll help you to get safely away from here.' Her eyes shining, she added, 'You are a Jacobite, are you not?'

'Now, why should you be thinking that?'

'We were told they were after a dangerous criminal,' said Francis. 'But, of course, we guessed you were a Jacobite. We'd never have dreamt of helping a criminal.'

'Our father is a Whig, and so is everyone else at home. But my brother and I are for King James.'

He looked from one to the other of them: Bella kneeling, her face eager and excited, and Francis standing by her, looking down at him expectantly; but he said nothing, and he saw the eager light in Bella's eyes begin to fade to puzzlement, and Francis's fine brows draw together in a wondering frown.

'You are indeed a Jacobite? We are not mistaken?' Bella gazed at him earnestly.

Francis said stiffly, 'You need not be afraid to admit it. You can trust us. I give you my word as a gentleman that not for any consideration whatsoever would I betray you.' It was a pompous little speech and delivered pompously, though it did not seem so to Francis. To him, it seemed merely fitting to the occasion.

There was a few seconds' silence.

'We'd be proud to help someone who had fought for the Cause,' said Bella.

The stranger glanced again from one to the other of them, then he smiled wryly. 'Faith! And what alternative have I but to admit that I'm a Jacobite, and I with nothing but the pair of you between me and the gallows?'

Bella glowed with approval, and Francis looked pleased.

'Bella is right,' he said. 'We shall be honoured to help you.' He suddenly remembered that the stranger did not even know their name. 'I am Francis Rimpole, son of Sir John Rimpole of Thorsby,' he said formally. 'And this is my sister, Annabel.'

In spite of the pain of his arm and his ankle, the stranger smiled and made each of them the best bow that he could from his seat by the ditch. 'Your servant, ma'am, sir.'

There was a moment's silence while Francis waited for him to give his name; but he made no move to do so.

Bella had less reticence than Francis. She said impetuously, 'You are a Scotsman from the Highlands, are you not? My brother and I guessed it from the way you speak.'

He looked at her. 'Sure and I am. Seumas ... Macdonald, at your service.' He managed another makeshift bow.

'Seumas Macdonald,' murmured Bella, the name conjuring up visions of tall, barefoot Highlanders, wrapped in tartan plaids, carrying huge claymores and striding across miles of heather towards Edinburgh to join their Prince.

Francis's voice broke into her thoughts, saying decisively, 'Bella, we should not delay. If we are not home soon, they will be wondering and asking questions.'

'But we cannot leave Mr Macdonald here like this!' she exclaimed, appalled.

'Of course not, silly. I only meant that we should have to think quickly of somewhere for him to hide.' He sat down. 'Now, come on, Bella, think hard.'

For the next twenty minutes they made suggestions, practical and impractical, racking their brains; and with the pressing necessity for speed impelling them, became several times quite irritable with each other. Meanwhile, Seumas leant against the hard wall, one leg stiffly before him, a hand clasping his hurt arm, his eyes closed and his brow furrowed, trying not to think of the pain in arm and ankle, and only half conscious of the words that were tossed back and forth by the two in whose hands his life rested.

At last Francis said, 'I have it! The Dower House!'

'But it is haunted,' objected Bella.

'Oh, heavens, Bella!' exclaimed Francis with exasperation. 'I do not suppose Mr Macdonald will care a jot for that. It is at least empty and dry and not too uncomfortable and no one goes there more than about once in six months, to clean it.' He turned to Seumas. 'You'll not mind a ghost, will you, Mr Macdonald?'

Seumas opened his eyes. 'A ghost?'

'Lady Alice, from the time of King Henry the Eighth,' explained Bella. 'She walks about the upper floor and the gallery, and cries.'

Seumas grinned. 'Better all the banshees in Yorkshire than a single militiaman, the way I am now.'

'What is a banshee?' asked Bella.

'Sure and isn't she the lady who is after crying when anything bad is going to happen?'

'The Dower House it is then,' said Francis, relieved that one, at least, of their problems was solved.

'But the Dower House will be locked,' Bella reminded him.

'Mrs Keighley has a key. And if we cannot take hers, there is another in the office. Mr Thompson has keys to everywhere.'

'Mr Thompson is father's agent, who looks after his affairs – the tenants and suchlike – for him,' Bella explained politely to Seumas.

Seumas opened his eyes. 'Is he now?' he said with a tired smile and closed his eyes again.

'Will you go and find a key, Francis, while I stay here with Mr Macdonald, or do you think I should go and fetch it?'

'Don't be such a fool, Bella! How do you suppose we could

take Mr Macdonald across the park to the Dower House in broad daylight? We shall have to hide him somewhere for now, and then take him to the Dower House tonight, after dark.'

'But where can he hide until then? It will not be dark for hours yet.' Bella stared about, and then suddenly exclaimed triumphantly, 'I know! In the copse.'

The copse, about three hundred yards farther on, and about that same distance from the walls of the orchard and kitchen garden, was a small artificial wood planted by Sir John's grandfather with trees and shrubs newly introduced into England: larches, spruce from Norway, and a tangle of cherry laurels which would provide a good temporary cover.

'We had better go there at once, if Mr Macdonald can manage it,' said Francis.

'I'm game for anything which will keep me away from Tyburn.'

They helped him to his feet – or rather, to his one good foot – then, Seumas leaning heavily on Francis with his good right arm around Francis's shoulders, and hopping on his left foot, while Bella carried rugs, basket, and the broom flowers, and kept a careful and continuous lookout all about them as they went, they made their slow and painful way towards the copse, staying close under the park wall. It was a nightmare journey for all three of them; and when at last they stopped in the shadow of the larches and spruces, they were all three thankful and exhausted enough to have wept with relief. They went a little farther among the trees to where the laurels – which, near the edge of the copse, had suffered from the cold winds off the moor – grew more thickly. Bella found one whose spreading, large-leaved boughs drooped slightly towards the ground. With difficulty she held the branches up while – with equal difficulty – Francis helped Seumas under the cover they offered, the dead, dry leaves of previous years crackling and snapping under their feet as they moved slowly in.

'Sure and I've never in all my life seen bushes the like of these.' Seumas was trying resolutely to conceal the fact that he was almost at the end of his endurance.

'They are cherry laurels,' said Bella helpfully. 'They have

berries which the pheasants eat. My father says that they give the pheasants a better flavour.'

'Do they now?'

'And Miss Proudfoot – she is my governess – says that the Roman god Apollo wore a laurel wreath. So, also, did one of the Roman emperors – I am afraid I have forgotten his name – as a protection against thunderbolts.'

'Gods and emperors, is it? I'm in a grand hiding place and all.' Seumas managed to chuckle, but he looked ready to faint, and he was clenching his fists to keep his hands from trembling, as he settled himself awkwardly against the branching laurel trunk.

Noticing his pallor, Bella asked anxiously. 'Will you do all right here, do you think?'

'Och, it's fine I'll be when I've had a bit of a rest.'

He appeared to her so gallant and forlorn, sitting there uncomfortably beneath the laurel, making the best of his perilous situation, that, on an impulse, Bella took one of the rugs, and slipping under the branches, put it around him; though she had no idea how she would explain its absence if questioned.

Francis made a protest, on the grounds that the fewer unnecessary odd things they did – and to lose a large rug in the park would certainly be reckoned as odd if noticed – the less likely they were to be suspected of having done all the other odd things they would be obliged to do if they were going to help Mr Macdonald.

'But he will be so cold there, once it is dark,' Bella insisted.

This was undeniable, so Francis gave way, only saying, 'Well, you will have to think of a likely tale yourself, to explain where the rug is, if we are asked, because I know I could not.'

After walking all around the laurel and deciding that unless someone were actually in search of him, no one would guess that anyone was hidden under it, they gathered up their belongings and then peered through the shiny leaves at Seumas.

'I shall return at about midnight, if all goes well,' said Francis.

'You'll no doubt be finding me fast asleep in my fine bed.'

Francis took this piece of courtesy literally and frowned

slightly. 'Of course, I should be glad if you were able to get some sleep while you are waiting,' he said dubiously. 'But I rather hope you will not be asleep when I return, because it will not be easy to find you in the dark.' He paused a moment. 'Oh, well, I shall have to hope for the best. Anyway, I shall hoot like an owl when I come, and if you hear me, you can answer.'

'I shall be answering every owl screech between now and dawn.'

Making haste to prevent such an unnecessary expense of effort, Francis said, 'I'm hardly likely to come before midnight. I shall have to wait until everyone else is in bed.'

They left him then, reluctantly; all three of them well aware that if the militiamen came back to search the park, the copse would be an obvious place to look.

5

As they walked to the Hall, they made their plans, sharing out the tasks that had to be done between then and bedtime. Francis would get the key of the Dower House from the office, and something for Seumas to drink; while Bella was to find some old linen for bandages and a basket in which to carry things. They would both save all the food they could from their supper and each contrive to remove one blanket apiece from his or her bed. All these various articles they would hide in their bedrooms; and then, that night, as soon as he was sure that everyone was in bed and probably sleeping, Francis would get up and dress, come to Bella's room for the things which she had collected, and go out by the side door of the Hall and so through the park to the copse. He reckoned, he said, that it would take him at least two hours to escort Mr Macdonald to the Dower House, settle him in there, and walk back to the Hall. Then, having let himself in through the side door and bolted it again, he would come up to Bella's room, both to report success and to give her the key of the Dower House. Since he was almost certain to sleep late after his night out, it would be her responsibility to get up early and return it to the office before Mr Thompson arrived after breakfast to deal with the estate accounts and other matters. As Sir John had at the moment no guests at the Hall, he was unlikely to stay up very late, so Francis had hopes of being able to set out soon after midnight.

They went through this plan of action several times and decided that they had forgotten nothing essential; and that, apart from accidents and unforeseen circumstances, all should go as arranged without too much difficulty or any undue risk of detection.

At home they found Miss Proudfoot feeling very much better and waiting for their return, sitting in the schoolroom, near the window, with her feet on a footstool and a book in her hands. They declared themselves delighted by her recovery and she expressed her pleasure on hearing that they had enjoyed their day; and these mutual protestations were quite sincere, as neither Francis nor Bella disliked Miss Proudfoot, for all her strict notions regarding the behaviour that was proper to the young, and they wished her well; while, on her part, she found little to dislike in them.

Straight-backed and flat as a board, her greying hair dragged up under a plain round-eared cap, from either side of her long nose Miss Proudfoot's large, dark eyes looked at the world with a melancholy which her brisk, efficient manner could never quite conceal; while the vertical lines between her fine, arched eyebrows gave her an unmerited appearance of perpetual crossness – unmerited since they were lines of anxiety rather than of ill temper. For though Miss Amelia Proudfoot knew it was sinful to doubt that the Lord was not unmindful and would surely provide, there were times when she could not help remembering both that there would come a day when Annabel no longer needed her and she would have to find another household where her French and her Italian, her playing on the harpsichord and her thin but pure soprano voice, her embroidery and her sketching, and all her other knowledge and many accomplishments were wanted; and that even a middle-aged gentlewoman whose appearance seemed not to have changed one jot in the past fifteen years, was yet growing older every day.

After Francis and Bella had washed their hands and faces and tidied themselves, the rest of the time between then and their light supper of bread and butter, cold meat and sticky, bottled pears, was spent in telling Miss Proudfoot how they had spent the day – or rather, in carefully not telling her how they had spent the day. Ordinarily, by this time, Francis would have been off somewhere, concerning himself with his own devices, leaving Bella with Miss Proudfoot; but, under the circumstances, he had considered it safest to remain with her, so that they could support each other's lies. Between them, they made much of all the beauties of nature which they had observed, and exaggerated shamelessly the number of birds' nests they had found. Miss Proudfoot was pleased with the bunch of, by then, rather wilted broom; and in order to keep her from questioning them, they questioned her at some length on the habits of broom, and whether it had any remedial or medicinal properties. This last question necessitated consulting a herbal, since Miss Proudfoot did not know the answer, and Francis was sent to the library to fetch Culpeper and Gerard, which gave him an opportunity to slip into the now empty office, which was next to the library, and take down off its hook on the wall, Mr Thompson's carefully and neatly labelled key to the Dower House and put it in his pocket.

During supper, which the three of them took together that evening, they managed to save only a very little food for Seumas. In practice it proved far from easy to transfer cold beef and ham and slices of bread and butter from the table or their plates to their laps or pockets, in spite of their prearranged scheme of alternately engaging Miss Proudfoot in conversation which would take her mind and her eyes completely off the behaviour and actions of the one whose turn it was to add to Seumas's rations. Afterwards, when they came to pool their contributions, they found that they amounted to a remarkably meagre meal.

'That will never last him until dinner-time tomorrow,' said Bella. 'He will starve on it.'

'You would starve on it, you mean. I doubt if he is such a greedy guzzler as you.' But all the same, Francis, also, considered it far too little, besides being a reflection on Rimpole hospitality; and he decided that something would have to be done about it. His conscience being, at this early stage, still quiescent, he was not yet taking it for granted that everyone would instantly be suspicious of anything – however innocent in appearance – which he did that was in the slightest degree out of the ordinary; and so he hesitated only a short time before going to the kitchen, where he explained that the day out had made him extremely hungry and that he had not had sufficient supper. He was quite a favourite with Cook, a buxom, kindly Yorkshirewoman, who was still apt to think of him as the sickly child he had been, picking at his food, and she was delighted by this sign of good appetite and gave him a plate of venison pasties.

On the way upstairs with this prize, finding the dining-room door open and the room empty, he helped himself to a decanter of claret from the sideboard and went up the stairs with it concealed awkwardly under his coat. He managed to reach his bedroom without either spilling the wine or meeting anyone on the way; and he hid it, together with the food, at the bottom of his clothes press.

After that, he remembered something which they both had forgotten – illumination for the Dower House – and he sneaked into the larger drawing-room, which was not used unless the Rimpoles had company, and removed two of the best wax candles from one of the branched candlesticks that were placed on the torchères which stood at intervals against the walls. Tomorrow, he thought, he would have to try to raid Mrs Keighley's store-closet, but for tonight, two candles would have to suffice.

Bella was equally fortunate with the things which she had to collect. The basket she got from Edward, the new young under-footman, who would not have dreamt of querying her need of it; and, searching on that shelf of her clothes press where her underlinen was kept, she found, at the bottom of a pile, a soft, well-worn shift of Dutch linen, which she felt sure that Old Nurse would not miss, and hid it under the bed, in the basket, for bandages.

Old Nurse, as she was always called, had been nurse to Lady Rimpole when she had been the eldest Miss Heston of Heston House in Devonshire. She was old, perhaps, but her eyes were still sharp enough when she pleased. Now that the younger of her two one-time charges was too old to need her oversight, she had an easy time, doing Bella's mending, lengthening her dresses and petticoats, trying to make her hair curl as prettily as her mother's had always done – 'You are like your aunt, Miss Elizabeth, Lady Norton as she is now,' she would grumble. 'No matter what I did, Miss Elizabeth's hair would be straight again by dinner-time!' – and complaining endlessly, as one who was Devon born and bred, of the ignorance of the Yorkshire folk and the barbarousness of the Yorkshire climate. Yorkshire, she insisted, was fit only for savages to live in, being nothing but bleak moors with cold winds blowing over them – conveniently forgetting that her own native Devonshire was not without its own moors and cold winds.

Old Nurse was small and bird-like and neat, and always smelt faintly of the sage with which she cleaned her teeth: fresh leaves in summer, distilled essence in winter. At sixty-nine, she had every tooth in her head, and ascribed this to her lifelong, liberal use of sage. She still saw Bella into bed every evening; and on this particular evening she bustled her off early, as she always did on Saturdays, because Saturday was bath night. As she said good night to Francis, Bella tried to convey to him, by what she thought of as a speaking look that she would be awake and expecting him later; but he merely appeared bewildered instead of understanding, and frowned at her warningly, while Old Nurse said, 'Oh, come along, do, Miss Bella. And stop pulling faces at your brother. You're far too old for such nonsense.'

While Bella undressed, Old Nurse tidied her clothes away tut-tutting over the mud and grass stains on the skirt of her pink dress, where she had knelt in the ditch beside Seumas; so that Bella was forced to invent a tale of having tripped over a hidden rock and fallen to her knees. Then, while Old Nurse twisted her hair tightly in rags – especially tightly, since tomorrow was Sunday and Bella had to look well in church – Bessie, the newest and youngest of the under-maids, plodded, panting, up and down the backstairs from the kitchen with pails of hot water to fill the wooden bath-tub which stood on an outspread sheet in front of the fireplace. In the winter, there was always a fire in Bella's room on bath nights, so that she did not catch cold; but Old Nurse did not consider that necessary in May, even in Yorkshire.

When twelve pails of hot water had been emptied into the bath and an extra jugful stood steaming alongside the big ewer of cold water by the tub, Bessie, her face crimson from her exertions and her hair straggling out from under her round-eared cap, gasped, 'That's twelve, m'm.'

Old Nurse glanced at the bath and was satisfied that it was indeed twelve. 'That will do, then, Bessie. You may go.'

'Thank you, m'm.' Bessie bobbed a curtsey in the direction of Bella. 'Good night, Miss Annabel.'

Unable to turn her head while Old Nurse was dragging the hair almost from her scalp, Bella rolled her eyes towards the girl. 'Good night, Bessie.'

Bessie fled, before Old Nurse should find her something else to do. There would be many more pails of hot water to carry upstairs that evening, and several more baths to fill before she could escape to her truckle bed in the attic she shared with five other serving-maids. Bessie always hated bath nights.

Bella, on the contrary, always liked Saturday evenings and usually tried to make her bath last as long as possible for the enjoyment of having Old Nurse scrub her back for her with the soap made in the still-room to Mrs Keighley's recipe, from fat and lye and scented with rosewater, and then pour scooped-up jugfuls of delightfully warm water all over her while she held a cloth around her head to prevent her hair from getting wet and the water from running into her eyes; until the water began to cool, and then it was pleasant to be rubbed dry and warm again with a large linen towel. But tonight she was impatient for it all to be over and Old Nurse gone; as though by being quickly into bed herself, she could make everyone else in the house equally prompt.

It seemed to her to go on for ever; but at last Old Nurse was saying, 'Now, into bed with you, or you'll catch cold.' And then she was between the sheets, only her rag-adorned head showing above the white linen, and two young under-footmen were carrying out the tub of tepid water to take it downstairs and empty it, so that it could be brought up again and set in Francis's room, ready for Bessie to fill for him, and Old Nurse was folding up the damp sheet from the floor and putting it, together with the empty hot water jug, outside the door for Bessie to collect.

Then Old Nurse was beside the bed. 'Sleep well, my lambkin, and pleasant dreams. And don't you touch those rags or I'll have something to say to you.'

Old Nurse always ended her good night wishes with this final injunction, and had done so ever since the time when Bella, then aged seven, unable to bear the discomfort of an over-tightly rolled curl, had undone all the rags and been well slapped for it in the morning. It had never occurred since then, but Old Nurse always seemed to think it might, hence her nightly threat.

She had already put out the home-made tallow candles on the chest of drawers, causing an unpleasant smell, and she now snuffed the one on the night-table beside the bed and, carrying her own lighted candlestick, made her way to the door and out, shutting it behind her, and Bella was left in the darkness. With great impatience she waited for what she judged to be half an hour, then she sat up and groped for the tinder-box on the night-table. Kneeling on the edge of the bed, after one or two false starts, she struck a spark and was able to light the candle on the table. Then she jumped to the floor, and with a good deal of tugging and pulling, got one of the blankets off the bed, folded it and put it under the bed beside the basket. The bed was by this time rather untidy, so she spent five minutes straightening it and trying to make it look as if all the blankets were still on it; then she collected together the clothes she wanted, including a warm, quilted dress in case it should be cold outside, her stoutest shoes, her scarlet cloak, and the largest of her everyday frilled caps.

After that she dressed herself, standing beside the bed near the candle, both to benefit from the light it gave and to be ready to scramble back into bed should anyone come in – which was, she considered, most unlikely. She dressed fully, except for the cap, shoes, and cloak, and then put on her nightshift over the top of everything else, which made it a rather tight fit. The cap she stuffed into one of the shoes, and the shoes she rolled up in the cloak, and the resulting bundle she placed under the bed with the blanket and the basket; then she climbed back into bed, leaving the candle alight, so that no time should be wasted in lighting it when Francis came, and settled down to wait for him. She might, without worrying, have gone to sleep, knowing that Francis would have to wake her; but she was far too impatient and excited, and could only lie there, fully awake, staring up into the shadows over the bed and wondering how Seumas was, hidden in the laurels, and daydreaming of taking part in daring rescues against enormous odds and of being loyal until death to the Cause.

On the other hand, Francis, waiting in his room two doors along, was sleepy, so sleepy that he was afraid to stay in bed. He knew he ought to get up in order to remain awake, but he kept putting off the moment of rising; and it was only when he had jerked himself awake from half-sleep for the third time and realized that on the next occasion he might not be so successful, that he sat up and lit his candle. He got out of bed, put on his dressing-gown and settled himself on a straight-backed chair with the candle on a table beside him and a book to read. But, persevere as he might, he was too tired to find any interest in the mishaps which beset Joseph Andrews and Parson Adams, though only two days before he had found them entertaining enough. Now, he kept finding himself re-reading the same passage – and making nonsense of it each time – and nodding over the page. Once he actually fell asleep, but the chair he had deliberately chosen was so hard and uncomfortable that he awoke after a quarter-hour or so.

The minutes ticked slowly by on the alarm watch – its silver pair-case pierced in a decorative pattern so that the alarm might sound clearly through it – which his father had given him on the day he had been fourteen, six months before, in October. When the hands had moved on its white enamel dial to tell him that it was eleven o'clock, Francis got up, and opening his door quietly, walked cautiously towards the front of the house. His, Bella's, and Miss Proudfoot's rooms were in the back of the building, but Sir John and Lady Rimpole had their bedrooms in the front, over the larger drawing-room. From the darkness of the passage and the narrow lines of light showing under the doors of his parents' rooms, Francis presumed that they were upstairs – otherwise the two candles which stood on the marble-topped console table at the head of the stairs would have been still alight – but not yet in bed, or their own lights would have been out. He returned to his uncomfortable chair and *The History of the Adventures of Joseph Andrews and his Friend Mr Abraham Adams.*

At half past eleven he looked at his watch again; and it was at this stage that he realized, for the first time, that he might have set the alarm for midnight and allowed himself to go to sleep. It had not occurred to him to do so because, although he had, on several occasions, during the months the watch had been in his possession, set the alarm ringing with the intention of trying it out, he had never needed to do so for any practical purpose. Marvelling at this singular lapse from intelligence, he dressed, yawning, and at a quarter to twelve he went out to reconnoitre once again. There was no longer any light showing under the two doors. More alert, now that the time for action had come, he collected blanket, decanter, food, and candles, putting what he could into his pockets, tucking the blanket under his arm, and holding the decanter carefully in one hand. Then he snuffed out his own candle, grabbing, at the last moment, as an after thought, his tinder-box and stuffing it into an already overfull pocket, closed the door of his room after himself very quietly, stood for a moment or two until his eyes were adjusted to the darkness, and then tiptoed to Bella's room and tapped lightly at the door. She heard him and jumped out of bed at once. As he opened the door, she was hurrying over to it. He hastily went in, almost dropping the decanter, and shut the door.

'Bella, why in the world did you keep your light on? Someone might have seen me coming in.'

'Have you got everything?' she asked.

'Yes, of course. Have you?'

'Yes.' She knelt down and pulled out from under the bed the things she had hidden. They put food, decanter, bandages, and candles into the basket, and folded the two blankets together. Francis was just picking up basket and blankets when Bella pulled her nightshift over her head, tossed it on the floor and grabbed her shoes.

'Whatever are you doing?'

'I am coming with you.'

'No, you are not. This is no time for a girl to be out.'

'I am coming.'

'No!'

It is difficult to argue in whispers, but they managed it, putting an intensity of feeling into their hissed words.

'I'm not letting you come with me. Get back into bed at once,' said Francis with determination.

Equally determined, Bella demanded, 'How do you suppose you will be able to carry all those things and help Mr Macdonald at the same time, all alone?'

This was something about which Francis had already been wondering, and while he paused for an answer, Bella completed her dressing by pulling on her cap over the curl-rags and picking up the basket and making her way to the door. 'Come on, Francis.'

She was already at the door, with her hand on the door-handle: further argument was useless. He capitulated – not too unwillingly – picked up the blankets and followed her. Half-way to the door he said, 'You idiot, Bella, what about the candle?' He put down the blankets and, to save himself a few paces, got on to her bed, reached over it to the night-table and blew out the candle. He almost fell over the bundle of blankets while trying to find it again in the darkness; but the two of them were finally outside the room and shutting the door.

'How dark it is,' whispered Bella.

They stood still until they could see, very faintly, the shape of the elegant banisters and newel-post at the top of the stairs; and then, saying into her ear, 'Keep close after me and walk lightly,' Francis led the way to the head of the wide stairway and began to go down. Clinging to the banisters with their free hands, they reached the hall safely and groped their way to the side door. The noise of the upper bolt of the door being drawn back seemed to echo through the house. Bella clutched at Francis's arm and they stood, frozen into horrified immobility, for two full minutes before they dared make a move to touch the lower bolt. Francis was almost afraid to lay his hand on it, but it proved less stiff than the other and therefore less noisy. Even so, it was noisy enough, and they again waited for a minute or so before opening the door and letting in the light of the rising moon. Francis urged Bella through the door and then suddenly hissed at her. 'Wait here. I'll be no more than a moment,' and disappeared into the darkness of the house.

Bella stood on the threshold, feeling very visible – and feeling, also, almost as though at least half the household were up and out and watching her from the garden – for what seemed like minute after minute; and then at last, when she had almost convinced herself that two of the darkest of the shadows under the wall of the stable yard, fifty feet away, were watchers and not shadows at all, Francis was back with her, so silently that she was startled. He thrust into her free hand one of their father's walking sticks, which he used when his gout was troubling him. 'For Mr Macdonald,' he whispered.

Bella was instantly delighted by his clever idea and stood, filled with admiration, until the sight of Francis closing the door quietly brought another thought into her mind. 'What will happen if someone should come down and find the door unbolted and bolt it, so that we cannot get in again?'

'We'll worry about that when it happens,' Francis whispered back. 'Come on.'

They walked quickly along the path towards the park, keeping close to the wall that encircled the kitchen garden and the orchard. The moon, a few days past the full, was not yet very high in the sky, but it was bright enough and very welcome. Where the orchard wall ended they turned to the right, diagonally across open ground towards the copse. They did not speak, but concentrated on hurrying towards their goal, Francis striding on so purposefully, that every now and then Bella, with her rather shorter legs, was obliged to give a little running step to keep up with him. Only once Francis spoke, 'Take care not to spill the wine.' And once, as they passed close by, in the shadow under a tree a cow heaved itself to its feet, hindquarters first, and Bella had given a little cry of surprise, 'What's that!' before she realized what it was and let out her breath in a sigh of relief.

Everything looked different when seen by the summer moonlight. So unlike the evening and early morning moonshine of winter, which might be considered merely as helpful illumination, this other was a transfiguration. Now, under its spell, ordinary things seemed mysterious and wonderful; and it was as though anything at all might happen in that strange, silver-leaved world, Bella thought.

6

IT was not long before they had reached the copse where the spruce and larch trees stood tall and still and dark; though the leaves of the laurels beneath them shone like little mirrors reflecting back the moonlight fiercely.

'It is in through this way, I think,' said Francis, although he, too, was discovering that everything looked different by moonlight when one was having to find the way for oneself. A few yards into the copse he stopped and gave a pretty good imitation of an owl hooting. There was no reply and they went on for a few yards more before he tried again. After his fourth hoot, there was a low answering whistle from somewhere to their left.

'We have come too far over,' Francis said. 'This way,' He pushed Bella in the right direction, so that she almost lost her footing and said accusingly, 'Take care of the basket.'

Two more owl hoots and two more whistles brought them to the side of the big laurel which they both recognized.

'Mr Macdonald, are you there?'

'I am.'

Francis ducked in under the branches to help him up and out. It was a lengthy and distressing process and could not be hurried; but at least Seumas was standing on one leg outside his temporary shelter, holding tightly to a branch for support. He saw Bella. 'Why, the two of you have come!' He made the faintest of bows in her direction. 'It's honoured I am, ma'am.' He spoke as lightly as he could for his discomfort; but Bella thought he seemed pleased.

'We have brought you a walking stick.' She offered it to him.

'Now, isn't that the clever notion?'

'It was Francis's notion,' admitted Bella, a little regretfully.

'Was it now? But I'll wager you have some good notions of your own?'

'Sometimes . . .' She sounded a little doubtful.

'Do you think you would be able to start off now?' Francis interrupted.

'Sure and I could. Just you be showing me which way to go.'

At the edge of the copse they paused for their first rest.

'Whereabouts is this Dower House of yours?'

'A little south of the west gate. Do you remember, the gate where you saw Bella yesterday? – or rather, it was the day before yesterday, now. It is about half a mile across the park from here.'

It was rather nearer a mile than half a mile from where they were, and Bella had opened her mouth to correct Francis before she realized why he had lied, and closed it again.

'Half a mile, is it? Well, we had better be going on if I'm to arrive there before dawn.'

They set off, Seumas leaning on Francis with his right arm, and with the stick in his left hand – he found the stick a great help, in spite of his stiff left arm, and said so, gratefully – and Bella carrying basket and blankets, as well as their picnic rug, which Seumus had found too awkward to wear wrapped about him while he walked. They made their way only slowly across the park, stopping every now and then for Seumas to rest, standing with his back against a tree, his eyes closed and his face quite ghastly in the moonlight. No one spoke much, even at first; and the farther they went and the longer their journey lasted, the less they felt like speaking and the more frequent and the more prolonged were the rests.

However, they came at last to the back gate of the Dower House, which opened directly into the park. The front gates, at the other end of the garden, after a short drive, gave on to the lane that ran past to the village and, as the house was empty, were at present padlocked, to deter possible trespassers. They passed through this wicket gate and made their way between a low box hedge and rows of fruit bushes towards the yard at the rear of the house. Unlike the Hall, the Dower House had neither been rebuilt nor modernized. Its little windows reflected the moonlight from their many panes like scores of hostile eyes, and the shadowed gables showed black and stark.

Bella shivered a little and wondered if Lady Alice were looking at them from one of the upstairs windows and resenting the intrusion of a stranger. They came slowly round to the front of the house and up the four steps to the front door.

'The key is in my pocket, Bella. Get it out and unlock the door.'

She groped for the key and fitted it into the lock. The lock was kept well oiled, in spite of the house's being empty, so the key turned easily. Bella opened the heavy door and a cold, unused smell came out to them. They went into the large, flagged hall which echoed emptily to their halting steps.

'You had better close the door before we strike a light, Bella. The candles are in the basket. Take one out while we can still see.'

Bella felt in the basket by the moonlight and found a candle. Then she shut the door and the musty darkness closed in on them. Francis, still supporting Seumas, who seemed by now incapable of standing unaided, even with the wall behind him, directed Bella to his right pocket for his tinder-box. Her hands were shaking – it was cold in the house after the mildness of the night outside, she told herself – so that it was more difficult than usual to strike a light with flint and steel and catch the spark on the charred linen rag in the box. But in spite of an excuse for it, for once Francis showed no impatience with her slowness; and at last she got a spark which grew to a glow and she could thrust into it the thin, brimstone-tipped match and light the candle.

She stood up holding the candle, her cold fingers clasped about the wax. Long shadows seemed to rush away from them, down the hall into everlasting darkness beyond which, invisible, rose the spiral staircase which led to the gallery and the upper floor, while above their heads the beamed ceiling of the hall – which rose the full height of the house – might have been a mile away for all that they could see of it by the light of their one candle. Bella turned to the others for the comfort of their presence: Francis's eyes were two black holes in his thin face, and Seumas looked like a corpse.

'Go and find the most convenient room for hiding in,' said

Francis, speaking now in a low, awed tone, as though he were in church. 'I think that much of the ground floor furniture is piled up in the dining-room, but there may be some in the drawing-room as well. Mr Macdonald would do best in a room with furniture, but it must still have its curtains up, Bella. Even if there's no furniture at all, the room must have curtains.'

Reluctantly, Bella left the others there, near the front door, and walked forward into the shadows, seeing them march before her as she held up her candle like a beacon to defy them. The little parlours, which opened off the hall on either side, had long ago been adapted for more comfortable living; and the large, chilly, Tudor hall itself had been rarely used, even for company, in old Lady Rimpole's time. Bella opened the first door she came to, on the right. It was the dining-room. The draught, as she opened the door, nearly extinguished the candle-flame, but she saved it just in time with a protecting hand. The low-ceilinged, dark-panelled room was piled high with white, ghostly shapes, and Bella had to go in among them with her candle before there was light enough for her to see that the windows were curtainless. She came out thankfully and closed the door.

'Furniture, but no curtains,' she said to the others.

The drawing-room opposite was in the same state, except that it contained hardly any furniture; and the morning-room beyond the dining-room, with its window facing north-east, had neither furniture nor curtains, but only dark panelling to throw back the candlelight. The thought came unwanted to Bella's mind that it was in such a room, against such a background and with no furniture to mask one's view, that the awful sight of Lady Alice in her white gown and gabled head-dress would appear most clearly to the beholder, and she hurriedly stepped backwards and out, trying to reassure herself with the knowledge that no one had ever seen Lady Alice downstairs.

The room across the hall from the morning-room, however, unlike the morning-room itself, contained several pieces of furniture shrouded under dust-sheets – one largish, central pile, ringed round by other, smaller shapes – and even from the doorway Bella could see that its curtains were still up. Bolder now, and triumphant at finding curtains which could be drawn – and in a room which was not bare of furniture, as might well have been the case – Bella stepped audaciously into the room with the candle, and immediately, from the shadows, a hideous monster, large as a hound, leapt silently at her with grinning teeth and huge, rolling eyes.

She recoiled with a cry, spilling hot wax on her hand and almost dropping the candle, and was back in the doorway again before she had remembered that this was the newly decorated Chinese room and that the monster could only be the pottery Chinese lion which used to stand by the fireplace.

'What's the matter?' Francis's startled voice asked from the hall.

'I ... I ... only burnt myself with the candle grease. Shaking now in earnest, she once more left the safety of the threshold and went fearfully towards the windows and drew the curtains across them, not daring to look about her in case of further horrors, and keeping her eyes averted from the window panes, for fear of seeing something looking in at her from the darkness outside. It took her a minute or two to pull the velvet curtains, because they were heavy and reached to the floor, and she had only one free hand.

'Are you all right, Bella?' came Francis's voice, filling her with the terror that a voice – even a known and friendly voice, and even if it is not entirely unexpected – can bring to one when one is alone in an unfamiliar room and the voice calls to one from outside.

'Yes! Yes!' she almost screamed back at him; then, calming herself with an effort, she called, 'There's furniture here, and I've drawn the curtains. Come on.' Although she wanted nothing more than to run from the room and join the others in the cold, musty hall – which now seemed a kindly refuge – she could not; her legs temporarily lacked the strength to carry her a single inch. She stood rooted there, hearing their limping progress along the hall: the stick tapping on the flagstones and their dragging feet. Just before they appeared in the doorway, she found the resolution to go and meet them with the light, the shadows trembling in the room as the candle wobbled in her hand.

'Get the covers off a chair, Bella.' Francis sounded exhausted.

With one hand Bella pulled the dust sheet off a pair of walnut chairs with outcurving front legs ending in paws – which gave them rather the appearance of bulldogs – and upholstered seats embroidered by the Dowager Lady Rimpole herself with a design in the Chinese manner. They were standing, one the right way up and the other upside down upon it. She managed to lay the upside-down one anyhow on the floor, spilling hot wax from the crazily-tilted candle in her other hand as she did so. Francis helped Seumas to the upright chair. Seumas sat down and the stick fell from his hands on to the carpetless boards with a startling clatter. He seemed very near to fainting once again.

Francis, relaxing his aching shoulders with relief, observed him anxiously. 'Is grandmother's couch still here, do you suppose? It would serve for a bed. Hold up the candle for me while I look for it.'

Bella held up the candle and Francis lifted corners of dust-sheets and peered underneath them. He finally gave an exclamation of satisfaction. 'Here it is. But there seem to be a great many things piled on it. Come nearer so that I can see what they are.'

The couch turned out to have on it, sharing its dust-sheet, a large mirror with an ornate, gilded frame, a bow-legged mahogany dumb-waiter with a claw clutching a ball at the end of each leg, a footstool, and, wrapped together in a cloth with bags of lavender against the moths, three silken cushions, also embroidered in the Chinese manner.

Francis moved these things to the floor and pulled the couch away from the main pile of dust-sheeted furniture in the centre of the room. 'Now the blankets. You will have to bring the candle.'

They went out into the hall, on the way passing Seumas who, seated sideways on the chair, was sagging in a disconcerting fashion over its back. With three hands between them, Francis and Bella managed to carry in from the hall everything they had brought with them, and Francis made up a kind of bed on the couch with the two blankets, the picnic rug, and the lavender-scented cushions, while Bella held the candle for him to work by.

Looking dubiously at the unconcerned Seumas, Francis asked him, 'Do you think you could manage a few more steps? Only from here to the couch. Then you could lie down.'

'We have made you a bed. You will be far more comfortable on it.' Still holding up the candle, as though supporting a ceiling of shadows, Bella, an anxious caryatid with curl-rags showing under her cap, raised it even higher, to encourage Seumas on his way.

Seumas roused himself to look up slowly. 'I'll try. You are taking a lot of pains over me, and it's grateful I am.' His voice sounded utterly weary.

Francis helped him up and Bella, bending carefully to do it, so that the candle might remain upright, picked up the walking stick, and put it into his hand.

Ten minutes later, his blue coat and his remaining boot off, Seumas was lying on the couch with the blankets over him and his head on the cushions.

'Are you comfortable?' asked Francis. There was no reply. 'I think perhaps he may be about to swoon again,' he said to Bella.

'What shall we do?' Bella held the candle closer and stared at the white, drawn face. 'Should we give him some of the wine?'

Francis had not thought to bring a cup or a glass, so he had to hold the decanter to Seumas's lips. Seumas managed to swallow quite a reasonable amount of claret without very much being spilt; and Francis and Bella waited solicitously to see if it would have any effect.

After a few moments Seumas's eyes opened and he smiled up at them. 'That's after being the best drink I've had in all my days, and I in great need of it, too.'

'It's my father's best claret. He is reckoned a good judge of wine,' said Francis, taking Seumas's praise literally.

Bella, also taking the remark literally, asked, 'Do you then not have French wine in the Highlands?'

'In the Highlands? Faith! And how should I be knowing? What's the Highlands to do with it, anyway?'

'All is well. We are friends,' Bella assured him. 'Do you not remember? You told us you were a Highlander.'

'Och, and so I did. I remember now.' Seumas's eyes closed again.

'I am afraid that we shall have to be going, Mr Macdonald. Do you think you will be all right?' Francis said apologetically.

The eyes opened. 'Sure and I shall. I'll do fine.'

'We shall leave everything beside you, where you can reach it. The wine, food, my tinder-box, and another candle. We'll come back tomorrow as soon as we can. I do not know when we shall be here, as it is Sunday and we have to go to church.'

'What about changing the bandage, Francis?'

'That will have to wait until tomorrow. He's borne enough for one day.' Francis looked at Seumas again. 'Would you like us to leave the candle alight?'

'I'd be glad of it.'

'We shall need a candlestick,' said Bella. She looked about her without much hope.

'All the silver was probably taken over to the Hall when the house was closed. There may be a candlestick in the kitchen.' Francis sounded equally unhopeful.

They went together to search, and there was, indeed, an old iron candlestick in one of the kitchen closets. With relief Bella put her candle in it and carried it back triumphantly to the Chinese room. She placed it on the floor near the couch with the spare candle beside it. 'You can light the other from it when it has burnt low, and save yourself the trouble of striking a light,' she said helpfully.

Seumas smiled at her. 'I'll do that if I'm not sleeping.'

'Is there anything else we can do for you before we go?' Francis asked him.

'Not a thing, thank you.'

Bella looked at the monstrous shapes of the shrouded furniture, now even more monstrous with what little light there was coming up at them from the level of the floor, and at the Chinese lion's horrifying head, and at the black shadows that darkened the farther corners of the room. 'Are you sure you'll not dislike being left alone with Lady Alice, Mr Macdonald?'

'Oh, Bella!'

'Lady Alice? Who is she?'

'Pay no attention to my sister, Mr Macdonald. It is only nonsense and village tales about Lady Alice.'

'It is not, Francis!' exclaimed Bella indignantly. 'Grandmother said she had seen her once, and she said that she often heard her.' She added reassuringly to Seumas, 'But she never comes downstairs, so she is not likely to trouble you.'

'Och, it's the banshee you're talking of.' Seumas grinned sleepily. 'Now is it not more probable that she'll be after disliking being left alone with me, poor lady, and she in her own home and I intruding, as it were? Now, good night to you both, and my thanks to you.' His eyes closed slowly.

Francis and Bella shut the door of the Chinese room after them, carefully crossed the pitch-dark hall to the front door and let themselves out.

'We shall have to consider leaving the front door open,' said Francis, as he locked it. 'We cannot bring the key with us every time we come here.'

The moon, just past its highest point, once again lighted their way across the park. Now that it was all over, and had taken far longer than they had expected, Bella was very tired. She tripped once over a tussock of grass and Francis steadied her with an arm about her shoulders. He gave her a little squeeze and said with unaccustomed affection and commendation, 'I'm glad you came with me. I'd not have managed alone.'

By the time they reached the Hall they were both stumbling with weariness. Just as Francis was opening the side door stealthily, the first cock crowed.

They bolted the door and crept up the stairs. Outside the door of her room, Bella whispered, 'The key! I was to return it early tomorrow.'

'It can wait. I've remembered – tomorrow is Sunday, so Mr Thompson will not be here.'

He saw her into her room and lit her candle for her. 'Can you manage now? For heaven's sake do not leave your clothes lying about for Old Nurse to find.' Then he remembered his tinder-box, on the floor at the Dower House, and crept to his room to fetch a candlestick. When he came back, Bella was undressed and in her nightshift. He bundled up her clothes and stuffed the bundle into her clothes press. 'You can sort them out tomorrow,' he whispered.

She climbed into bed, and he lit his candle from hers.

'Good night.'

'Good night, Francis.'

'Shall I leave your candle alight?'

She gave no answer. Her eyes were already closed.

He snuffed the candle, stifled a yawn, tiptoed out with his own candlestick and along to his room. He, too, was asleep the moment he got into bed.

7

ON Sunday morning, as usual, the family and household went to the little church in the village, the family bowling along ahead in the large, new, best carriage, smart and recently repainted for the summer, with the Rimpole crest upon its doors, drawn by six fine match bays; Sir John with Lady Rimpole beside him wearing a yellow quilted brocade gown in the latest London fashion and a shallow-crowned, narrow-brimmed chip hat, and Miss Proudfoot opposite them in her black bombasine, with Francis and Bella one on either side of her. Both the ladies carried fans as well as prayerbooks.

After the family, in the old, now second best, carriage, behind three bays and an elderly grey, came the six upper servants of the Hall, Keighley and Mrs Keighley, Old Nurse, her head nodding sleepily, as it always did in a coach, Cook, stuck-up Miss Stubbs, Lady Rimpole's dresser, and Sir John's valet, fussy little Fowler; all in their Sunday best and all packed in tightly together in distasteful and wary proximity – as always, the three Yorkshire folk resentful and suspicious of the two Londoners, the Londoners scornful of the rustics, and the Devonshire farmer's daughter resentful and suspicious and scornful of everyone else – but not for anything would a single one of them have given up the privilege of riding in the carriage and thereby asserting superiority over all the other servants who followed after them – a good way after – in a farm waggon which jogged along to the accompaniment of much chattering and giggling from the younger lads and girls.

It was always the same each Sunday, variety being provided only by the weather and the season of the year; and the day after Francis and Bella had had their great adventure was no exception. The carriage came round from the stable yard to wait for them in the drive, conveniently near the front door; the family party, which had gathered in the portico, came out on to the terrace, carrying prayerbooks, and descended the steps to the drive; Sir John handed Lady Rimpole and Miss Proudfoot into the carriage, Francis handed in Bella, and Sir John and Francis themselves climbed in; the steps were lifted up, the coachman in his livery whipped up the horses and away they trotted, down the drive, past the Lodge where Rigby the head-gardener lived, out through the tall, wrought-iron gates and along the road.

Usually Bella and Francis, with Miss Proudfoot between them, her Sunday expression on her face, looked with interest through the windows of the carriage in search of anything worth noting to enliven the journey; but today each was tense and thoughtful and in no mood to be diverted by happenings in highway or lane. They were both looking out of their respective windows, it is true, but taking no interest in what they saw; their minds were too busy wondering how Seumas was, and how they could contrive to get to him again, and when; and whether they would be able to take with them enough food for him.

As the carriage approached the spot where the park walls gave way, for fifty yards or so, to a high, clipped yew hedge on either side of the gates of the Dower House, Francis averted his eyes from the window and instead looked fixedly opposite him at the blue velvet squab against which his father's shoulder rested. Only when they were well past the Dower House did he turn his eyes again to the window.

On the other hand, as soon as she caught sight of the three cottages which stood close together on the opposite side of the road, a little before the Dower House, Bella turned from her window to look out of the window beside Francis, leaning forward a little and anxiously scanning hedge and gates to see if all seemed the same at the Dower House as on any other day. It did. Tall, trimmed yew hedges, wrought-iron gates, closed fast; and through the gates a sight of the short drive up through the front garden of the Dower House, and, at the end of the drive, a very brief glimpse of the house itself, behind its trees and shrubs. There was no time to see more as the carriage passed by. Everything appeared to be as always: no militiamen trying to force a way in through the padlocked gate, that they might enter and search the garden; no disturbed villager standing in the lane, his arms flung wide to stop the horses, that he might tell the squire there was a traitor hidden in the Dower House. Bella's taut muscles relaxed, and before they had reached the west gate of the park, three hundred yards or so on, she had turned again to her own window and was watching the sunlight on the grey stone of carpenter Tuttle's cottage, and then on the other cottages at the outskirts of the village, and seeing the cottagers and their children, who were gathering before their doors or walking along the lane towards the church, step aside as the carriage went by, with a bow or a curtsey for the squire and his family – a mark of respect which Sir John and his lady never failed to acknowledge.

Then they were in the village itself and, soon after, outside the grey, square-towered church and stepping down from the carriage to be greeted by the vicar and to make their way to the family pew. In church, throughout the long service and Dr Mortlake's even longer sermon, behind the high walls of the squire's pew, Sir John and Lady Rimpole always set their children and any guests who might happen to be staying with them, as well as the villagers, a good example. Unlike so many of the gentry, Sir John did not talk with his friends, lay bets, play cards, smoke a pipe, or drink sherry during the sermon. The worst he ever did was to lean back and go to sleep when Dr Mortlake's rambling digressions became too involved and obscure; while Lady Rimpole usually sat straight up, as though listening intently, her face a mask of polite interest, her mind occupied with the news of any recent London scandals and the latest fashions, about all of which her many friends in the south, and in particular her sister, Elizabeth, Lady Norton, who had a house in Berkeley Square, kept her well informed. The worst she ever did, when the sermon went on too long for even her to bear it and all recent scandals and latest fashions had been contemplated *ad nauseam*, was, still with an interested expression and an admirably straight back, to glance downwards to where her hands, in their elbow-length gloves, held on her lap, not her prayerbook, but the newest French romance or volume of English verses, or whatever her current reading might be, which she had brought along with her in case of emergencies.

Usually Bella sat very straight and still and tried to be as much like her mother as possible – though, rather plump and not particularly pretty, she quite despaired of ever achieving Lady Rimpole's charm and poise and grace; and usually Francis, ignoring Miss Proudfoot's frowns, surreptitiously passed the time by reading the forms for special services in his prayer-book. In this way he had already worked through, on successive Sundays, the Form of Solemnization of Matrimony, the Order for the Visitation of the Sick, and the Ministration of Baptism to such as are of riper years.

But on that particular day both he and Bella were too much occupied with their thoughts to need any other diversion. The Prayer for the King's Majesty – since their respective conversions to the Jacobite cause, Francis and Bella always mentally substituted *James* for Dr Mortlake's *George* – at the conclusion of which their parents and Miss Proudfoot had united in a loud and loyal 'Amen!', had added to their troubled thoughts of Seumas, the beginnings of a guilty conscience; as yet faint – though soon to increase – with Bella, but stronger already with Francis, who was even then reflecting that, however right he might consider his action to be, to his father and to everyone else in his acquaintance except Mr Marivel, helping Seumas to escape from the militia and offering him shelter was aiding and comforting the King's enemies – in short, it was treason; and that by hiding Seumas at the Dower House, he was involving in his treason his father, who, as a Justice of the Peace, a well-known North Riding landowner, and a member of the old and respected Rimpole family, ought to be above suspicion. If the unthinkable worst happened and Seumas were discovered and captured, would anyone believe that Sir John had had no part in harbouring him, Francis wondered.

When they came out of church a number of parishioners made their bows and their curtseys to the squire and his lady, among them Mr Thompson the agent and his young wife, who lived in a small house in the village. Mr Thompson was an earnest, conscientious man and, Sunday or not, he wished to ask Sir John if he should ride over, the first thing on Monday morning, to look at the roof of a certain farm about which he had just received a complaint, or whether he should leave it until later in the week. While Sir John was good-naturedly listening to him, Lady Rimpole, with that charm of manner which made her so much admired and liked in any society, was complimenting Mrs Thompson – as one woman to another and without any trace of condescension – on the new straw hat she was wearing, and expressing her astonishment that not only the trimming, but the hat itself, was all her own work. Shy young Mrs Thompson, her cheeks glowing, was stammering out her thanks for the compliment, made happy for the day by her ladyship's kindness.

Miss Proudfoot, presuming that their elders would not wish them to be idly standing by while they spoke to the Thompsons, shepherded Francis and Bella into the carriage, and they sat waiting in it with her for the next ten minutes, until their parents joined them. Thus it was that they missed all mention of the presence of a fugitive in the district and the excitement of the militia's chase after him – the village's first topic of interesting conversation since old Widow Peel had tripped over her own dog and broken her arm six weeks before – and as Sir John and their mother said nothing of the matter on their return to the carriage, Francis and Bella had no idea whether they knew of it or not; and, having to feign ignorance themselves, they were unable to ask and find out.

As Sunday passed and afternoon succeeded morning and early evening followed afternoon, it became obvious to Francis and Bella that they were not going to be able to visit the Dower House before dark. They had both feared that it might be difficult to do so, but it was, it seemed, going to prove impossible, even for Francis. In one of several hasty, whispered consultations which they managed to snatch at intervals throughout the day without arousing suspicion, they were finally, at around five o'clock, obliged to admit this.

'We shall have to go in the night again,' said Francis. This time he made no suggestion of excluding Bella from the expedition, even though, without Seumas to manage and little to carry, Bella's support would not be essential. But Bella, having proved her usefulness on their previous midnight excursion, had earned the right to accompany him on any others that became necessary; and Francis was not sorry for this.

That there would be little to carry with them seemed, unfortunately, undeniable. Their attempts to collect food for Seumas had, by five o'clock, failed miserably. Indeed, their attempts had not so much failed as hardly been made at all, owing to lack of opportunity; and dinner had nearly brought them to disaster.

On Sundays, if there were no guests at the Hall, Sir John liked to enjoy an informal dinner with all his family. Both Francis and Bella, therefore, had their meal in the dining-room with their parents and Miss Proudfoot. To Francis, who quite often dined with his parents, Sunday dinner was not so much of an occasion; but Bella usually thoroughly enjoyed the grown-up feeling of sitting at the big dining-room table with its shining silver, so well polished with whitening-powder, and its sparkling glass, set out on the snowy cloth of fine Flanders linen – all, silver, glass, and table-cloth alike, engraved or embroidered with the Rimpole crest, a stag's head above the words: *Durat honor meus* – and taking part in the family conversation, almost as though she were already out and in society.

But on this Sunday all her enjoyment was wanting, because she deplored the fact that it would be impossible to collect for Seumas any of the food which was so lavishly displayed on both dining-table and side table. It was a particularly good dinner, with two chickens and a large veal pie as well as a sirloin of beef; followed by a grateful-pudding made from eggs, raisins, bread, flour, and milk, and flavoured with ginger, and a large fruit tart with damsons preserved by Mrs Keighley. Bella was especially fond of chicken and Francis of roast beef, yet they kept thinking of Seumas, growing hungrier and hungrier in the Dower House; and as they saw dish after dish being taken from the table unfinished – each dish still holding enough to provide Seumas with one or two good meals – their spirits sank lower and lower.

With a boldness brought on by desperation, Francis did indeed attempt to glean something from all this wasted plenty, but he was caught by his mother in the very act of trying to transfer a slice of veal pie and a potato from his plate to his pocket in his table napkin. Vastly surprised, since Francis was not a greedy boy, she asked him what in the world he was doing. Blushing furiously, he mumbled some excuse about perhaps feeling hungry later on; and, the attention of the rest of the table having by then been attracted, Lady Rimpole informed everyone with much amusement of what she had observed her son to do.

Miss Proudfoot was shocked, and exclaimed at this piece of ill-bred conduct on the part of someone for whose polite behaviour in public she felt herself at least partly responsible, having given Francis, as a little boy, his earliest lessons in deportment; while Bella was appalled at the rashness and imprudence of Francis's action, though at the same time admiring and envying the courage which had enabled him to take it.

But Sir John seemed to find the whole matter a rather good joke. After at first exclaiming, 'Heaven forbid that anyone should find himself hungry in my house, especially my own son!' he laughed heartily and continued to tease the wretchedly embarrassed Francis for the next five minutes.

Francis was, in his father's opinion, in many ways over dignified and staid for his age – the natural result of too much concern and care in his early years and the lack of boisterous friends of his own age with whom he could have forgotten dignity; and Sir John was rather pleased that he had been caught out in a piece of childishness, and therefore made much of the opportunity to bring Francis down to the level of his years by means of a good deal of rather heartless ridicule. Then, noticing Bella's expression, her father chaffed her on being mortified by her brother's lack of company manners, so that she felt herself obliged to divert any possible suspicion, either of her collusion or of Francis's real motive, by pretending a want of sympathy with him; so she joined in the teasing until he was thoroughly and miserably uncomfortable, and even serious and sober-minded Miss Proudfoot was amused by the spectacle of his discomfiture and ceased to be so shocked by his lapse.

After dinner, Francis very naturally tried to salve his hurt dignity by rounding on Bella as soon as he could get a word with her alone. 'There was no need for you to have jeered at me, Bella, since you knew why I had done it. A fine sister you are! But then, it was exactly the sort of thing a girl would do!' he said bitterly.

'What else could I have done, Francis? I was so afraid that they would try and find out why you had really taken the piece of pie. It was so brave of you to have tried – I would never have dared to do it myself – but indeed you should not have run such a risk.'

He well knew that Bella had only been acting for the best, as she saw it, and eventually allowed himself to be mollified, though his humiliation still rankled and he firmly made up his mind to take no such chances again, even at schoolroom meals, and he said as much to Bella. 'I'll be hanged if that is not the last time I attempt to save anything for Mr Macdonald during mealtimes – not even during schoolroom dinner. I'd wager half a guinea that old Haughtyhoof will be watching me like a hawk from now on. You may try if you like, but for heaven's sake be careful.'

When he had had a short after-dinner nap, Sir John, who was not strict in his sabbatizing, rode in the park for an hour or so, and Francis had to accompany him – something he would normally have enjoyed, but which, on that day, was thoroughly frustrating.

At six o'clock, when Francis and Bella, having given up all hope of being able to reach Seumas before dark, had also almost given up hope of obtaining any food for him, Miss Proudfoot proposed that she and Bella should stroll around the garden for an hour or so, as the sunshine was by then less strong.

This gave Bella a sudden idea. 'May we walk by the lake and feed the swans, please?'

Thorsby Lake, lying between the road and the Hall, to the east of the drive, was very small, being little more than a large artificial pond, made by Sir John's father for his first wife, who had admired water scenery. There was little natural water scenery in the immediate vicinity of Thorsby, so Sir Charles had had a small beck diverted to form an artificial lake for her, planted its margin with willow trees and stocked it with water fowl and a pair of swans, which had bred and increased. On a summer evening it made a pleasant short walk to stroll around this little lake, and Bella always enjoyed feeding the ducks and the swans, although on this occasion she had an ulterior motive for her request.

'Of course you may, dear. Ring the bell and ask for some stale bread.'

This was not what Bella wanted to do, and if she failed in her next move, she foresaw herself walking beside Miss Proudfoot all around the lake, surreptitiously breaking off two bits of bread each time, throwing one into the water to the swans, and concealing the other somewhere about her for Seumas's supper.

'As it is Sunday, Miss Proudfoot, would it be kind in me to go down to the kitchen and fetch the bread for myself?'

Miss Proudfoot, rather surprised and quite pleased by this offer – mor for its signs of pious observance of the day of rest than for its indications of thoughtfulness for the servants – readily gave her permission; and Bella, before the governess could change her mind, hurried off to the kitchen, where Cook gave her half a stale loaf. It was really very stale, and fit only for the swans and ducks; but she supposed that Seumas would find it better than being hungry. And anyway, she told herself, he must often have eaten worse, and less, since the battle of Culloden.

She thanked Cook and took the bread; then, once out of the kitchen, hastily broke off a portion for the birds, meaning to run upstairs with the remainder and conceal it in her room. But as she approached from the back part of the house, she saw Miss Proudfoot already waiting for her in the hall near the foot of the stairs, a light shawl over her Sunday gown. Miss Proudfoot was facing the front door and had not seen her coming. Bella stepped aside into the shadows beside the tall grandfather clock which stood against the wall and thought rapidly. Then, the proximity of the clock bringing the idea to her mind, she tiptoed quickly from her hiding place, and with one eye on Miss Proudfoot, opened the case of the clock, dropped in the bread and closed the case again. Then she walked forward demurely to Miss Proudfoot, holding her rather small offering for the swans. 'Here I am, ma'am. I have the bread.'

'Very well, Annabel dear. Come along.'

They went out through the front door, along the terrace and down the steps, Bella a little breathless from her narrow escape.

When they returned from their stroll, Francis managed to convey to Bella that he had been unable to collect any food at all since their last, few, hurried words at five o'clock; and Bella told him to fetch, at the first opportunity he had, the bread which she had hidden in the clock.

'In the clock!' he whispered. 'Lord, Bella! Are you out of your mind? You might have stopped it. Then there would have been a fussation.'

'There was nowhere else,' she whispered back.

Later, Francis told her that he had just made a vain attempt to pick the lock of Mrs Keighley's store-closet to get at the candles which, among many other things, were kept there; and so, had been obliged to take another two expensive wax ones from the larger drawing-room. Also, he told her, he hoped, before bedtime, to collect some more wine.

8

As on the previous night, they made ready in good time for their walk to the Dower House. Bella dressed and put on her nightshift over her clothes and slipped back into bed to wait; and Francis sat up with his book. This time he was not as tired, so he found the adventures of Joseph Andrews and Parson Adams rather more amusing, and the minutes did not seem to pass so slowly. Being less tired, he had decided not to set his alarm watch and go to bed; and as there had been no need to undress for bath night, he had not bothered to take off his clothes. He had merely removed his coat and put on his dressing-gown, in case, by a most unlikely chance, anyone should enter his room.

Once again, no one was late to bed, and Francis was tapping at the door of Bella's room slightly before midnight. A little less excited tonight, and sure that Francis would not fail to rouse her to go with him, Bella had allowed herself to doze off. She was fully awake and sitting up in bed, alert and eager, however, as soon as Francis had opened her door. Getting downstairs and out of the house proved as successful as on the previous night, though it was every bit as nerve-racking to accomplish.

They had little enough to take with them this time, though Bella had put into the basket a jar of salve for cuts and bruises which Old Nurse prepared regularly from woundwort, houseleeks, burdock leaves, and prunella when they were in season, and, on Francis's suggestion, her tinder-box, so that they might have a light immediately on arrival at the Dower House. But as well as the bread and another decanter – this time of brandy – there was a round, flat cheese in the basket. Francis, inspired by the sight of Bella's half-loaf as he had brought it out from its hiding-place in the clock, had made his way cautiously to the dairy to look for cheese. In the Sunday-evening emptiness of the well-scrubbed dairy, he had hurried to the shelves where the newly-made cheeses were set to ripen; flat discs laid out in order of age. Carefully moving several others to conceal the traces of its abstraction, he had taken one of them, hoping that neither of the two dairymaids would remember how many there had originally been. Bella was delighted by this addition to Seumas's meal, and full of praise for Francis's cleverness, which did much to blunt the still painful memory of his dinner-time humiliation.

He had also had another good notion, as he now informed Bella, while they were walking quickly across the park in the darkness, for the moon had not yet risen. 'We cannot leave the front door of the Dower House unlocked for many days, in case someone should try to get in. And we cannot possibly keep the key from the office, for it would most certainly be missed during the daytime if it were not there on its peg. You know how fidgety Mr Thompson is: I would not mind betting that he counts all the keys every time he goes into the office. But neither can we continually be taking the risk of borrowing it. So I thought that if we were to unbolt the back door tonight, we could use that in future. From the park, it is quicker and more convenient to enter the house by the back door, so it would be an advantage to us. It's a pity that Mr Macdonald cannot bolt the back door after us and then let us in when we come – we could have a special signal knock, so that he would know it was we who were there – but, of course, so long as he cannot walk easily, that would be impractical.'

'Perhaps that could be done when his foot is better,' suggested Bella. 'If he felt truly safe here, he might stay a little longer – perhaps until it is possible for him to go back home to the Highlands.' She let her thoughts drift off into a daydream of months-long, thrilling aid to the fugitive, culminating in the return of a fully recovered and happy Mr Macdonald to his rejoicing Highland family, calling down blessings on her and Francis for having restored to them the master of the house.

Her thoughts were broken into by Francis's saying, 'I hope all is well with him and that his arm is not worse. It is unfortunate that we did not have the time to take another look at it last night.'

'And I hope he does not think that we have deserted him and do not mean to come again,' said Bella. 'We have had to leave him alone for so long.'

'Of course he will not think that!' Francis was scornful. 'I told him that we would come back.'

This seemed to Bella hardly reason enough for unquestioning confidence in their return; but she said nothing to Francis, not wishing to provoke his further disdain.

Whether or not Seumas had believed himself deserted by them, they never knew, for he made no mention of the long time they had left him alone. When they had let themselves in through the front door, Francis, kneeling on the flag-stones of the hall, lit with Bella's tinder-box one of the candles he had brought, while Bella felt her way cautiously along the wall to the door of the Chinese room, gently opened the door a crack and called into the pitch darkness, 'Do not be afraid, Mr Macdonald, it is only my brother and myself.'

Seumas called back to her loudly and gaily and in a strangely excited voice, 'Why, it's glad I am to see you – or shall be when there's a glim to see you by.'

'I am sorry we are so late, but we could not get away before. I hope you have not been hungry and lonely, all by yourself in the dark.'

'Och, it has not been dark all the time. And it's not hungry I am, but thirsty. I have a raging thirst on me, I could be drinking up the Thames. And why should I be lonely in this fine house, and I with the banshee to keep me company? And were you not here yourselves not long since to bring me food and drink? And we talked, too – though of what we talked I'll be confounded if I can remember now. What was it, will you kindly be telling me?'

His voice, cheerful as it was, sent cold shivers down Bella's spine, coming out of the darkness at her; and she was thankful when Francis got a spark and lit the candle and the shadows surged forward in a vain attempt to put it out. She hung back and let Francis go first into the room with his light and set it in the kitchen candlestick on the floor by the couch.

Seumas was sitting up in his improvised bed. The blankets were rumpled and awry, the rug and two of the cushions had fallen to the floor, where the decanter lay on its side, empty.

'Sure and it's good to see you again. I watched for you from the glaze, you know. Faith! It's a fine view you have from this window, right across the river and the sun shining on it fit to dazzle a man.' He talked on a little wildly, his eyes catching the light of the candle and glittering, his lean cheeks no longer pale, but flushed now, and his tongue darting out to moisten his dry lips after every few words.

Francis and Bella looked at one another. With the help of the stick and the furniture piled in the middle of the room, he might well have reached the window and looked out between the curtains: but there was no fine view from that window, only a corner of the garden – certainly no river.

'He is feverish,' whispered Francis. 'It must be the bullet wound troubling him. We had best take a look at it immediately.'

Bella started to unpack the things out of the basket and set them on the floor. She glanced up. 'Would you care for some bread and cheese? I am afraid that it is all we could bring you.'

'It's not hungry I am. But is that drink you have there?'

'Yes, brandy.'

'Then give it to me, for the love of heaven. And be quick about it. My throat's afire.'

She hesitated and said in a low voice, 'Francis, if he is feverish, ought he to have brandy? Is it not unwise to drink wine when one is in a fever?'

Francis shrugged his shoulders. 'I believe it is, but that is all there is for him to drink. Give it to him, Bella.' He added, 'After all, if you are going to dress his wound, he will need to drink something strong.'

Half reluctantly, Bella removed the stopper and offered the decanter to Seumas. He grabbed it, stretching out his good arm, and raised it with both hands, gulping down the brandy in great draughts. When he paused for breath the decanter was empty and he all but dropped it on the floor as his fingers unclosed from about it. Bella rescued it and replaced the stopper.

'Och, that was rum booze and no mistake, and I needing it and all.'

'It was brandy, not rum,' said Bella kindly; but he paid her no attention.

'It's all bowman everything seems after it.' Seumas went on talking, but they could make little sense of it, and his voice became more and more blurred and indistinct, until he lay back, his head sprawled across the remaining cushion.

'He's drunk,' said Francis. 'Let's take the bandage off now.'

He held up the candlestick while Bella unknotted the napkin which she had tied around his arm. It had stuck to the edges of the wound and would not come away easily. She hesitated.

'Pull it off quickly,' advised Francis.

'I cannot. It will hurt him.'

'It hurts less if one does it quickly,' he urged.

But Bella could not bring herself to do it. With an impatient exclamation, Francis handed her the candlestick and pulled off the napkin himself. Seumas gave a groan and attempted to twist away, and he mumbled something about their trying to do for him. Bella held the light closer. The long scratch was inflamed and swollen.

'You will have to wash it and put on Old Nurse's ointment and tie it up again with the bandages you brought yesterday, Bella.'

'I . . . I cannot,' faltered Bella. 'I would not know how to manage. You must do it, Francis.'

'Not I! I would not know either. But, anyway, it's nonsense about your not knowing. Of course you know. Girls always know such things. It's one of their few uses.'

'But what shall I wash it with?'

'I'll fetch you water from the kitchen while you make the bandages ready.' As Francis moved to take the candlestick from her, Bella pleaded, 'Don't leave me here in the dark.'

Francis lit the spare candle from the one in the candlestick and handed it to her, then, taking the candlestick, he went out to the kitchen, beyond the hall, at the back of the house. There, after a search in all the closets, he found a basin and took it to the well in the middle of the large, stone-flagged room. A cold current of air – even colder than the kitchen, but fresher and cleaner, somehow – came up the shaft of the well when he raised the lid. He lowered the bucket and brought it up full. He poured water into the basin and then found a jug and filled that, in case Seumas wanted to drink later, as he probably would. He was rather doubtful as to whether Seumas, even in his present condition, would be ready to drink water, that last resort of the thirsty; but, with the brandy finished, there was nothing else for him to drink.

Having taken care to replace the lid of the well and to leave the kitchen looking as undisturbed as possible, and having taken the opportunity of walking along the narrow passage between kitchen and still-room to unbolt the door to the back yard and kitchen garden while he was in that part of the house, he returned to the Chinese room, having to make two trips because of needing a hand for the candlestick each time. 'I should have had you go with me,' he said to Bella.

Bella made one final attempt to get Francis to undertake the dressing of the wound, but he declined firmly. 'Get on with it, Bella. What do you think girls are for if it's not for this kind of thing?'

So she got on with it, while he held the candle for her; and she managed, on the whole, not too badly, though she wavered when Seumas groaned and said, 'What in the world is it you're after doing to my poor arm, you fiends, and it almost shot away? Is it trying to do for me you are? And who may you be, anyway, and where am I?'

At last, however, the wound was washed as well as possible with cold water, liberally plastered with Old Nurse's salve and tied up with strips of Bella's worn-out shift.

Unquiet, but half-stupefied from having drunk on an empty stomach almost three-quarters of a decanter of best smuggled French brandy – for Sir John made a point of never inquiring too closely into the source of the brandy he purchased at such a reasonable price, being inclined to turn a blind eye to smuggling, so long as it benefited himself and his friends – Seumas had borne it remarkably well, all things considered; and between them Francis and Bella tidied up his bed, replacing the two fallen cushions under his restless head and covering him with the blankets and the rug – which he immediately tried to throw off again. They left the water and the tinder-box and the food near him; but, after a consultation, decided to put out the candle, in case, tossing uneasily, he should drop a cushion or a blanket on it and so start a fire. When they told him that they were going, he did not even seem aware of it, so they blew out the candle and groped their way to the front door. As arranged, they locked it after them. Just as they had done this, Bella exclaimed, 'Oh, we never remembered to unfasten the back door, so we shall have to bring the key again next time.'

'I remembered. I did it when I went to fetch the water.'

Bella, who had been afraid that Francis would have wanted them to return into the dark, silent house, that they might feel their way to the back door and unbolt it as planned, was very relieved.

They walked across the park by moonlight, both of them thoughtful and not a little concerned for Seumas.

'He really needs an apothecary,' said Bella after a long silence. 'I wish we could fetch Mr Seton to him.'

'Well, we cannot, so there's no use in wishing it.'

After another pause, Bella said hopefully, 'Mr Seton is a Scot, too. Perhaps he may be a Jacobite.'

'He is not. I know, because I heard him talking to Keighley when he came in January to bleed everyone. He was saying that the Stuarts were popish trouble-makers and as good as foreigners and that we did not want them over here.'

Bella was instantly indignant at Mr Seton. 'King George is a foreigner, too. And a trouble-maker, usurping King James's throne.'

'But not a papist as well,' said Francis drily. This was incontrovertible, and Bella could think of no reply to it.

'Poor Mr Macdonald,' she said after yet another worried pause. 'Do you think he'll . . . he'll . . . recover?'

'He'll recover, you will see,' said Francis determinedly, going on to say, with kindly reassurance, 'You managed very well, Bella. I wager Seton could not have done it better – under the circumstances,' he added, truthfulness getting the better of his good intentions.

9

On Monday everything promised to be much easier for them. It was decided that Francis should set off for the vicarage in very good time, looking in at the Dower House on his way, and taking with him anything that they had collected for Seumas by then; and that later, instead of going to meet Francis at the west gate, Bella should go to the Dower House and wait for him there. They further decided that as it was impossible to save enough food for Seumas from their meals, and since they would in future be able to go to the Dower House at other times than after dark, they could raid the Hall larder every night for food which could then be hidden in their rooms until Francis went to the vicarage the following morning. This seemed to them a very good plan, and one that could be put into operation every day except Saturdays and Sundays, and for those two days something else could no doubt be contrived.

Early on Monday, before Mr Thompson rode up from the village, Francis replaced the Dower House key in the office. He also returned the two decanters to the sideboard in the dining-room, thankful that, so far as he knew, the one day's absence of the claret had not been commented upon, and hoping that the emptiness of both decanters would not be noticed.

There was also the pressing necessity for candles to be dealt with that morning. Since Mrs Keighley always opened the closet where certain of the stores were kept, without fail on Monday mornings, to get supplies for the week, while waiting in the schoolroom for Miss Proudfoot to join them for breakfast, they planned a concerted assault upon the closet while the housekeeper had the doors unlocked. In the past, one or both of them had often enjoyed ten or fifteen minutes at the store-closet on a Monday morning with her, both for the fun of seeing all the rows of good things which lay upon the shelves – great jars of preserved fruit in syrup, each jar with a little brandy poured in at the top to prevent the fruit from going bad; small spice and herb and pepper jars; the stocks of Bohea tea; potted pigeon, chicken, venison, and tongue, all ground in a mortar and pressed into jars under a protecting layer of clarified butter, so that the meat would keep; quince marmalade, almonds, currants, and sugar loaves – as well as for the pleasure of receiving the handfuls of raisins, the figs, and dried apricots which she could usually be prevailed upon to give them. And so, though neither of them had done so for several months, she would see nothing strange in their turning up at closet-opening time that day.

But when the moment came, although they both knew she would not be surprised by it, they were nervous of exciting her suspicions, and they both tended to over-act their casualness; so that Mrs Keighley, no fool where young people were concerned, guessed at once that something was afoot. But – again, knowing young people – she presumed that they were after a substantial amount of titbits for themselves, and she was amused and ready to be generous.

They had approached her, Francis carrying three or four books and his riding cloak rather awkwardly – though nothing could have been more natural than that he should have been holding books and a cloak, since he was due to leave for the vicarage shortly. These he set down on the floor by the wall beside the closet when he and Bella crowded nearer, one on either side of the housekeeper, watching what she took out and asking questions about everything.

Mrs Keighley always had with her one of the maidservants and two big trays when she went to fetch large quantities of supplies from the store-closet and, as she took out the things which she wanted, she would lay them on a tray. When the tray was full, the girl would carry it to the kitchen and unload it on to the kitchen table, returning with the empty tray to find the other piled high with good things and ready for her.

After five minutes' chatter, designed to lull any doubts Mrs Keighley might have of their honest intentions, and a certain amount of help in taking from her hands various jars, sugar-loaves, and suchlike, and laying them on the tray for her; when the maid had just started off for the kitchen with her third heavy load, Francis stationed himself in front of that part of the closet which held, besides the neat piles of old linen for charring for tinder, the supply of candles made each month in hundreds and used – in winter, anyhow – in almost the same number. For special occasions – otherwise only for the exclusive use of the squire and his lady – there were candles of beeswax, those for Lady Rimpole's room being pleasantly perfumed; and for everyday use – and for everyone else but the master and mistress – rather smelly tallow candles made laboriously by dipping wicks into melted fat. In the long, light days of summer, the rate of consumption did not keep up with the rate at which they were made, so there were in the closet a great many candles laid away against the short, dark winter days, all tied together neatly in bundles of twelve, which were piled on top of each other on one of the shelves.

Francis gave Bella a nod and she moved casually along to the farthest end of the closet, looking at all the things it held, her eyes moving slowly downwards from top to bottom. Suddenly, as her glance reached the very lowest shelf of all, she gave a little scream, 'Oh, Mrs Keighley! I saw a mouse!' She whisked her skirts away and backed a pace or two.

Mrs Keighley instantly put down the jar of almonds of which she had just taken hold. 'A mouse? In my store-closet? Nonsense, Miss Annabel.'

'But there is one there. I saw something move, just here.' Bella pointed to the extreme corner of the bottom shelf and peered down at it from a safe distance.

'There's never been a mouse in here since I can remember. You're dreaming, Miss Annabel.'

'I'm not, truly. It was there. Or if it was not a mouse, then it was a huge spider or a little rat.'

'A rat! Eh, now, Miss Bella, you never did see a rat in my closet.' Mrs Keighley was so shocked by the possibility of a rat among her stores, that she quite forgot the refined speech she habitually affected when speaking to the family or to the lower servants, and lapsed into her comfortable, natural Yorkshire, the use of which she normally confined to her husband and to friends, like Cook. 'Happen it was a big spider – they get in everywhere – or even a dratted mouse, but not a rat. Never.'

She moved along the closet. 'Here, miss, let me look. If there is a mouse, me and t'cat will soon be shut of it, t'wretch.' Ponderously and rather creakingly she knelt down and peered at the bottom shelf, shifting bags of oatmeal and dried peas; while Bella, apparently bolder now that she had an ally against the enemy, knelt down beside her and made herself helpful.

Mrs Keighley's attention right off him, Francis swiftly took down a bundle of candles in each hand and laid them on the floor against the wall behind the open closet door at his end. Three times he did this, one eye on Mrs Keighley all the while, until he had six bundles safely captured. More he dared not take, in case she noticed the gaps he had made. The candle problem was now settled, but Bella still seemed to be holding Mrs Keighley's attention fully with her non-existent mouse. Quickly he scanned the shelves for something else which might be of use to Seumas; but the anxiety of the moment had dulled his wits and he was quite unable to make a choice. At random he snatched down four jars and laid them by the candles before he heard the maid's footsteps slip-slopping on the flagstones as she returned from the kitchen.

By then Mrs Keighley had decided that since there was no trace of mice, and since none of the stores at that end of the bottom shelf appeared to have been nibbled, Bella must either have seen a large spider or been imagining a movement on the shelf. Puffing, and with stays and hoop creaking, she heaved herself to her feet and was standing, her usual picture of respectable, black-clad dignity – though slightly out of breath – by the time the girl reached them.

Francis and Bella remained with the housekeeper until she closed and locked the closet door. While she turned the key in the lock, Francis kicked his cloak over the stolen goods and stood in front of them. Then with two last prunes apiece to nibble, following the maid with the fifth and final trayful, they escorted Mrs Keighley as far as the kitchen door, thanked her for the titbits, said good-bye to her and, safely alone, fled back to their prizes. Francis spread out his cloak and they laid everything on it, working with frantic speed. Then, holding his books in one hand and catching up his bundle by the cloak-ends, Francis hurried along the passage and dashed for the side door and the stable yard, where the grey pony, Sultan, should by now be waiting for him, with a gasped, 'I'll see you later. Remember where!' to Bella.

Bella made her way slowly upstairs to the schoolroom. Now that their raid for candles was over and successful, she felt as exhausted as if she had just taken part in some prodigious feat of physical endurance; and she was not at all sorry to have to sit down with her embroidery while Miss Proudfoot read to her an ode by Mr Cibber the Poet Laureate, whom she had once met and of whom, therefore, she thought very highly; though Bella considered the ode very tedious – as well as distasteful, being all in praise of the Hanoverian usurper.

Francis did not find it at all easy to mount Sultan while still keeping a firm grip on his bundle, but he dared not let it out of his hands. He snapped at the stable lad who offered to hold it for him, and he was distant and unsmiling towards old Robert, who had been groom to his grandfather and had watched Sir John grow up, because he was afraid that the old man – who often displayed a familiarity which would have been considered impertinent in any of the other outdoor servants – would otherwise comment jokingly on his bundle and ask him what it contained. He got away without mishap, however; though he had one very bad moment when he nearly lost hold of a corner of the cloak and his heart gave a sickening leap at the thought of its contents showering to the ground before the eyes of Robert and young Ben.

The old man and the lad looked after him as Sultan trotted into the park with Francis awkwardly clasping his bundle to him.

'Eh, but we are tutty today,' remarked young Ben. 'You'd have thought my hands were too mucky to touch his precious books or whatever they were. Nay, then, he can fitter, for all I care.'

Robert shook his head. 'He's nowt but a lad, for all his grown-up ways. Happen he'll leave all that behind soon. His father was never that road at his age. He was a real boy, he was, Sir John. Up to tricks and mischief any time and always one for a joke or a kind word – and he still is that, bless him. But Master

Francis, now, he never does owt wrong. It's not natural, not at his age, that it's not. But it's all on account of his being so sickly, like, when he was a bairn.' He shook his head again, sagely, and Ben nodded in agreement.

'Aye, happen you're right.'

Francis had been a good deal concerned as to how he would find Seumas; and it was with considerable trepidation that he made his way from the back door of the Dower House to the Chinese room, carrying the booty from the store-closet. But to his great relief Seumas seemed very much better. No longer so flushed and restless, and speaking quite rationally, he replied a little weakly but very cheerfully to Francis's rather hesitant, 'Good morning, Mr Macdonald. How are you today?'

Francis drew back the curtains from the middle of the window, enough to let in some light for Seumas, but not enough to allow anyone standing outside to see anything he was not meant to see. 'I think we should do best never to draw back the curtains any more than this, Mr Macdonald,' he said earnestly. 'And they must always be drawn across again, without fail, before a candle is lighted.' He then opened his bundle. 'I cannot stay long, as I have to go to the vicarage for lessons, but I have brought a supply of candles for you, enough for several days, and these jars of preserves.' Now, for the first time, he had an opportunity to see what was in the jars he had brought, and he was a little surprised to discover that he had seized a jar of cherries in syrup and some picked walnuts, as well as two jars of potted venison. He was rather inclined to frown over the cherries and walnuts as wasted efforts; but Seumas seemed amused and said he was partial to both.

Francis tidied Seumas's bed and fetched fresh water for him, with apologies for being able to offer nothing better for the moment and with promises of something more drinkable to follow. He then settled him, propped against the cushions, with a breakfast of cheese and stale bread and one of the jars of minced venison, before hurrying off to the vicarage. 'We shall both be here again after midday,' he said as he left. 'My sister should be there the first.'

'I shall be looking forward to seeing you both,' said Seumas, with his mouth full of cheese. Francis noted with relief that his appetite seemed good and that he appeared to be enjoying his breakfast.

As soon as the morning's instruction with Miss Proudfoot was over, Bella hurried out and made her way to the Dower House. She, too, was very apprehensive as to how she would find Seumas; but she let herself in through the back door and walked resolutely along to the Chinese room. She tapped on the door and turned the handle and then stood, reluctant to push open the door, afraid of what she might find on the other side of it. 'Mr Macdonald?' she called out anxiously, not really expecting an answer.

'Good morning to you, Miss Bella. Come in, ma'am. Your brother said that I was to be expecting you.'

Bella, overwhelmingly relieved, went in eagerly. 'You are better!' she exclaimed. 'Oh, I am so glad of it!'

'I had a good breakfast and then a good sleep and now it's fine I feel.'

He certainly did look and sound much better, she thought, remembering how he had been twelve hours before. 'How is your arm?' she asked.

'Not throbbing as it has been, thank you.'

Much bolder now than she had felt the night before, Bella unwrapped the bandage to see for herself. The wound appeared to be greatly improved.

'That will be due to the salve I put on it. My old Nurse makes it, you know, and she always says it will heal anything. She will be so pleased to know how well –' She stopped. 'Oh, no! Of course I cannot tell her, can I?'

He grinned at her. 'I doubt if she'd be all that pleased, if you did.'

'She would have a spasm. She is always threatening to do so, if ever I provoke her, but she never does have one. If she were to find out about you, though, I think she really would have a spasm. Do you not agree?'

'It's certain she would have a spasm. But for all her threatening, I promise you, there's no one who'd be more surprised by it than she.'

They laughed together over this; and in their laughter Bella's remaining fears for Seumas were swept away. No one who was going to die of his injuries could possibly laugh like that, she was sure. She put on more salve and bandaged his arm again. Then she looked at his ankle. It was still swollen and discoloured and very painful, but there seemed to be nothing she could do about it, as she admitted.

'Och, never you be worrying. Just a few days and it will be as good as ever.'

'When Keighley – he's the butler – fell off a ladder and sprained his ankle, he could not walk properly for four weeks,' she said dubiously.

'Now, would I not be out-doing a butler easily? I'll be running like a hare in no more than three weeks, you'll see.'

She hunted out some china which was packed away in baskets in one of the kitchen closets, and brought in two plates and a cup, and Seumas ate a dinner of bread and cheese and sticky cherries speared out of the jar on the end of his pocket-knife.

'I am sorry that it is such an odd dinner,' said Bella.

'Why, fit for a king it is, and I sitting up on as good as a throne in my fine palace.' He offered her a cherry, and though she felt that it was a little like taking food out of the mouths of the poor, to take it from someone who could so ill spare it, she was unable to resist, being particularly fond of preserved cherries.

Seumas looked about him. 'Sure and it's a fine house I'm in and no mistake, now that I've enough light to see it by. It is a shame such a house should be standing all alone and empty and no one in it but a banshee.'

This reminded Bella of the nocturnal horrors of the Dower House. 'Oh! Have you heard Lady Alice?'

'I have not.' He paused. 'Well . . . Let us be saying that I have not – not to be sure that it was she and not the mice. But it's only a short while I've been here, and I not feeling too lively for much of the time. So I may see her yet.'

'Grandmother saw her.'

'Did she now? Was it living here the old lady was, maybe?'

Bella nodded. 'All this furniture was hers. She had this room decorated in the Chinese manner. It is the very latest style in London, she told us. She did not like Francis and me very much: she considered children were a nuisance. She was not really our grandmother, you see, but only grandfather's second wife, our father's stepmother. She died about a year ago. She had a pug-dog and a grey parrot which talked – and pecked, if one were not careful.'

'And now the house stands empty? Would you care for another cherry?'

'Thank you.' She helped herself. 'When father dies and Francis inherits and he marries, mother will be able to come and live here.' She paused and reflected. 'But I somehow doubt if she will, because she likes London best. She will probably go and live in London. My aunt Norton lives in London, she is mother's middle sister. Her youngest sister is our aunt Bradshaw. She lives in Bristol, because our uncle Bradshaw has concerns there. He comes to see us sometimes, but Lord Norton says that Yorkshire is too far away for him, and so mother goes to stay with them in London instead, which she enjoys.'

By the time Francis arrived they were on the best of terms, chatting together about the peculiarities of the late Dowager Lady Rimpole and her rather unlikeable pets and sharing the cherries. Bella had a momentary qualm lest Francis should be annoyed to find her eating the provisions which he had obtained with such pains and daring for their guest; but he was far too pleased by Seumas's satisfactory improvement to care if Bella ate all the cherries and half the candles as well. Besides, he was well aware that, without her help, he could have managed to take nothing from the store-closet. Altogether, she had proved herself an invaluable ally in time of crisis, and his new-found respect and admiration for her were increasing daily.

That night they made the first of what were to become, for a time, their regular raids on the larder. Francis sat up reading until it was safe to go down to the kitchen; but Bella had not even tried to keep from falling asleep, and Francis had to wake her when he went to her room. They crept downstairs together, Bella carrying their ever-useful basket, and Francis a branched candlestick. As they were not leaving the house, they had both undressed and were wearing their dressing-gowns. It had been decided that if, by mischance, anyone should catch them, Bella was to try and hide herself in the shadows and hope to pass unnoticed, and to leave it to Francis to answer questions. He was going to pretend that he had been unable to sleep and had come down to the library to find a book. However, there was no one about and they reached the kitchen safely. Bella stood by the door while Francis took the candlestick over to the fire and lit the three candles from the embers. A shape detached itself from the darkness, inspected Francis and then moved over to Bella, two eyes glinting greenly in the light from Francis's first candle.

Bella bent down and stroked it. 'Puss, puss. Good puss.'

The cat, reassured by the fact that they were not strangers, but otherwise aloof and quite uninterested in them, faded away into the shadows again as Francis crossed the room to Bella with the lighted candles. Copper pots and pans winked at them from the walls and there was a brittle scrunching underfoot as they moved towards the larder, where Francis gave the candlestick to Bella. As he unlatched the door, Bella looked down at the flagstones. Cockroaches, black beetles and woodlice were scurrying away, disturbed by their crushing feet.

'Ugh!' Bella dropped the basket and drew up the hem of her dressing-gown.

'What is it?' Francis asked.

Bella pointed to the floor.

'They'll not hurt you.' He opened the larder door. 'Come on.'

Inside the larder it was cool and there was a strong smell of food of many kinds – not altogether pleasant a smell, since food keeps fresh for a shorter time in warmer weather – and the choice was so wide that it was difficult to know what to take and what to leave.

'No, not that,' said Francis, as Bella's hand hovered over an open custard pie. 'We must take only things which it will be possible to carry to the Dower House comfortably. Nothing which is easily squashed and spoiled will serve.'

In the end they decided on a large slice of veal pie, a leg of chicken, and four small pasties; and Francis, who had fetched a carving knife, cut a piece from what was left of the cold sirloin – while he was gone to look for the knife, Bella had taken the opportunity to break off and nibble a tiny morsel from the corner of a large uncut piece of freshly-baked parkin, and had found it delicious – and then, as an afterthought, when they left the larder they opened the bread bin and took half a loaf.

'I hope they do not notice that all these things are gone,' whispered Bella, putting the bread into the basket. 'We have taken a great deal, I am afraid.'

'How could they notice? There is so much here. Besides, each of them will think one of the others has taken it,' Francis whispered back.

Neither of them had more than the very vaguest notion about housekeeping, so Bella accepted Francis's statement and was reassured. And of some households it would indeed have been true; but Lady Rimpole was singularly fortunate in having a housekeeper and a cook, each of whom was conscientious and thrifty. On the following morning, both Mrs Keighley and Cook thought that certain things were missing from the larder, but neither said anything about it. After the third of the midnight raids, however, when each was quite convinced that she had not been mistaken, they mentioned their suspicions to one another, found they were in perfect agreement and decided that in future they would together look through the larder the last thing every evening to see what was in it, and again the first thing in the morning, to see if anything were missing: an arrangement which, eventually, had disastrous results.

Francis and Bella, quite unaware that their depredations had been noticed, continued their raids successfully and unchecked for several nights, to their great satisfaction and to the benefit of Seumas, to whom Francis, having hidden the food, wrapped in a napkin, under a layer of books in the basket, carried it every morning on his way to the village.

10

On the Tuesday morning, when Francis delivered the proceeds of the first night's raiding, he asked Seumas if there were any particular thing he would like brought to him. With the whole of the contents of the larder from which to choose, he was really thinking of food; but Seumas passed his hand across his face and said, 'Well, now, the thing I'd be most glad of is a razor. And, if you could manage it, a comb. I must be looking a scarecrow by now, and I once one of the bowman boys –' Abruptly Seumas stopped speaking, his eyes warily on Francis, who, having missed his last words, presumed that Seumas was suddenly concerned lest he had asked for too much, and made haste to promise to do what he might as soon as possible.

That very afternoon he made the attempt. The comb had been easy. He had a spare one of his own which still had most of its teeth; but the razor would, he was sure, prove far harder. At a moment when he was certain that Fowler, his father's valet, was not even on that floor, he slipped into his father's bedroom. He found Sir John's pair of razors lying in their case on his dressing-table. A thorough and rather nerve-racking search with his ears strained to listen for sounds of anyone approaching the room, failed to bring to light another razor. It would be impossible, he knew, to attempt to take one of the two in the case. It would be missed instantly the next morning; and Fowler, being Fowler, would have the whole house upside down and inside out while he looked for it. It was unthinkable that he would wait quietly and hope that it would turn up again. The only thing to do, Francis decided in the end, was for him to borrow the razor from its case after Fowler had shaved his father the next morning, carry it to Seumas on his way to the vicarage, explain the position and the need for haste, and bring it back with him at dinner-time and return it to its case. And then, on Saturday, if it proved possible, he would ride over to the little market town of Thirsk and buy Seumas a razor of his own – the purchase itself would provide no difficulty since, in this first week of June, he had a whole month's spending money to spare. This settled, Francis made his way with relief towards the door.

At the door he thought that, while he was there and the coast was clear, it would be an opportunity to take a clean shirt for Seumas, as his own was bloodstained and filthy, and Bella had all but torn the sleeve off it while dressing the bullet wound. Francis opened his father's clothes press. Sir John seemed to have numerous shirts, all laid neatly on top of one another in a pile, and would therefore be hardly likely to miss two, Francis thought. He took two from somewhere near the bottom of the pile, and then, for good measure, helped himself to an armful of underlinen as well. He had just closed the press and was picking up his booty, which he had temporarily laid on the floor, when he heard a hand on the door-knob. He had been aware of no footsteps approaching and he was taken by surprise. He bundled up the clothes, gave a wild look around him for a hiding place, and dashed for the bed. He flung the clothes under the bed and dropped down to the floor out of sight of the doorway just as the door opened and Fowler appeared, carefully balancing a pile of clean shirts in his arms as he shut the door behind him. A small man, hardly able to see over the top of his towering pile of shirts, he crossed the floor cautiously with his precious burden, stepping softly and deliberately – which accounted for Francis's not having heard his approach – and humming a little tune to himself. For Fowler loved his work and was happy only when he was busy; and having just finished ironing thirty-seven shirts – he always ironed his master's shirts himself, being convinced that anyone else would neglect the ruffled cuffs – he was supremely happy.

Francis was safely under the bed by the time Fowler reached the farther side where the press stood. The valet came to the bed – Francis could see his neatly shod feet only inches away from his nose – and laid the shirts down on it while he went to open the press. Then Francis heard the happy humming stop as Fowler gave an exclamation of surprise on examining the shelf which held shirts. He had obviously noticed that someone other than himself had been to the press. Oh, heavens! thought Francis with exasperation. Fowler would be bound to notice what no one else would notice. And I left it all so tidy, too.

But, as Francis, by lying flat upon the floor-boards, could see from beneath the edge of the brocade counterpane, which did not quite reach to the floor, it was not any disturbance caused by Francis in the press that was troubling him, but the fact that the pile of shirts, tall as it was, was smaller than he thought it should be. I might have known, Francis said to himself. I might have known.

Fowler was the one person in the household whom it would probably be impossible ever to deceive in his own domain. With his finicking meticulousness, he would instantly notice any change, however slight, in the precise order which always prevailed in his kingdom of Sir John's room.

Francis was suddenly seized with an overwhelming urge to sneeze, as he took in an unguarded breath and a speck or two of dust from the floor tickled his nostrils. He was only just in time to clap his hand over his face, stifling the impulse. His eyes began to run and he felt that at any second he would choke; but at last the sneezes were conquered and he was able to breathe normally – though cautiously – once more. By this time, Fowler was carrying all his master's shirts to the bed and spreading them out on it in twos and threes, as he calculated which were the missing ones, tut-tutting to himself as he did so. When he had satisfied himself, not that two shirts were indeed missing – he had known that since the moment of opening the press – but exactly which ones they were, he proceeded to look for them.

First he searched the whole of the press, taking out everything and laying it on a clean towel spread on the floor at his feet; and then putting it away again, shelf by shelf. He did the same with the chest of drawers and the drawer of the dressing-table. After that, having exhausted all the likely spots where two shirts might have been misplaced – not that it was at all probable, with Fowler in charge of them, that two shirts would ever be misplaced – he started on the unlikely spots: under the cushions on the window-seat, in the powder closet, in the cupboard of the night-table, even peering into the tiny little drawers

under Sir John's dressing mirror, though they would have been far too small to hold more than the ruffles of a shirt, and lifting up, one by one, his wigs on their stands – two bob wigs, two tye wigs, a bag wig for wear with full dress, a scratch wig for sporting occasions and two pig-tail wigs – though there could not possibly have been a shirt folded up under any one of them. Finally there remained only the bed. This had been left until last, because to search it would necessitate first removing all the shirts which had been laid out on it.

By this time, certain of eventual discovery – since Fowler would be bound to look under the bed, even before stripping it to look in it – Francis, who had been desperately racking his brains for some excuse for being found hidden beneath his father's bed with a bundle of clean linen taken from the press, had concluded that the only thing for it was to pretend that it was all a childish trick to annoy Fowler. He had decided that, when Fowler approached the bed to begin collecting the shirts, he would stretch out his hands, grab hold of both of Fowler's skinny ankles, shout 'Boo!' and leap – or rather, owing to his position, crawl – out from under the bed. What the result of this piece of madness would be to his fourteen-year-old dignity, he dared not think. Even if word of it got no further than Fowler – who might just possibly, to save his own dignity, not report it to Sir John – he would never, he was sure, in all his life, be able to see Fowler again without blushing. But a desperate situation needs desperate measures. If the existence of Seumas were to be kept secret, then Francis was ready to do even this, hard though it might be, and sacrifice dignity for the Cause.

But he was, miraculously, spared. Fowler was still four feet away from the bed when Sir John entered the room. Francis heard his surprised voice from the doorway.

'Good lord, Fowler! What are you doing, man?'

'Two of your honour's shirts are missing, and I have been trying to find them.' Fowler spoke as though he were announcing some immensely tragic disaster. 'I cannot think what has become of them. Nothing like this has happened to me since I have had the privilege of serving you, sir.' He sounded almost in tears.

'Heavens, man! All this pother over two shirts. What nonsense! They are probably in the wash.'

'No, sir, they are most certainly not in the wash. Your honour has eleven shirts in the wash and I have just returned seven-and-thirty clean shirts to this room, which means that there should be four-and-twenty shirts in the press. But I can find only two-and-twenty. I have searched all the room except the bed, and I am about to strip that and search it.'

'Why in the world should there be any shirts hidden in the bed!'

'I have no notion, sir. But then, nor have I, neither, any notion why there should be two shirts short in the press.' Fowler seemed to have plucked up his spirits a little and he now sounded almost accusing.

'And nor have I. But never mind about the shirts, Fowler. I want my grey camlet riding coat, the buckskins, and my riding boots.'

'But I must mind about the shirts, sir. It is a very serious matter indeed if your honour's garments are allowed to vanish in this mysterious manner. I–'

'Oh, confound the shirts, Fowler! I want my riding clothes and my scratch wig.'

'Yes, sir, but –'

'Fowler, I do not want to hear any more about those shirts. Nor do I want to see any more shirts. Put those shirts away and bring me my buckskin breeches.'

'Sir –'

Sir John was suddenly struck by an idea which he afterwards told his wife he considered both providential and brilliant. He said with elaborate casualness, 'I gave Lady Rimpole some things the other day for her poor basket.' He paused.

'Yes, sir?' Fowler's voice was brittle with apprehension.

'It is possible that those two shirts were among them. Indeed, now that I come to think about it, I am almost sure that is what I did with them,' lied Sir John glibly.

'Two of your honour's second best shirts in her ladyship's poor basket!' Fowler's voice rose to a wail. 'Oh, sir, how could you?' He was utterly overcome and repeated, 'Oh, how could you?'

Sir John suddenly roared, 'Fowler, put those confounded

shirts away this moment or I'll give them all to her ladyship, and fetch me the grey riding coat and everything else I want.'

There was complete silence for a few seconds, then Fowler said coldly, 'Very good, sir,' and proceeded, slowly and deliberately, to return the shirts from the bed to the press, two by two; while Sir John sat down on a chair and waited, half exasperated and half wanting to laugh; and Francis, lying full length under the bed, bit his wrist agonizingly as he felt the hysterical laughter rise up in him almost irresistibly.

Eventually the shirts had been put away to Fowler's satisfaction, Sir John had been dressed and had departed downstairs, and Fowler, after tidying away his master's discarded clothes, had, without a backward glance at the room where he had been so disgracefully slighted, walked out and off to his own quarters for an hour's enjoyable sulking; and Francis was at last able to come out from under the bed, bringing his booty with him. As he stood up, he sneezed violently, three times.

Safely back in his own room with the door shut, he dropped the shirts and underlinen on to a chair and began to smile. Then suddenly there presented itself to his inner vision the spectacle of himself, had Fowler been one yard nearer the bed, grabbing the little man's legs and shouting 'Boo!' just at that very moment when his father entered the room. His smile died at the harrowing thought, and he sat down, trying to shut the appalling picture out of his mind; and then relief flooded over him. All was well: he had not been caught. He began again to smile and, a moment later, to laugh. He laughed and laughed, uncontrollably, rocking on the chair, his hands over his face.

However much talk there might have been in the village on the engrossing subject of the fugitive and his pursuers, Francis heard none of it on his way to and from the vicarage each day. Unlike his father, he was not one for chatting amiably with his inferiors. Although, with those older, upper-servants at the Hall, under whose affectionate eyes he had passed his fourteen and a half years of life, he did, to an extent, relax his reserve, his intercourse with the villagers of Thorsby was mainly confined to acknowledging their greetings. So that now, although he would have found it helpful to have known what was being said about Seumas, and whether it was supposed that he had left the district or not, Francis dared not question anyone, lest he should thereby arouse suspicions regarding his motives. As it happened, in spite of the distance he customarily maintained, there was not one of his father's tenants who would have thought it other than the most natural thing in the world that even Master Francis should show interest in the first really exciting thing that had happened in Thorsby for months; and though normally quite intelligent enough to have realized this, under the present circumstances, with his conscience troubling him, Francis was unable to view his own behaviour objectively. For the same reason, he dared not ask questions at home, but waited for someone to bring the subject up in his presence – which no one happened to do. Dr Mortlake, also, was no help. He was far too scholarly and unworldly to be interested in so mundane a matter as the pursuit of a Jacobite or any other man by the militia or anyone else, and he would have paid such a pursuit scant attention had it been going on right under his straight, thin nose. As a result, not offered the information he wanted, and not daring to ask for it, Francis finally persuaded himself – and Bella, as well – that, if everyone else had not supposed that the fugitive had left the district, he would have been bound, by that time, to have heard someone say so. As it was, this was exactly what everyone else did believe, though this did not prevent the villagers from continuing to discuss the topic among themselves, or from remaining hopefully on the lookout for the return of a suspicious stranger.

On the Wednesday of that first week in June, the morning after Francis's ordeal in his father's room, Seumas insisted that if Francis drew the water from the well for him and filled a basin and left it on the table in the kitchen for him, he could make his way there without mishap. 'Better the kitchen than here,' he said. 'For I'd not want to be splashing water on your grandmother's furniture.'

'There will be no hot water for shaving,' said Francis dubiously.

'Och, I can manage with cold, and not for the first time, neither.'

'And you'll be careful and not fall along the passage?'

'I'll be taking it at a snail's pace. Have I not all the time in the world to be doing it?'

Hoping for the best, Francis left him; and he must have managed successfully, however long it took him and whatever difficulties he encountered, for when Bella arrived, soon after midday, he was sitting on the couch, washed and shaven, with his hair combed and tied back and wearing his clean shirt – or rather, Sir John's clean shirt.

'Oh, Mr Macdonald! How different you look!' Bella was surprised into exclaiming.

'Do I not!' he laughed. 'Indeed, it's a new man I feel.'

'I like you better without a beard.' She knew that personal remarks were impolite, but she had said it without thinking, and then, realizing what she had done, hoped he would not mind.

'I like myself better without a beard,' he retorted gaily.

'You look much younger.'

'And why should I not look younger, and I only four-and-twenty?' He chuckled. 'Though I do not doubt that four-and-twenty seems very old to you, Miss Bella.'

She considered four-and-twenty. 'It is not as old as father, and it is exactly ten years older than Francis. I am only eleven, and I expect that eleven seems very young to you.'

'Eleven is a fine age to be, and one is only eleven once, so one should make the most of it.'

'Can you remember what it was like to be eleven, Mr Macdonald?'

'Faith! Can I not? But I remember fourteen better, for that's when I left home, and I never went back again.'

She waited for him to go on, but he seemed to be lost in his thoughts. After a while she prompted further speech by asking, 'Was your home in the Highlands at that time?'

He looked up. 'In the Highlands?' He seemed suddenly to recollect what they had been talking about, for he said, 'Sure and it was in the Highlands. Where else would it be and I a Highlander?'

'What is it like in the Highlands?'

'Och, it's all hills it is. And . . . and heather . . . and mist and . . . and sheep.'

'Do you love it very much?'

He looked at her thoughtfully before replying, 'Well now, is not a man always supposed to love his own home and the place where he was born?'

She thought it over and then said, 'I think that perhaps I love Yorkshire, though I love it more in the summer than in the winter. My mother loves London best, though she was born in Devonshire. She would like to live in London, as our aunt Norton does. She says that it is always gay in London, and there is so much to do and to see and to talk about. And the Court is there and all the latest fashions and Mr Handel's oratorios.' She was silent for a while, contemplating all these delights which she had not yet known; until consideration of the Court at St James's sent her thoughts off like an arrow. She looked up. 'Mr Macdonald, have you ever seen the Prince?'

Her eyes, eager and shining, were willing him to say he had. He smiled into them. 'I have.'

'What is he like?'

'Och, a fine young man he is and all. You'll not be finding many like him in this world.' Starting hesitantly, he seemed to warm to his narration. 'Sure and it's noble and handsome he is, and every inch a prince. About my height, he'd be, and all dressed in crimson when I saw him, and riding a great white horse. He had gold buttons on his coat and diamond buckles on his shoes. So brave and bold he looked, that a man just seeing him would have been ready to follow him to hell – and farther. And he holding his shining sword aloft till the sun could be catching it as though it had been dipped in blood, and all the clansmen gathered round and shouting out for him. Och, it's drawn the heart out of you it would, Miss Bella, and the tears from your eyes, so that you no longer cared whether you lived or died – so long as you lived or died for him, the darling man.'

When he had finished, his voice sinking down low and fading away, there were indeed tears in Bella's eyes, and all she could say was, 'Oh, how I wish that I could have been there to see him.'

When Francis arrived, a few minutes later, the magic of the scene was still with her. 'Oh, Francis,' she said, 'Mr Macdonald has seen the Prince, and he has been telling me about him.'

'Did you really, sir? Do tell me! What is he like?'

Seumas told them again, while they both sat enthralled; Francis as moved as Bella. And this time Seumas added some details which he must have forgotten the first time.

Walking back to the Hall for dinner, they talked about the Prince all the way, envying Seumas the glory of having fought for him.

After that day, they questioned Seumas often on his experiences with the Prince's army. At their request he told them of the battles of Prestonpans and Falkirk, and of the bloody disaster of Culloden. After starting diffidently and a little hesitantly – perhaps as though loath to remember those things – once launched upon his subject, his rich, warm, lilting voice would carry them spellbound with him at will, up the heights of honour, glory, and triumph or down to the depths of sorrow, despair, and defeat; until the vibrant tones died away into silence and, the spell broken, they found themselves back in the Dower House, dust-sheeted furniture all around them and ten minutes to go till dinner-time, so that they had to scramble to their feet with hasty farewells, and run down the back garden path to where Francis's pony waited patiently, tethered to one of the gnarled old apple trees in the little orchard. Hastily Francis would lift Bella on to Sultan's back, mount himself, and urge Sultan into a quick trot across the park towards the everyday, prosaic world which consisted of such things as Miss Amelia Proudfoot and schoolroom dinners.

Francis had taken to tethering Sultan in the orchard of the Dower House, so that, hidden by the garden wall, he would be out of sight of anyone walking through the park. By the end of that first week of June, Sultan had cropped a circle of grass around six of the trees, and Francis and Bella were beginning to wonder what one of the gardeners from the Hall would think of it, when he came with his scythe in July, to cut the grass at the Dower House; as someone was sure to do, now that there was no longer a gardener attached there.

But that was one of those problems about which they only

worried themselves when they were not with Seumas. When they were with him, questioning him and listening to him, any risk seemed worth the running, and any lies worth the telling, for his sake.

11

DURING the course of that week, various articles had found their way from the Hall to the Dower House, to the increased comfort of its occupant. They included soap and a towel, Francis's watch, a steady supply of wine, several books and two old copies of the *Gentleman's Magazine*.

It had been about halfway through the week that Francis had considered how dull it must be for their guest, all by himself with nothing to do. A few books would be the very thing to help to pass the time, he had thought. He had almost taken one with him on next going to the Dower House; but then he had remembered hearing of the ignorance and illiteracy of so many of the Scottish Highlanders, and he had decided that it might be tactless to take Seumas a book to read without first finding out whether he could read or not.

As it turned out, his tact had been unnecessary. In reply to his casual, 'Would you care for it, Mr Macdonald, if I were to bring you a book to read?' Seumas had replied promptly, 'It's very grateful I'd be for something to read.'

'Have you any preference?'

'I have not. Any book at all would be welcome, though I'd rather it were nothing too pious or too learned, since I am neither, myself.'

After that, in the days that followed. Francis was to take him, in succession, all the volumes of Clarendon's *History of the Rebellion*, and *A Journal of the Plague Year*; then, fearing that he might possibly have considered both these works too learned, *The History of the Life of Mr Jonathan Wild the Great* – over which Seumas smiled a good deal to himself – *Hudibras*, *Memoirs of a Cavalier*, *The History of Colonel Jack*, the two copies of the *Gentleman's Magazine*, and *Pamela, or Virtue Rewarded*.

On the Saturday morning, under the pretext of buying a book needed for his studies, Francis obtained his father's permission to ride over to Thirsk with a groom. In Thirsk he bought a razor for Seumas. That afternoon, at their earnest request, Miss Proudfoot said that Bella might walk with him in the park. As soon as dinner was over, they hurried to the Dower House and spent the afternoon with Seumas. It was an enjoyable afternoon; they all talked and laughed a lot – Seumas quite as much as the two of them.

The Monday following was Lady Rimpole's morning for driving around the village and the neighbouring cottages, visiting the poorer tenants and distributing among them food and discarded clothing and comforting words; at doing all of which she was very adept and gracious. She often took Bella with her on these monthly rounds, and on Sunday she had expressed the wish that the next day should be one of those occasions.

Accordingly, after breakfast on Monday, when she was ready, wearing her blue damask round gown and a wide-brimmed hat tied on with blue ribbons, Bella went to her mother's room as she had been bidden and found Lady Rimpole still in the hands of Stubbs, her dresser, who was putting the finishing touches to her coiffure. Stubbs had a remarkably deft hand, and seemed to know instinctively just the right effect to aim for in her mistress's toilet upon any given occasion, and hardly ever needed a word of instruction in the matter. The ravishing and fashionable results of her ministrations to hair and dress accorded strangely with her own sour, puritanical temper and with the pursed-up expression she habitually wore because she considered it gave her an appearance of gentility.

Lady Rimpole offered a cheek for Bella to kiss, while at the same time tweaking one of Old Nurse's carefully contrived curls into place and smoothing the tucker at her neck. 'Good morning, Annabel, my dear. I'll not be above a minute or two longer. Go and sit down and be patient for a moment until Stubbs has finished with me.'

Bella sat down and watched. Her mother had on one of her plainest gowns, of mulberry damask, so that she might not appear too finely dressed by contrast with those whom she was to visit; and, bearing in mind the width of cottage doorways, she was wearing it over her narrowest hoop.

Three minutes later Stubbs stepped back, her head on one side, to survey her handiwork. 'That, I think, is satisfactory, my lady,' she declared.

Lady Rimpole looked at her reflection in the mirror. 'Perfectly, thank you, Stubbs.' She reached for her gloves from the dressing table, and Stubbs took up the scarlet cloak which was lying across the back of a chair. At that moment there was a knock at the door and, on being bidden, Mrs Keighley came in, her round face flushed, her expression perturbed and her spotless white mob-cap very slightly awry.

'Oh, my lady, I know you are about to go out, but if you could spare me a minute before you go, I'd esteem it an honour and be grateful. I'd not keep your ladyship above five minutes.' In her agitation the Yorkshire accent was beginning to show through more than usual, though her choice of words was still genteel.

Stifling a sigh, Lady Rimpole took off the glove which had been half on and laid it on her lap. 'Willingly, Mrs Keighley. What did you wish to tell me?'

Mrs Keighley hesitated, with a half-glance at Stubbs; and Lady Rimpole, understanding, said, 'There is no need for you to wait, Stubbs. I am sure you will wish to start ironing my riding habit for this afternoon.'

She smiled, but Stubbs's tone was icy with disapproval when she replied. 'Very good, my lady.' Her nose in the air, she stalked past Mrs Keighley and out of the room her demeanour showing plainly what she thought of being turned out of a room to oblige a Yorkshire rustic.

Mrs Keighley ignored her and advanced farther into the room, a comfortable Yorkshire body who was at the moment well on the way to being uncomfortable.

'Oh, my lady, do forgive me for troubling you like this, but I thought you could tell me what I should do. It's this new girl, Bessie Barnsley, my lady, and I'm sure I don't know what to do about her.'

'Barnsley? Which one is she? The plump, fair one who has

not been here longer than two months?' Lady Rimpole recollected perfectly well which was Bessie, but she fully knew the value of pretending absolute reliance on a good housekeeper.

'That's Bessie. Been here just the two months, she has. Oh, I know I should not have taken her on in the first place and her with a lazy good-for-nowt as a father, who never does a stroke of work and has been suspected of poaching often and often, though he's never yet been caught, so well does the devil look after his own – if your ladyship will pardon my saying so – but she begged me to give her a chance and I thought it unchristianlike to hold it against her that her father's what he is, so I took her on, my lady, and now I wish I hadn't, though she's the best worker I've had for the good Lord knows how long and willing and all, and I had great hopes of her, my lady.'

She stopped for breath and Lady Rimpole asked, 'Why, what has the girl done?'

In low, shocked tones, Mrs Keighley replied, 'She's been stealing, my lady.' Then she burst out. 'Oh, my lady, nowt of t'sort has been at t'Hall since Keighley and I have been in charge, and I'd not have had it be for the world. She denies it, of course, my lady, though I have talked and talked to her and so has Keighley – I even said I might be willing to overlook it this once if she confessed – but she still swears she did not do it, t'little slut. But that I cannot believe, my lady, because there's never been owt like it here before, and she's the only new one – save young Edward and he's been here a six-month besides being too gaumless to steal a crumb – so it must be her.'

She stopped again, seemingly quite overcome and at a loss to express adequately her regret and distress at the calamity; and Lady Rimpole had a chance to inquire, 'But what has she been stealing?'

'Food, my lady. Food. Good food as was meant for his honour's own table. Every night it's gone from t'larder. Cook and I, we've kept an eye on t'larder ever since we first noticed, and she can bear me out in what I say.'

Bella, who had been listening with interest to the details of this domestic crisis, suddenly stiffened. Her jaw dropped slightly and her interest changed into appalled incredulity. She hardly heard Mrs Keighley's next few words as she contemplated the disaster which had overtaken her and Francis.

'It's not as though we're not well fed here, as your ladyship knows. The servants lack for nowt – not like in some houses I could name but won't – and each time she takes far more than she could eat, even for a growing girl. It's not in her room, neither, because I've looked. I thought that happen she might be giving it to that father of hers, but she swears he's off on one of his ploys and she's not seen him since she's been here and, indeed, Will Bradford says that Barnsley's not been seen around t'village for weeks. But it must be Bessie who's taken the food, because who else could it be?'

'How long has this stealing been going on?'

'About a week, my lady.'

'Has she stolen anything before?'

'Nowt. Nowt at all.' She shook her head vigorously, then she remembered and added, 'Her first week here, I caught her finishing half a custard which was not meant for her, but I gave her a good scold and she promised not to do it again and I believed her, the more fool I – if your ladyship will pardon the manner of speaking. But then new young lads and lasses very often do try to take any food they can lay their hands on, the first week or so, my lady. It's often the first time in their lives that they've had enough to eat and they are making sure of it while it's there, so to speak. It soon stops, once they know there's always going to be plenty for them.'

Lady Rimpole nodded, and then she brought Mrs Keighley firmly to the point of all her rigmarole. 'It is a pity she has not admitted it, but you seem satisfied that she is the thief. In what way do you wish me to help you, Mrs Keighley?'

'Tell me if your ladyship thinks I'd do best to turn her off, as I want to do. Keighley says give her another chance because she's a right good worker, and willing and clean. But I say she does not deserve another chance, sticking to her lies and denying it and all. So I said to Keighley that I'd ask your ladyship, and do what your ladyship says.'

Bella held her breath while her mother considered the matter.

After a minute or so of deliberation, Lady Rimpole said, 'I think I agree with you, Mrs Keighley. Give the girl the rest of her first six months' wages – the family probably needs it – and send her home.' She smiled in dismissal and began once more to put on her gloves.

Bella, unable to bear it any longer, jumped to her feet. Bessie might be only a village girl and one of the under-servants and of no importance at all, but it seemed very unfair that she should be blamed for something she had not done. 'No, mother! Please give her another chance!'

Lady Rimpole's lovely brow wrinkled in surprise, and Mrs Keighley's mouth opened into a startled gasp. Her mother had for the moment forgotten Bella was there, and Mrs Keighley had not even noticed her.

'Mercy! Are you here, then, Miss Bella? You fair startled me, springing up like a jack-in-a-box.'

'Why ever not, Annabel?'

There was a pause while they both waited for her to speak, Lady Rimpole amused and Mrs Keighley incredulous.

Bella opened her mouth and shut it again, several times, struggling for a reason. The true one it was impossible to give. She found words at last, though they were very inadequate. 'Because ... Oh, because ... she is a pleasant girl ... cheerful and polite and ... and ... Oh!' She turned to Mrs Keighley 'You are not truly certain she took the food, are you? You never saw her do it, did you?'

'No, miss, that's right enough. Only that once, the first week. And, as I said, that I don't regard.'

'Supposing it were all a mistake and she did not steal the food? She will be ruined for ever and all because you thought she was a thief when she was not.' She turned back to her mother, by this time almost in tears. 'Oh, please give her another chance and I am sure she will not do it again.'

Lady Rimpole smiled and then gave a little laugh and held out her hand to Bella. 'Why, Bella, what a soft-hearted little goose you are! When you have a home of your own, your husband will not thank you for taking pity on thieves. I hope for his sake you will have learnt better by then, or his household will be in a sorry state. Very well, my dear. For this once we shall do as you wish.' She looked at Mrs Keighley, still smiling. 'Miss Annabel is pledge for her, so give the girl another chance. But make it plain to her that if it happens again, she goes instantly and without any wages.'

'Very good, my lady.' Mrs Keighley, glad to have the difficult decision made for her one way or another, curtseyed. 'Now I'll not be detaining your ladyship any longer, and I thank you for hearing me out.' Another curtsey and she was gone, and Bella was left shaken and white-faced beside her mother.

'Rub your cheeks, Annabel dear. You look a fright with no colour in them. What a to-do about a Bessie Barnsley! You are an odd child, are you not?' She gave Bella's shoulder a little pat and smiled; then she said briskly, 'Now, come along. The carriage will have been waiting quite fifteen minutes for us.'

Bella somehow got through the morning, following her mother into one small, dark, two-roomed cottage after another, smiling kindly at the curtseying, grateful tenants as they received their dole of cast-off clothes from the poor basket and pounds of cheaper-quality tea; joining Lady Rimpole in commending the industry of tired wives, grown old before their time, and little girls, all of whom spent their brief leisure in spinning, that they might add a few pence to the meagre wages of their menfolk; and looking as interested at their answers to her mother's questions as she knew her mother would wish her to look; while all the time her mind kept slipping back to her guilty thoughts of the unfortunate Bessie, whose character she and Francis had ruined, and for whom they could do nothing without betraying Seumas to his death – which was unthinkable. It was useless comfort to tell herself that Bessie, too, was suffering for the Cause, since Bessie did not know, and could not be told, of this honour, and therefore could not enjoy her martyr's crown. And anyway, she probably did not care two straws for the Cause, and would without a doubt have stoutly refused to suffer for it.

Because it had been arranged that Bella was to accompany Lady Rimpole that morning, she had known that she would not be able to meet Francis after his lessons, and she had warned him of this. He therefore went alone to the Dower House on his way home and was pleased to find Seumas, with the aid of the stick, practising walking up and down the hall between the front door and the Chinese room. It was taking him ten or twelve minutes to make the double journey of some twenty yards, and his left arm, which was still stiff and painful, was a hindrance rather than a help, but he was persevering gallantly, and he said cheerfully, 'See what fine progress I am making. Why, soon it's running up and down the stairs I'll be, exchanging greetings with the banshee herself.'

When Francis arrived home he found Bella, with a long face, waiting for him. 'Oh, Francis,' she cried, 'something terrible has happened.'

Since he had, not fifteen minutes before, left Seumas alone and safe, the most terrible thing of all could obviously not have happened; but Bella's distress was quite sufficient to give him an unpleasant sinking sensation. 'What has happened?' he asked, a procession of secondary misfortunes presenting themselves before his mind's eye.

She told him, and he was as appalled as she. 'Oh, heavens! I'll have to go at once and tell them it was we who did it.'

Bessie Barnsley was only a servant-girl and a poacher's daughter into the bargain, and it mattered very little to him what became of her; but no gentleman ever let another – not even a servant – take the blame for his misdeeds, and Francis was ready in that instant to rush off and find someone to whom he might confess.

Bella caught hold of his arm. 'Francis! Francis, you cannot! What explanation could we give for taking the food? They will ask questions and we shall have to tell hundreds of lies and it will all be so difficult. And supposing that they find out about Mr Macdonald?'

The first impetuous moment over, Francis saw the reasonableness of this. 'You are quite right. What a devilish coil! Whatever are we going to do about it? That wretched girl! Which one is Bessie, anyway?'

'The new one with the yellow hair. She carries up the bath water.'

'Oh, that one.' He paused and thought. 'We shall have to do something about her – but what?'

They considered it. Then Bella said, 'Listen, Francis. Could we not give her something, a present of some kind, to make it up to her for having everyone think that she's a thief? And we could tell her that you and I, at least, believe she's honest.'

Francis brightened. 'That's a good notion. I have that guinea which old Lord Barton gave me when father and I rode over to see him the other day. Would that serve, do you think? She could buy herself something with it, a cap, mittens, buckles, or some such Sunday finery – whatever trumpery it is that girls like to buy themselves.'

'Of course it would serve! What a capital thing, Francis! Let's see to it at once.'

'If I give you the guinea, Bella, will you convey it to her and tell her we think that she is honest and so on?'

'I'll do it as soon as I can after dinner.'

A few minutes later he handed her the guinea with a final warning. 'Whatever you do, Bella, do not let her suspect that it was we who took the food. Be discreet, for heaven's sake. Do not go and blurt it all out like a silly girl.'

'Of course I shall not!'

'Well, just remember, that's all. If you do let her guess, she's not likely to keep quiet about it, and then it will be the end for us. Or rather, it will be the end for Mr Macdonald – quite truly the end.'

With this horrid thought in mind, Bella determined to be discretion itself, no matter how sorry for Bessie she might feel.

After dinner she waited about on the stairs until she saw one of the footmen in the hall below and asked him to send Bessie to her. Soon Bessie came, looking thoroughly woebegone, her eyes red and swollen, her face tear-stained and her mouth sullenly drooping. At the sight, Bella's conscience gave her trouble, but she resolutely thought of Seumas and the Cause. She went straight to the point.

'Bessie, we heard that you were in disgrace, and I want to tell you that my brother and I do not believe that you stole anything. We are very sorry for you and we are sure – quite sure – that you are not a thief.'

Bessie sniffed. 'That's main kind of you and Master Francis, miss. I only wish as there was others that thought the same as you.'

'If you ... If you work hard and ... and give satisfaction, they'll soon forget all about it.'

'Happen they may, miss. But, again, happen they may not,' said Bessie dubiously.

'I heard Mrs Keighley say that you were the best worker she'd had for a long time and that she had great hopes of you. And Keighley thinks you are a good worker, too.'

Bessie brightened a little. 'Did she that, Miss Annabel? And does the old man think so? I must say that she's always been very good to me, and Mr Keighley, too, to now. So happen it may not be held against me for ever. But it's a right shame, miss, that it is and all, for a lass to be accused when she's done nowt, and –'

Bella quickly interrupted this outburst, before it should move her to rashness. 'Yes, yes, Bessie. I know. But I am sure that they will forget about it in time. Meanwhile we thought, Master Francis and I, that you might like to buy yourself something to cheer yourself up.' She pressed the guinea into Bessie's unexpecting hand.

Bessie stared at the coin as if she could not believe her eyes. 'A yellow George! A whole yellow George!' She looked at Bella. 'For me, miss?'

'Yes, from my brother and myself. To buy yourself a present from us.'

Bessie's face slowly lighted up into incredulous joy. 'Eh, miss, I never had a whole golden guinea before, and I never thought to, barring when my year's wages come to be paid to me, and then I'll have to give that up to them at home. Why, I've never even held a guinea in my hands before, let alone had one of my own. Thank you Miss Annabel, thank you. And Master Francis, too.'

'I am glad you are pleased, Bessie. I hope you enjoy spending it.' Her mission carried out, Bella turned to fly, before anyone should come and catch her talking on the stairs with the suspected thief. And then, suddenly remembering, she turned back again and said urgently. 'You will keep it to yourself, will you not, Bessie? There's no need to say anything to anyone about Master Francis and myself giving you a present.'

Bessie's ecstatic expression turned gradually to a broad grin which split across her flushed face. 'Nay, then, what do you take me for, miss? I'm not daft. Let on about this' – she lifted her fist with the guinea clenched in it – 'and they'll be saying as I stole it, they will and all. Besides, it's mine and I'm not letting my dad get his hands on it. He's brought too much trouble on me already, I reckon. Don't you fret nor fash yourself, Miss Annabelr. I'm keeping it to myself, I am.'

Reassured, Bella grinned back at her and ran up the stairs.

12

IT was left to Francis, arriving empty-handed at the Dower House on his way to the vicarage the next morning, to explain to Seumas that no more kitchen raiding would be possible, and why. He was very apologetic about the fact, and rather diffident over their excuse for it, thinking that the reputation of a poacher's daughter – or even the honour of a young gentleman – would seem of very little consequence when weighed against the freedom and the life of a fleeing patriot.

But to his surprise, Seumas, after frowning slightly for a moment, said, 'Och, the poor girl. What's to become of her now?'

'Oh, Bella says that our housekeeper thinks well of her otherwise, so I dare say it will all blow over soon and she will do all right.' He spoke casually, deliberately making light of the matter, and then went on to a more important question. 'I'll be bringing you something to eat from the village on my way back at dinner-time. I am sorry that you will have to wait so long for your breakfast.'

Seumas brushed this aside and persisted, 'But meantime, until it's blown over, how will it be with her? It's a bad time she'll be having, I'm thinking.'

Surprised by this concern with the affairs of Bessie, Francis said, 'Bella and I gave her a guinea for herself – as a kind of compensation, you understand – with which to buy herself something. Bella said that she was as pleased as could be and went off smiling.' Francis had not meant to mention the guinea for fear of making their guest feel under even more of an obligation to them than he must be feeling already; but he thought that he should do so, as Seumas seemed to be taking the girl's plight so hardly.

Seumas's brow cleared a little. 'It's glad I am to hear it, for I'd not be wanting the poor girl to be unhappy at being misjudged on account of me.'

'I must leave you now, Mr Macdonald. But I shall hurry back with some food as soon as I can after lessons. I only hope you will not be too hungry by then.'

Seumas smiled reufully. 'It's a deal of trouble I'm after causing you one way or another, I'm afraid. Is it not?'

With absolute sincerity and without a trace of that air of self-consequence which too often seemed to mar his better nature, Francis said, quite simply, 'We are proud to do anything we can to help someone who has fought for the King, Mr Macdonald.'

To Francis's surprise, Seumas frowned again, abruptly and on an instant this time, and turned his head away, so that he was no longer looking at Francis. He said nothing for a very long moment, and Francis wondered whether he had done the wrong thing in reminding him of Culloden and his sufferings and the King's lost cause and the Prince who might, even at that very second, be facing his captors; and for a while he stood, at a loss, waiting for Seumas to speak.

At last Seumas half turned to him, still frowning, and said, 'Will they not be expecting you at the vicarage?'

'I have still a few minutes to spare.'

Francis made no move to go, and Seumas suddenly threw out his good arm in a gesture of impatience. 'Och, be off with you now, or it's late you'll be for your lessons.'

Puzzled, and a little hurt, Francis went.

When Bella arrived, some three hours later, carrying on a cabbage leaf the first of the season's raspberries which she had picked from the rather overgrown canes in the Dower House garden as she passed by them – 'To keep you from feeling too hungry until Francis brings your dinner from the village,' as she explained – Seumas was unusually silent and seemed in poor spirits; though he smiled at her and thanked her for the raspberries and insisted on her sharing them with him. At first she refused, on the grounds that she had had breakfast and he had not; but he said, 'I'll not be enjoying them alone.'

She gave way then, thinking, as she did so, that virtue is sometimes rewarded; for she had, with the greatest self-control, refrained from eating a single one while she had picked them for him.

'Did my brother tell you of what happened yesterday?' she asked him, in between raspberries.

'He did.' Seumas did not seem inclined to discuss it, which suited Bella, who did not particularly want to talk about it herself, and had only mentioned the matter to make sure that Francis had not shirked giving Seumas the explanation due to him for their failure to supply his breakfast. But after a moment or two, Seumas asked, 'That servant-girl, will it truly be well with her?'

'I am certain it will,' Bella told him. 'Mrs Keighley is a very kind person really. And I saw Bessie this morning, not to speak to, but in the passage as I was coming out, and she seemed much happier than yesterday. You see,' she explained, 'no more food will have disappeared in the night, so they will believe she has stopped stealing it.'

'That's that, then; and the worst over,' said Seumas; and they smiled at each other with surface satisfaction. But Bella knew – and she knew that Seumas knew that she knew it – that neither of them was really satisfied by the outcome of the whole sorry affair.

'Those were good raspberries,' Seumas commented as the last one was finished.

'Do you have raspberries at home in the Highlands?'

He did not reply for a moment, then he said lightly, 'And why should raspberries not grow in the Highlands?'

'I thought that perhaps it might be too cold and bleak for them.'

'Well now, would raspberries not be growing anywhere at all?'

'I do not think so.' Bella was rather unsure of this. 'I fancy they might not grow in the very hot countries or in the very cold ones. Miss Proudfoot would be able to tell us. Should I ask her and let you know?'

'You be doing that.'

Seumas certainly seemed depressed that morning. Perhaps it was because he was hungry, she thought, and wished that

Francis would hurry with whatever it was he was going to buy in the village.

She broke a long silence at last to say, with a view to cheering him up, 'Has your home a garden, Mr Macdonald?'

Again he did not reply at once, then he said, 'Sure and it has.'

'A large garden, or a small one?'

'Och . . . middling, I suppose.'

'Do you grow flowers – roses and so on – in it, or only vegetables and things to eat?'

'For the love of heaven, must you be always asking questions?' he cried suddenly. He was instantly contrite, even before he had seen the look of pained bewilderment that came to her face. 'Och, I'm sorry. I never meant that, Miss Bella. Forgive me.' He impulsively took hold of one of her hands. 'It's a bad, black, dumpish mood I'm in this morning. Will you be forgiving me now?'

'Of course.' She put her other hand on top of his. 'There's nothing to forgive, Mr Macdonald. It's my fault for asking too many questions.' She smiled at him, though she could not see him properly for the tears which had sprung into her eyes.

'Not a single one too many. It's flattered by your kind interest I am. It's only that . . . Och, as I said, I'm in a bad mood today.'

'Did you have a restless night, perhaps? Are your arm and your ankle still giving you much pain?'

He slipped his hand out from between hers. 'That's it. I did not sleep so well last night and I'm a little in the dumps this morning as a consequence. It's having a sleep after my dinner I'll be, and then I'll be as merry as a grig.' He smiled at her and said, 'Now, let me be asking you some questions for a change. I've long been wanting to hear more about this banshee of yours. What do they say she looks like, those who've seen her? Is it an old lady she is, or a young one?'

Bella, who regretted that there was no romantic ghost attached to Thorsby Hall, had always envied the Dower House its White Lady, and she needed very little encouragement to talk about her. By the time that Francis arrived with a small cheese and a large cake and ale in a jug from the village alehouse, she was deep in the story of unfortunate, deserted Alice Rimpole, whose handsome lover had ridden away and never come back again, leaving her to pine away into first madness and then death.

'Oh, Bella! At it again! You must forgive her, Mr Macdonald!' But he was, these days, so much in charity with his sister, that on this occasion he was merely amused by her predilection for the fantastic, and not exasperated, or even downright contemptuous, as he would have been only ten days before.

By now Francis and Bella were finding that one lie usually leads to another, if even a single fabrication is to be maintained successfully. They were also learning that, in upholding one set of values, it often happens that one betrays all, or most, of the others; and that in order to keep faith honourably with an ideal, it is sometimes necessary to disregard honour. They had managed to buy their way out of the Bessie affair, and though they had come out of it undetected, they could hardly be said to have come out of it without any shame to themselves. However, they were both still comfortingly bolstered up and heartened in their efforts, both honest and dishonest, by the thought that what they were doing for Seumas, they were doing also for the Jacobite cause.

Francis now regularly bought pies, cakes, cheeses, and ale in the village on his way to or from the vicarage – something he had, in the past, never before done – each time giving an elaborately casual explanation of why he was doing so. Since he had never been a particularly talkative boy outside his own home, and certainly not one who considered that anything he did needed to be justified in any way to his inferiors, his sudden ingratiating garrulousness appeared far more suspicious to the villagers than if he had followed his natural inclinations in the matter and merely been arrogantly silent.

Soon all the goodwives of Thorsby, and not a few of their menfolk, too, were discussing with interest – and watching for its next manifestation – Master Francis's extraordinary appetite which seemed to need such inordinate amounts of food to sustain it between breakfast and dinner; some of the gossips saying indignantly that what he ate in between two meals would be enough to keep a poor bairn – one of the speaker's own poor bairns, of course – in victuals for two days; and others declaring that they were right sorry for the young master that he was always so hungry and he a growing lad, and that it was a mickle shame if the rich folk could not feed their bairns enough to keep them from hunger at ten o'clock in the morning.

In this way, as well as in the purchase of the razor, his spending-money for the whole of June was rapidly being used up, and he had none left over from the previous month; so that he soon began to regret even the purchase, early in May, of *Joseph Andrews* from the bookshop in Thirsk, as well as his rash generosity to Bessie. Bella was quite unable to help him, the contents of her purse providing only two pennies, a lucky pebble with a hole through it, a piece of jet from Whitby and three pins. He took the pennies, remarking that they would buy Mr Macdonald remarkably little, and adding, 'There's nothing else for it, I shall have to sell something. Quite apart from food, Mr Macdonald needs a new pair of boots before he leaves here. We cut off one of his and left it in the ditch, if you remember.'

He assembled a collection of saleable articles, including a spare riding whip which he did not often use and several books which he had already read, and decided gloomily that they would not fetch much. Matters becoming pressing, with no idea of when he would be able to pay them back, he borrowed half a crown off Keighley and another off his father's valet, choosing those two out of all the servants because, on the one hand, he knew he could trust Keighley not to betray him, and on the other, because he knew that Fowler considered himself above mentioning such a sordid transaction to Sir John.

He even brought himself to ask his father for an advance, not merely on next month's spending-money, but on his first half's Eton allowance. Sir John was surprised at this, since Francis was not, in the ordinary course of affairs, an extravagant boy and always lived within his means; and he knew, moreover, that Francis had, only a fortnight or so before, been presented with a guinea by his old friend, Lord Barton. But he was always ready to listen to petitions and always pleased to be indulgent up to a point; and remembering his own youth and its occasional shifts when he was out of funds – for his father, Sir Charles, though ready enough to spend a small fortune on making a lake for his wife, had firmly believed that the young should not be pampered – Sir John was prepared to be helpful to his own son. But, reasonably enough, he first inquired why Francis wanted the money. To this Francis was quite unable to give an answer. He did murmur something about a gift for Bella, in celebration of her twelfth birthday, to which Sir John said, 'But, my boy, your sister's birthday is in November. You have plenty of time to think of that – and to save for it. Come now, for what do you really want the money?'

Francis still could not answer. He merely looked embarrassed and wished that he had not been such a fool as to approach his father. As the silence between them lengthened, he completely lost his normal poise and began to scuff with the toe of his buckled shoe at a medallion of roses on the Aubusson carpet beneath his feet, looking anywhere but at his father.

Sir John, still remembering episodes from his own youth, asked knowingly, and, it must be confessed, not unhopefully, 'Have you been laying money on the cocks and the horses and losing more than you can pay?'

'Of course not, sir!' Had Francis but realized it, one good lie at this point would have brought him any sum within reason that he had liked to name, and at the price of no more than a lecture on the foolishness of wagering more than one could afford to lose and his own promise to be more circumspect in the future. For Sir John believed that debts of honour should be immediately paid – no matter what happened to tradesmen's bills – and, if the truth were to be known, he would not have been sorry to have found Francis getting into a natural and foolish scrape, such as gambling rashly, and learning better from it. But Francis's indignant denial had an unmistakable sound of truth, and Sir John stifled a regretful sigh. Further probing having failed to elicit the cause of the need for an advance, Sir John lost patience, refused the request and dismissed Francis. But before the door had closed behind him, Sir

John, with more understanding of his son's temperament than Francis would ever have given him credit for, took pity on the pride that had demeaned itself to make a difficult request, only to be refused. He called Francis back and gave him two half-crowns. 'Here, these may help tide you over until next month.'

Francis, fully aware of the tolerant, half-amused pity that had prompted the gift, found it almost as difficult to accept the coins gracefully as it had been to accept the refusal of an advance with fortitude. But, as he said to Bella afterwards, two Georges were a great deal better than nothing, and would buy Mr Macdonald a fair quantity of food.

Towards the end of the week, Francis rode over to Thirsk with his father and a groom. In his pockets he had first carefully stowed away most of the various articles which he hoped to sell. The spare whip, together with Seumas's remaining boot as a pattern for size, he had concealed in his folded cloak, which he was not wearing as it was far too warm.

In Thirsk Sir John went to the home of a friend whose house stood in the centre of the town. The groom was sent to sample the beer in the kitchen, and, having made his bow to his father's friend and having answered all the kindly questions asked of him by the old gentleman – which included such nonsensical inquiries as, 'And how is dear Miss Bella? Growing prettier every day, I'll be bound. Remember to give her my respects, my boy, and tell her that I am hoping to see her again soon' – Francis was sent off to stroll about the town, and Sir John and his friend settled down in the library with a bottle of brandy between them, to have, for the next three hours or so, a companionable talk about the political situation and the prospects for the hunting season.

Francis had ample time in which to dispose of all that he wished to sell. He went to a bookshop first, since that would, he felt, probably prove the easiest of his transactions, as he was well known to the bookseller, and because the books were the most cumbersome items he had brought with him and were weighing down his pockets. He sold them all easily enough; though, having been basing his reckoning on the prices asked from customers for books, he had put too high a value on them, forgetting that a shopkeeper expects to get a profit on his wares. And he had a slight argument over the two small volumes of *The History of the Adventures of Joseph Andrews*, with which he was sorry to part. Having bought them so recently as the beginning of May, he now expected to get his money back on them, and was inclined to cavil when the bookseller offered him sixpence less than he paid.

'But they were worth sixpence more, only five weeks ago.'

'I know that. But they have had five weeks' use since then.'

'I take good care of my books. They are in exactly the same condition as when I bought them from you.'

The bookseller did not deny this. Instead he asked, 'Have you read them?'

'Yes.'

'Did you enjoy the tale?'

'Yes.'

'It's an entertaining tale, is it not?'

'A very entertaining tale,' agreed Francis.

'Then it must be worth sixpence to you to read it. Take my offer or keep Joseph.' The bookseller's eyes twinkled at him triumphantly, and he took a pinch of snuff while Francis disgustedly made up his mind to accept.

He sold the riding whip at the saddler's, and for the price he asked: but only because he was young Mr Rimpole from Thorsby Hall and it was as well to keep on good terms with him, and not because the man wanted the whip at all. None of this did he attempt to hide from Francis, who found it very distasteful to have to refrain from throwing down on the counter the saddler's grudgingly given coins, taking up his riding whip, and stalking out of the shop.

After having managed with considerable difficulty to dispose of the remainder of the saleable items – an old penknife, a cricket ball, and several articles which had, in earlier years, given him pleasure, two whip tops and a peg top, and six marbles – Francis salved his pride by going to the best cobbler in the town and ordering a pair of boots to be made to the size of the one he had brought with him, and by choosing leather and style with lordly disregard for price. When he was given a rough estimate of what the cost was likely to be, he was shocked; but being too proud to admit that the boots might well

prove beyond his means, he said that the price would do very well and he would call for them himself on Saturday. The cobbler made a protest over the short time allowed him for the job; but Francis, who did not know when he would be able to come into Thirsk again, should he miss a chance on Saturday, insisted. The cobbler gave way, and Francis, too late, foresaw another shilling or so being added to the cost of the boots, on the grounds that they had been an urgent order.

'What name, if you please, sir?'

'Rim –' He saved himself just in time, '– pelby. Mr Rimpelby. My brother.'

'And t'address, sir?'

'I have told you, I shall fetch them myself. There will be no need to deliver them.' He made to leave the little shop before there were any more questions.

The cobbler, a fine old craftsman who prided himself on his skill, was distressed by this casual attitude to his workmanship. 'Nay, then, what of fitting t'boots, sir? Will t'gentleman be coming here to try them on?'

'If you make them the exact size of the boot I have given you, there should be no need for a fitting,' said Francis quellingly, and escaped before the cobbler could raise any further protest, shutting the door of the shop after him and leaving the old man shaking his head over the odd behaviour of some of the quality – for, in spite of the battered appearance of the boot brought him as a pattern, the young gentleman was obviously quality.

13

THAT week had brought a change in Seumas. He was still gay and cheerful enough for most of the time – although at moments the gaiety and the cheerfulness seemed to be achieved only with an effort – and though just as friendly towards them as ever and just as welcoming as he had always been, each day when they arrived at the Dower House, he now talked to them much less; and if there were still occasions when he would rattle on amusingly about nothing at all in his old manner, there were also times when he would be completely – and, it seemed, thoughtfully – silent.

He ceased telling them about the Prince and the battles and his own experiences in the campaigning, and he did not respond to their attempts to draw him on to speak of those days; and though never actually preventing their questions about himself, he in no way encouraged them, and gave only short and all but evasive replies. Then, almost immediately, he would turn the talk to less personal matters, or ask them about themselves and have them tell him about their doings and interests. They missed his tales and his exploits in Scotland, of the Prince's progress into England, and of the clansmen who had followed the White Cockade, of how the streets of Manchester had looked to one in the Prince's army, and all the other matters with which they had been so enthralled; for his talk had opened another world to them, a world unfamiliar and wonderful, a world in which they had long been waiting for a chance to share – the world of courage against great odds, of faith kept, of stirring deeds and of loyalty which expects no reward.

When they found that he no longer seemed to want to speak about his past experiences, but appeared instead to be deliberately building a barrier between themselves and those former days of his, they were both distressed. Francis, after due thought, decided that Seumas's exile must be beginning to weigh too heavily upon his heart; so that he now preferred not to remember what must, after all, bring him grief to recollect; and he respected his silence, even while regretting it.

But Bella, far less sure of herself than her brother, was afraid that they had inadvertently affronted Seumas in some way, or that he was for some reason disappointed in their conduct, and so had withdrawn himself from them. She said as much to Francis one day when they were walking slowly back from the Dower House, leading Sultan – since on that day there was ample time to spare before dinner, Seumas having been even less talkative than he had been of late.

Francis frowned, staring at the grass under his feet. 'I wondered that for a time, too,' he admitted at last. 'But I could think of no way in which we could have offended him unintentionally. After all, we have done our best for him, even if we have not always been successful – as with the supply of food from home for instance. But he is far too magnanimous a person to hold it against us that we cannot any longer bring him so much to eat, or in such variety.'

He paid no heed when Bella broke in at this point to exclaim, in heartfelt agreement with him, 'Of course Mr Macdonald would not care a straw for such a thing!' and went straight on, 'No, Bella, it must be that he is missing his own home and his country, and he is worried about the future and whether the Prince will ever manage to escape and so on. Lord! He has enough to be unhappy about, poor Mr Macdonald!'

'Yes, it may, perhaps, be that.' But Bella was not entirely convinced. 'Why do we not ask him what is the matter, Francis?'

'Good heavens, Bella! One cannot ask people things like that and go prying into their feelings in such a fashion. It would be most unmannerly. I would not dream of doing so.'

But Bella had no such reticence. To her mind, if they had done, or were doing, anything to give offence to their guest, then it was only sensible that he should tell them what it was, so that it could be remedied.

The following morning, which was Friday, arriving as usual at the Dower House before Francis, and finding Seumas smiling but hardly talkative, she asked him outright, 'Mr Macdonald, you have been so quiet lately, and you never seem to tell us about yourself and your adventures any more. Have we done something to displease you? Francis says that I should not ask you. But if there is anything amiss, I think we ought to know about it, so that we can put it right.'

Seumas stared at her, with, for once, no easy answer ready on his tongue. At length he said, 'Is it thinking that you've been? I'd not have had such a thing happen for the world. It is nothing at all that you have done. Haven't you and your brother been kindness itself to me, and I nothing but a burden to the pair of you? No, no, Miss Bella darling, it's only that I am – Och, it's the moody fellow I am, sometimes up in the clouds and laughing fit to burst with the sun all shining in my eyes, and other times down at the bottom of the sea and crying fit to break your heart. It's deep down I am now, and I'm sorry for it if it's caused you to be anxious.'

'Then it is truly only because, as Francis said, you are sad and troubled, and not because of anything we have done?' she insisted earnestly.

'Of course that's the way of it. How could you be thinking that it was anything you'd done? And here was I, glooming away, letting you have such thoughts in your pretty head. Will you be forgiving me now if you can?'

Very cheered and elated to think that her boldness and disregard of Francis's scruples had been rewarded, she smiled happily at Seumas. 'I'm so glad that all is well again.' Then her face fell. 'But it is not well for you. You must be so lonely for your home and your family and your friends. I wish that we could do something to help you to return to them soon.'

'I shall one day be doing that, never fear.' He looked at her solemn face and said, 'Come now, Miss Bella, smile again. Do not be grieving for me.' With sudden vehemence he repeated, 'Do not ever be grieving for me, Miss Bella, I beg of you. It's not worth it I am.'

'Of course you are worth it! And I cannot help it if I am sorry for you and want to help you.' She screwed up her brow in concentration. 'I suppose we could not contrive somehow to send a message to your home, to say that you were alive and well?' she asked after a few moments' silence.

'Och, that would be difficult and ... And none too safe, perhaps?'

'I suppose you are right.' It was disappointing. But of course, she told herself, it would really have been impossible. One could, after all, hardly use the services of the Post Office to send comforting messages to King George's enemies in Scotland. 'Will your family and your friends be very concerned for you?' she asked.

'No doubt my friends will be thinking that I'm well able to be taking care of myself – though I wager they'd never guess that I'm being taken care of by two such good Samaritans as you and your brother.'

She was silent again for a long time, while he watched her wanting to say the right thing to cheer her and make her happy once again, but strangely at a loss to know just what the right thing might be.

Behind her solemn expression, she was picturing to herself – as well as she could for her lack of first-hand knowledge – a Highland home and a tall Highland woman wearing a tartan shawl which was blowing in the wind, looking out into the sunset, watching and waiting; ever watching and ever waiting, patiently and hopefully, for the return of Seumas Macdonald, her – Would he be her son, or her husband?

Bella could not complete her picture of the scene without knowing. Would the face be that of a sad, grey-haired woman, or a young one with red hair? The Scots were often red-haired, she knew. She looked up. 'Mr Macdonald, you have never told us. Are you married?' It would make, she felt, a far lovelier and sadder picture if the woman were young and red-haired.

'No, it's not married I am, nor ever likely to be.' He appeared to be amused by the question.

She was disappointed. It seemed to her almost sadder that there should not be, somewhere, a broken-hearted young Scotswoman weeping for him, than that there should be. She tried to save her picture from complete destruction. 'Then you are not even betrothed? You have no sweetheart at all at home?'

He knew then what he had to say to please her. She had shown him the right answer herself. 'Och, I suppose you might say I have a sweetheart, in a manner of speaking.'

She was, as he had guessed she would be, instantly pleased. 'Oh, I am so glad for you! What is her name?'

'Her name? It's ... it's ... Mary. She is the daughter of ... of a farmer who lives near-by.'

'Is she pretty?'

He laughed. 'Faith! And how would I be knowing that, and I prejudiced, as you might say? Sure and she's pretty. She ... she has yellow hair and ...' He warmed to the subject, became less hesitant and plunged on with enthusiasm, '... and grey eyes and a mouth that's always laughing, and she's nothing but a little slip of a thing such as a man could be easily putting into his big pocket. It's the fine seamstress she is and her needle always busy making shirts for her father and her brothers. It's a good cook she is, too, and her plum cake is fit for any lord to eat.'

For her tall, red-haired Highland girl, Bella rapidly substituted dainty, slim little Mary, the farmer's yellow-haired daughter. 'Oh, I like the sound of her! I do hope you can marry her when you are home again.'

'Maybe I'll be doing that.'

They smiled at each other, very well pleased with one another; and they were still smiling when Francis came in with a jug of ale and some pies.

'Mrs Cotter at the alehouse looked at me so oddly today when I insisted as usual in carrying this off with me instead of drinking it there and then. She kept on hinting that I should tell her why I wanted to do so – As though I have not had to tell her enough lies already! – She is really a most provoking and impertinent woman. What business is it of hers what I choose to do with a jug of ale?'

On Saturday Francis rode over to Thirsk to fetch the boots. They were ready and waiting for him as promised. The cobbler had sat up, weary-eyed, long after midnight to finish them by the meagre light of two stinking tallow dips, made from scraps of rancid waste fat. As Francis had feared, their price was considerably more than the first estimate, largely owing to the haste in which he had demanded that they should be made. Francis had prepared for this contingency by bringing two shillings more than the sum mentioned as the possible price; but he was considerably taken aback and put out to find that all the money which he at the moment possessed, was less than he owed the cobbler.

Had he protested and blustered, it is possible that the old man would have given way and dropped his price to very little more than the earlier, suggested figure; but to Francis, chaffering in such circumstances was unthinkable and an admission of inadequate means. One should either pay without quibbling the price that was demanded, or one should refuse the goods. In this case, as the boots were for Seumas, and Seumas needed them, they could not be refused.

Had he looked schoolboyishly rueful, admitted that he had not enough money with him, and asked with a pleasant smile what he should do about it, the cobbler would undoubtedly have been trustful and co-operative; but Francis, concealing his discomfiture at the vastly increased price, said high-handedly, 'I have not enough money with me. I'll take the boots now and bring you the remainder of the money next week.'

'There's no need for you to fash yourself, sir. I'll send my grandson round with t'boots later today, and he can collect t'money then. That road you'll be spared both coming back here next week, and carrying t'boots home yourself.' He glanced at the several other purchases for Seumas with which Francis was already laden – a cheese, two loaves, and a bottle of wine.

Francis inwardly cursed the fact that he had bought these things first – he had left fetching the boots until last in order not to have to carry them around with him – because otherwise he would probably have had just enough money to have paid the cobbler.

'I will take them myself, now,' he said firmly.

The cobbler pretended not to have heard this. 'If you'll kindly let me have your direction, sir, they'll be delivered within an hour.'

'I said that I would take them myself.' Francis glared intimidatingly at the old man, much in the same fashion as when he had demanded that they should be ready by Saturday. On this occasion it had no result.

Still polite, but very stubborn – for he was by this time thoroughly suspicious of a customer whose attitude had been, all along, very odd – the cobbler said, 'I'm right sorry, sir, but I cannot let you have t'boots until they've been paid for.'

Francis said stiffly, 'Are you accusing me of trying to cheat you?'

'Nay, sir, that I'm not. But I'm sure that t'gentleman would not wish to be owing t'money, and I'm sure he'd prefer me to see that t'boots were delivered and spare you t'carrying of them. My grandson shall run to your brother's home with them this very minute.'

'Then he will have a long way to run,' Francis snapped. 'My brother does not live in the town. That is why he particularly requested me to take them for him.' Previously pale, Francis was now becoming flushed.

'If that's so, sir, of course you'll wish to take t'boots for him. But if you'd be so kind as to give me your brother's direction, happen I'll be able to collect t'cash when I'm next going by, to save him t'trouble of sending it.'

Francis was at a standstill. The cobbler was only being reasonable, and he had now either to invent an address which the cobbler, being old and probably very familiar with the district, would know at once to be false; or he had to retire defeated. Having already had as much as he could stand, he chose the latter. With as much dignity as he could still call upon, he said, 'Since you seem determined to be disobliging, you had best keep the boots until Monday, when I'll come back for them.' He turned and made for the door. At the top of the step up to the street, he turned and sent a parting shot at his victorious antagonist. 'My brother will be very displeased to learn of how unaccommodating you have been.'

The cobbler bent his grey head. 'My humble apologies to t'gentleman, sir, and my regrets.'

Francis, with a glance he hoped was withering, went. The cobbler, looking after him, decided he was never likely to see him again. It had been, no doubt, some boyish prank on the young gentleman's part, and he had never meant to buy the boots at all. The old man, turning to the boots and thinking of a half-night's sleep lost on finishing them in time, and wondering if and when he would be able to find another customer for them, sighed deeply and went back to work he had neglected during the two days he had spent on the ill-starred boots.

Francis smarted all the way home. To be suspected and worsted by a cobbler was bad enough; but, even more mortifying than that, it was now imperative that he should have the price of the boots by Monday, so that the cobbler would know that he could really afford them and was not having to raise the money with which to pay the extra amount – as, of course, he was.

Indignantly he told Bella about it when he reached the Hall. Her ready sympathy saw nothing humorous in the spectacle of her normally self-reliant brother being routed by a cobbler.

'Oh, Francis, I am sorry! How uncomfortable for you!' She placed a hand on his arm, thoroughly concerned for his feelings.

'Uncomfortable! I should think it was!' Then he smiled ruefully and said with unusual candour, 'I don't mind admitting to you, Bella, that I felt devilish embarrassed. To have my honesty doubted by an old fool of a cobbler and not to be able to tell him who I was and have him eat his words, was pretty humiliating, I can tell you.' He paused and then said determinedly. 'I must not fail to go to Thirsk and collect those boots on Monday. I cannot have that miserable old wretch thinking I haven't the money to pay for them and am having to chase all over the North Riding to scrape up enough to settle the bill.' He stopped, grinned unexpectedly at her and added, 'Which is, as it happens, almost exactly what I shall be doing.' After a moment, frowning once more, he said, 'Where the money is to come from, I cannot think, because there will be food and so on to buy during all next week. I suppose I shall be forced to have another attempt at touching father for an advance. If I make up some tale or other, he might possibly give me July's spending-money now. Though I doubt it,' he added gloomily. 'He made things very difficult for me the other day.' He stared despondently before him. 'Have you any good notions for raising money, Bella? Possible ones, mind, not some hare-brained scheme or other. And ones which would not take for ever to carry out.'

They sat down and considered the matter thoroughly.

'We shall have to sell something, as you did the other day,' said Bella at last.

'Yes, I already know that. But what? We cannot sell any of our things if they are likely to be missed. And it's not all that easy to sell things, either. It's only easy if the buyer wants them.'

He remembered with revulsion the saddler and his grudging obsequiousness; and then he also remembered that, of all the things which he had sold on that day, the books had been disposed of the most easily and satisfactorily and – in spite of the little argument over *Joseph Andrews* – with the least embarrassment. But he had not so many more books of his own, apart from study books which he needed for his lessons.

Slowly he said. 'There are hundreds of books in the library and I'd wager father never reads half of them. What's more, I'd wager some of them have not been opened since grandfather's time.'

'Francis! That would be stealing!'

'Yes, but – Hang it all, Bella! They will be mine one day. Where's the harm in anticipating that day?'

'But it would be stealing. They are still father's now.'

'It would not be for ourselves, but for Mr Macdonald and the Cause.' He spoke a little over defiantly; and when she did not answer, he challenged, 'Well, what do you say?' She still said nothing, and he remarked, 'We have already done some pretty ... odd ... things for the Cause, so why should we boggle at stealing?'

After a struggle between her sense of honesty and the thought of the Cause and Mr Macdonald, Bella said, 'Very well, I suppose it is the only way.' Having accepted the path of crime, she proceeded to walk down it circumspectly and with sound sense. 'How can we be sure of taking ones which father does not read, so that they will not be missed?' Warming to it, and without waiting for his answer, she went on practically, 'And we shall have to move every book upon the shelves a very little farther from the next, to fill the gaps where the ones we have taken were used to stand. It should not be difficult to manage, provided that we are able to spend sufficient time on it. And if we do have the misfortune to take a book which father reads, why, he may well think it has been misplaced. There are so very many books in the library, after all.'

Francis, listening to her, was already mentally in the library, standing on the portable library steps, selecting books for sale, seeing them in their calf-bound rows before him. 'The devil take it!' he suddenly exclaimed. 'It would be hopeless. They are almost all of them in matching bindings, with our crest on them. No, stealing books can be discounted.' He sounded irritated and disgruntled; but inside he could not prevent a feeling of relief. It was just as well, perhaps, he decided after a moment. They would have to go on racking their brains: there must be some honest way of raising money.

There was, it seemed. Ten minutes later, on an instant, Bella cried out excitedly, 'I have it, Francis! The very thing! The gold locket and chain which aunt Norton gave me three years ago. It lies in its case in my clothes press and no one ever looks at it, and I am not to be allowed to wear it until I am older. By that time it will surely not seem at all strange if it has apparently been lost. No one will ever dream that it has been sold. Not the locket, of course, because that has grandmother Heston's hair in it, but the gold chain. Is it not the very thing?'

'Bella, you really are the cleverest girl! Of course it is the very thing. It should keep us in funds for days.' His triumphant satisfaction dimmed a little, temporarily, as he said, more soberly, 'Though I do think it's a shame that you should have to sell your jewellery to get me out of debt.'

Bella giggled delightedly. 'Jewellery! You make my gold chain sound so important. And it's not as though it were for you to spend on yourself. It's for Mr Macdonald. Only he must never know,' she added urgently. 'It would distress him.'

'Of course he must never know!' He gave a deep sigh of relief. 'Well, that's settled, thank heaven. I'll take the chain over to Thirsk on Monday.' The problem being now resolved, he stood up, stretched his arms above his head and yawned. Relaxed in both mind and body from the constriction of the last hour or so, he looked down at Bella with for once unconcealed admiration and an unusual degree of affection. 'I must say that you are a capital sister, Bella. I do not know where I would have been without your help these last two weeks – or where Mr Macdonald would have been, either.'

She smiled up at him, proud and happy. 'What nonsense, Francis! Don't be so stupid! You have had all the difficult things to do.'

They were at that moment closer to each other than they were ever to be again in all their lives. They were united in a common aim, they had achieved the goodwill of a mutual interest and the solidarity of a shared enterprise – just as, a week later, they were to be briefly united in righteous anger. But after that they were to grow steadily and rapidly apart again, until Eton flowed, like an unbridgeable gulf, between them, to leave them severed and completely separate for years. A long time later, when they were both grown-up and had families of their own, they were to become moderately good friends – friends who sometimes smiled together over the callow ways of youth which they had left behind. But that was in the days to come, and a long time hence. And, even then, they were never again to be as close as they had been in that June of 1746.

14

On the Monday afternoon, once again on the pretext of going to the bookseller for a work recommended by Dr Mortlake, Francis rode to Thirsk with Bella's chain in his pocket. To avoid any possibility of being spied upon, he gave the groom who accompanied him the price of a tankard of ale and left him with the two horses at an inn, saying that he would return there for him when he had completed his business with the bookseller.

There was about to begin in the inn yard a private, hastily arranged cockfight to settle an argument between two of the patrons of the inn, as to the merits of their respective champions. It had attracted the attention of most of the inn-servants and the inn's customers, including several prosperous farmers and four elegant young gentlemen from a travelling carriage which sported a coat of arms on its panels, who had been breaking their journey southwards with dinner and a change of horses in Thirsk. These and several others were all eagerly gathering round to appraise the rivals' birds, a red and a grey, and bets were being laid. The betting was heavily in favour of the red cock, the victor in many earlier mains.

Francis, well aware that he should be on his way to the goldsmith's shop, stopped to watch. He would have liked to lay a wager – only a small one, for he was a cautious boy – on the red bird, but he resisted the temptation for fear of losing even a shilling of the money that was so badly needed for Seumas. However, he soon wished that he had risked at least a shilling, since the red cock was by far the better bird, and the winnings would have been a way of augmenting their funds by a little. He watched for several minutes, until it was obvious that it would be the red's victory, since it was still fresh and fierce, while the grey bird, though defending itself gallantly, was bleeding in a score of places and had, moreover, by this time lost the sight of one eye. Francis wished he could have waited until the finish, which promised to be a killing – always the most satisfactory conclusion to a main – but he did not know how long he would need for his transaction over the chain, or, indeed, how much persuading the goldsmith would need before he even decided that he wanted to buy a chain at all, so he reluctantly tore himself away and headed for the shop.

As things turned out, Francis might with perfect safety have waited until the end of the cockfight – and then remained to watch two or three more, had there been two or three more to watch – for he was able to dispose of Bella's chain in an unbelievably short time.

Mr Russell, the goldsmith, had a good memory for faces; and though he had seen Francis only once, and that twelve months before, he knew him immediately as the son of Sir John Rimpole of Thorsby; though, as he tactfully waited for Francis to make the first reference to this fact, Francis never realized that he had been recognized.

Around a year earlier, Lady Rimpole had broken the clasp of a favourite necklace on the very morning of the day on which she had particularly wished to wear it, and she had sent Stubbs to Thirsk in the chariot-and-four to have it repaired in a hurry. A few days later, having driven over to the town to visit a friend, Lady Rimpole had, with her usual graciousness, requested the coachman to stop before the goldsmith's shop, so that she might thank him in person for the speed and efficiency with which he had carried out the repair. He had come from his shop to receive her thanks, and as she was speaking to him from the carriage, he had noticed Francis and Bella, who were with her, and been enchanted by them.

For Mr Russell was an elderly bachelor without any children of his own to disillusion him, and he therefore believed, most erroneously, that all children were innocent and well-behaved little angels who, although they might at times have high spirits, never did anything really wrong. And so, when Francis, elaborately casual, said, 'I want to sell this chain for my sister,' Mr Russell immediately presumed, for no good reason at all, that young Mr Rimpole and his sister were raising money secretly in order to buy a present for their charming mother, a sentimental misapprehension which touched him so deeply that Francis was out of his shop within five minutes, with a good price for the chain in his purse, and feeling very well pleased with himself.

He made his way at once to the cobbler's shop, where, so that the cobbler might have no doubts at all about his solvency, he made sure that the old man saw that he had more than enough in his purse to pay for the boots.

The cobbler was very pleasantly surprised by his return, and he bowed Francis – carrying the boots under his arm – from his shop with many declarations of being honoured to have served him, and protesting his readiness to serve him again at any time in the future.

On arrival at the Hall, Francis had the satisfaction of being able to refund the loans made to him to Keighley and Fowler; and the next morning he gave the boots to Seumas. Seumas was obviously moved and pleased; though they both made a point, for different reasons, of making light of the matter, and Seumas only said, 'I've put you to so much expense since the day I came into your life, I only wish that I had more than the threepence left in my pockets, that I might be helping with the spending.'

Francis immediately insisted that none of this was of the slightest importance, and hurriedly started to ask Seumas if he were nearly finished with *Colonel Jack* and in need of another book to read. But when, soon after, Francis left Seumas for a few moments to draw a pail of fresh water from the well in the kitchen, he returned to find Seumas gesturing with the knife with which he had cut them off, to a pile of silver buttons from his coat.

'Do you think perhaps you could be selling these somewhere? They might be helping to swell the funds, maybe?'

Francis was very pleased. Their resources seemed to be prospering, what with Bella's chain and now Mr Macdonald's buttons. 'I hate to take them from you,' he said. 'But they will indeed be useful, especially as you will need some ready cash when you leave here.' He collected the buttons carefully and knotted them in his pocket handkerchief.

'I should have thought of them before,' said Seumas apologetically.

'It has completely ruined your coat, I am afraid.' Francis eyed the despoiled garment dubiously. 'That is, it has ruined what Bella had not already ruined by tearing your sleeve half off.'

'Och, it was very much the worse for wear days before I met you.'

'I'll find you another coat before you go,' promised Francis. 'You can count on that.' And he went on his way to the vicarage that morning with his mind running on schemes for outwitting Fowler's vigilance and rifling his father's clothes press undetected.

When Bella arrived at the Dower House that same Tuesday morning, Seumas was practising walking with the new boots on.

'See, is it not the perfect fit they are? And am I not walking finely in them?'

Bella's first pleasure in this was almost immediately clouded by another thought that came too quickly into her head. She said slowly, 'Your ankle is so much better, I suppose that you will soon be leaving us.'

After a second's pause, he replied easily, 'Well, it's on my way I must be soon, if I'm ever to be home again.'

'How many days do you think it will be before your ankle is quite healed?'

'Why, five or six, maybe. In a week, by next Tuesday, I should certainly be off your hands.' He smiled at her, but she looked away.

She stood fidgeting with the carving on the back of one of the chairs which they had unshrouded for Seumas's use, running a fingertip round and round a mahogany acanthus leaf; and then suddenly all her fingers tightened to clutch on the wood and she looked straight up at him. 'I shall miss you when you are gone, Mr Macdonald.'

For a long moment they looked at each other seriously; then he smiled again, made her a bow and said, 'And it's missing you, too, I'll be, Miss Bella. Sure and it's been a privilege to know you, ma'am.'

The smile he gave her was deliberately carefree and gay, his bow urbane and elegant, and the tone of his voice was light and carefully nonchalant: but he meant every word he said.

All that week Seumas was his old self once again, talkative and cheerful. His temporary mood of melancholy and silence seemed to have gone as suddenly as it had come, and – to Francis, at any rate – as inexplicably. For Bella did not tell her brother that it was she who had achieved this transformation. Pleased as he was by it, he would yet have been shocked by her temerity and her lack of respect for the private feelings of another.

The week passed pleasantly for them. There were no alarms or dangers to threaten their guest; there was, thanks to Bella's gold chain, enough money to buy him generous supplies of food and drink; and Francis had also sold the silver buttons profitably to Mr Russell – who, presuming the buttons to be his, had been charmed by the thought that Francis was matching his sister's generosity in sacrificing a treasured possession for the sake of giving pleasure to his mother – so that there was now even some money in reserve as well. Seumas's ankle and arm were improving rapidly and daily; and though this was, to Francis as well as to Bella, a far from unmixed joy, they could not but feel pleased when they reflected on how greatly they had contributed to this recovery, and remembered that, but for them, Seumas Macdonald might well, by now, be in the gaol at York or elsewhere, waiting to be hanged for a traitor.

By the Friday of that week it had been agreed that Seumas would be fully recovered and well enough to leave Thorsby on the following Monday, exactly three weeks and two days after he had entered their life to change it so immediately and so completely from dull, ordered propriety to outrageous, dangerous and deceitful – but delightful – conspiracy.

15

On the Friday they had found Seumas in particularly good spirits. He had told them, at considerable length, about the Prince's siege of Carlisle; and afterwards, as they returned home through the park, they planned how best Bella might contrive to get permission to spend the whole of Saturday morning ostensibly walking out with Francis in the park, so that they might, in actuality, be for as long as possible with Seumas at the Dower House.

On arrival at the Hall, Bella went straight indoors, while Francis took Sultan round to the stables to hand him over to a groom. In the stable yard, chatting idly to the grooms, were two militiamen. The shock to Francis was so great that he could not trust himself to ask the lad who came forward to take the pony, what they were doing there: he was afraid lest his agitation should betray him. As Sultan was led away, he turned and almost ran to the house with some idea of acquainting Bella with the disturbing news and warning her to be on her guard; but, immediately on entering, he was informed that his father had a guest for dinner and was expecting him to join them.

He changed his coat and tidied himself for dinner with his mind in a turmoil of misgiving; and he did not have an opportunity of seeing Bella before having to present himself in the library, where his father was awaiting him. The guest proved to be a young officer of the militia, whose face seemed to Francis very faintly familiar. He was, it appeared, a nephew of Lord Barton and he greeted Francis with great goodwill.

'We have met once before, you know, at my uncle's house, though I doubt if you will remember the occasion. It was several years ago. I was up at Oxford then, or maybe I was even still at Eton, and you were – Oh, I'll not remind you of how young you were!' He laughed cheerfully. 'As I recollect, your health had not been good, but now Sir John tells me that it no longer gives cause for any anxiety, and that you go to Eton in the new year. May I say how glad I am to know that you are recovered, and wish you every success at Eton and as much happiness as I had there? I swear, I almost envy you, having it all yet before you!'

His good-natured, youthful exuberance should have made him appear a likeable person to anyone; but Francis, politely replying to his kindly greeting, could only think of him as a deadly enemy, and one to be foiled at all costs. Of just how deadly an enemy he was, Francis was not long left in doubt.

'Mr Barton is here with a few men to recommence the search for the criminal who gave his captors the slip at an inn somewhere near Osmotherly and Thimbleby three weeks ago, when he was on his way to stand his trial at York. As you no doubt heard, Francis, he disappeared from sight then, but now old Abigail Peel swears she saw him on Tuesday night, raiding her henroost: so Mr Barton is back again,' explained Sir John; and even in the appalling moment of having his worst fears realized, Francis experienced a second's indignation at hearing Seumas once again described as a criminal.

'Two score militiamen were called out to scour the countryside and find and bring him in, and I had the ill fortune to be chosen to be in charge of them.' Charles Barton grinned ruefully as he said it. 'We failed to catch him, and the Duke was in a fury.'

Francis supposed that he was speaking of the Duke of Cumberland, and wondered fleetingly why Cumberland should concern himself with a single fugitive Highlander – unless, of course, Mr Macdonald was someone of greater importance than he had admitted?

But there was no time for further reflection; Charles Barton was continuing, 'It was the more galling, as my corporal and half a dozen men came upon him near here. They almost had him, and then the fools let him slip through their hands. One of the men swears he shot and hit him, but either he must be boasting or the fellow can have been no more than grazed, for he got clean away.'

One tiny portion of Francis's mind which was still able to

reason, weigh up, and calculate, decided that the truth would be safest at this point. He heard himself saying – and marvelled at the calmness with which it was said – 'Yes, I was in the park with Bella, my young sister, and we heard shots and saw a part of the chase.'

'You did? I trust your sister was not distressed?'

Sir John laughed heartily at this suggestion. 'Not Bella, I'll wager! She is a girl of spirit. It would take more than the sight of a militiaman to make Bella swoon.'

'I wish I might say that of my two sisters, sir! I offer my most respectful compliments to Miss Bella.' He turned again to Francis. 'My corporal told me that there had been a little girl who had called out to them the direction they should take, and a young gentleman who had helped him. Might that have been you and your sister?'

'Yes, sir.'

'You both have my thanks for it. Please convey them to Miss Bella. I only wish that the fools had profited from your help and taken O'Leary.'

'O'Leary?'

'The man for whom we are searching. James O'Leary. He is an Irishman, wanted in London – as well as in York – for highway robbery, coin-clipping – Oh, there is a list of charges against him from London as long as my arm, enough to hang him ten times over. I cannot begin to remember them all.'

It was impossible that it should be the same man. This Irish criminal – the word fitted, here – could not be their Mr Macdonald. Yet it had been Mr Macdonald whom the militiamen had hunted across Farmer Bly's cornfield, and shot.

Francis asked as indifferently as he could manage, 'This O'Leary, is he a Jacobite?'

'Like our neighbour Marivel, eh?' Sir John broke in with a laugh; adding with a look of sly amusement in the direction of his son, 'And like someone else nearer home!'

Francis was too perturbed even to notice his father's teasing; besides, Charles Barton was answering his question, appearing mildly surprised.

'A Jacobite? Not that I know of. In fact, I'd say that treason is about the only offence not mentioned on the list!' He laughed.

'You forget, Barton. You mentioned coin-clipping. That is reckoned as treasonable.'

'Lord! So it is. I had forgotten.'

Francis, with a supreme attempt at sounding casual, said, 'What is he like to look at, this man?' Hastily thinking to add, lest his motive in asking should be queried or his interest in James O'Leary arouse suspicion, 'In case I should see him around at any time, sir, and could report it.'

His father said, 'I doubt strongly that he is within fifty miles of Thorsby by now, Francis. I give little credence to Widow Peel's egg-thief. I think our good Abigail is mistaken. She more likely saw Barnsley, or another of the parish ne'er-do-wells. I have no doubt, myself, that this O'Leary got clean away three weeks ago and is now safely in Durham or Manchester.'

'So do I, sir,' agreed Charles Barton. 'But, because of the Duke's personal interest, we were forced to investigate the rumour.' He turned to Francis – who decided at this juncture that the duke of whom he spoke must be the Duke of Shale, the Lord Lieutenant, and not Cumberland, after all – and continued, 'Even if I cannot remember all his crimes, I have his description, at least, by rote – though small use will it be now to either of us, I fear. He is said, by an accomplice, to be about five-and-twenty, of tall to middling height, dark complexioned, with black hair and blue eyes. He speaks with an Irish brogue and has a polished and most plausible manner. He dresses well and fashionably, and at times, I understand, when he finds it to his advantage, he can ape the gentleman successfully.' He broke off for a moment to grin at Francis and remark, 'You see how pat I have it all in honour of the Duke. But, I regret, to no purpose.' He went on with his recital, 'When he escaped from the inn he was wearing his own hair, powdered – wherever he is, he'll have acquired a wig by now, without doubt – a blue coat with silver buttons and a grey waistcoat embroidered in blue and white. But none of that last is of the slightest importance, for he will certainly have disguised himself in some way, days ago. Well, that is all I can tell you about James

O'Leary, but he sounds, in short, a most damnable rogue and he deserves hanging – even if only for putting me to the embarrassment of failing to catch him for the Duke!'

He ended with a laugh in which Sir John joined, so that Francis's reaction to this indisputable description of Seumas went unremarked. There was no more talk of the matter, for, a few moments later, Lady Rimpole joined them and, soon after that, they went in to dinner.

How Francis got through dinner, he did not know; but since neither at the time nor later, did anyone comment on anything strange in his behaviour, they must have noticed nothing; and both his silence throughout most of the meal and his brief, subdued replies when he was spoken to and could not avoid an answer, were no doubt ascribed to a becoming modesty and a courteous respect for his elders.

After dinner he excused himself and took his leave, creditably enough, of the young officer who, once again, wished him well at Eton, recommending him – 'should the old curmudgeon still be there' – to keep out of the black books of a certain master, who was, as he put it, 'a very Tartar'.

Pale, and feeling rather sick, Francis made slowly for his room, finding it necessary to drag himself up the stairs from step to step, holding to the banisters. Bella was waiting for him halfway up; but he was almost upon her before he was aware of her. She flung herself at him, whispering frantically, 'Francis, Francis! There are militiamen in the garden. I saw them from the window. Oh, Francis, what shall we do? Are they searching for Mr Macdonald, do you suppose?'

He answered her in a flat, incredibly calm voice, 'No. They are searching for James O'Leary, a criminal who escaped when he was on his way to York to be tried and hanged.'

'Oh! Then all is well! Oh, Francis, I am so thankful! I have been so worried, you cannot imagine what it has been like.' In her happy relief she babbled on, 'When I saw the militiamen from the window, I was ready to swoon, knowing I could not reach you because you were having dinner with father and mother. I must have gone as white as a sheet, because Miss Proudfoot asked me if I felt unwell. I could hardly eat my dinner, though I had to try, so that she should not suspect there was anything amiss. Oh, Francis, what a terrible scare it was.' She was suddenly conscious of his grim, set expression and the paleness of his cheeks. She stared at him, her own expression beginning slowly to reflect his. In a changed voice she said, 'All is not well, is it? Francis, what has happened?'

He told her. He did not mince matters nor attempt to break the cruel news gently. It had come brutally to him, so he saw no reason why she should be spared. Besides, by this time he was beginning to be angry – with Seumas – so he was ready to hurt someone.

Naturally, as soon as the first shocked numbness had gone and she was able to realize exactly what it was that he had told her, she did not believe it, and said so. 'There is some mistake, Francis. Or else you have misunderstood.'

'No, there is no mistake. And I did not misunderstand.' At the sound of a burst of laughter – Sir John's and his guest's – from downstairs, he took hold of her arm. 'Come on. We cannot stand talking on the stairs.'

On to the next floor, to avoid all possibility of finding Miss Proudfoot in the schoolroom, where she would undoubtedly detain Bella if she saw her, Francis pulled her with him into the empty larger drawing-room, and there he told her exactly why it was that there could be no mistake about the identity of the fugitive; and, in the light of Charles Barton's exact description of Seumas, how it was impossible for him to have misunderstood. He half expected her to cry – he had supposed it to be something which girls always did on such occasions – but she did not. Instead, after her first broken exclamations had been uttered, she looked as white and stricken as he himself did, for all the anger that was now burning in him.

Later, her anger was to match his, but for the moment she was feeling only shame and pain that they had been so cruelly deceived; but she made neither protest nor comment when Francis said, 'Whatever the consequences, I am going to tell father.' A moment or two later he added, 'I do not care what father does to me, so long as . . . so long as O'Leary is taken.'

Bella still said nothing, and she did not even look at him until he said, again after a pause, 'I shall have to wait till Mr Barton is gone and father is alone, even if it means that he has to send after Mr Barton and the militiamen to bring them back. I could not face telling father with a stranger still in the house.'

At that Bella looked at him and said quietly, 'When you go to tell father, I shall go with you.'

He was surprised. 'No, no, Bella. There'll be no need for that. I'll not mention you at all and, with luck, no one will ever know you were involved.'

'But I was involved, Francis. And I shall go with you to father.' She still spoke quietly, but her determination was obvious and, somehow, formidable, and he offered no further argument.

It was some minutes later that, from somewhere among the bitter, shaming memories that jostled each other in their eagerness to torment him, there came into his mind the picture of himself looking down at Seumas in the ditch below the stone wall of the park and swearing on his honour as a gentleman that not for any consideration whatsoever would he betray him. Not for any consideration: not for revenge, not even to see justice done on a deserving criminal. And yet, the Seumas Macdonald to whom he had given his word was not the James O'Leary who was a coin-clipper and a thief. Or was he? Was not the man the same, unchanged in himself – unchanged in his corrupt, deceiving heart? To whom, Francis began to wonder, did one make a promise: to a man himself, or to the man one believed him to be?

They must have been standing there, in the middle of the bright pattern of the Persian carpet, in silence, for quite a long time when the door was half-opened and Miss Proudfoot looked perfunctorily around the edge of it. She was so little expecting to find Bella in there, that she had already begun to withdraw her head before she caught sight of her. She stopped and opened the door wider.

'Annabel! I have been searching for you everywhere. You have kept me waiting for half an hour. Will you please to tell me what you are doing in here?'

They were carried back suddenly, by her entrance, to the ordinary everyday world of which they had once been a part before their misdeeds had brought them to this pass; that everyday world which had flowed on, unchanging, day after day, until the gay and gallant stranger had come to change it all for them; and which would go on again, unchanging as before, day after day, when that stranger had been led out of their lives, to prison and the gallows.

In a flat little voice, Bella said, 'I beg your pardon, Miss Proudfoot. I did not know that I had been so long.' This much, at least, was true.

'You have not answered my question, Annabel. What are you doing in here?'

For three weeks she had been so practised in falsehoods and evasions and half-truths, that it was without a qualm that she now lied glibly. 'Francis has been telling me about Lord Barton's nephew whom he met at dinner. Mr Barton is an officer in the militia, ma'am. Is it not interesting?'

In an hour, perhaps less, Miss Proudfoot and everyone else would know their secret. Until then, let it continue to be their secret. There would be time enough later, she thought, for the truth and for the penalties which it would bring.

'Very interesting, Annabel, I have no doubt. But hardly interesting enough to justify your discourtesy in keeping me waiting for a half-hour,' remarked Miss Proudfoot drily. She stepped aside, holding the door wide open, and gestured to Bella to precede her, as though, now that she had found her, she was going to take no risk of losing her again.

In the doorway Bella paused and turned to look at Francis. What did it matter now what Miss Proudfoot thought? Let her think what she liked of her. 'Francis, you will not fail to take me with you?'

'No.'

'Promise?'

'I promise.'

Only then did Bella go on, out of the room, followed by Miss Proudfoot, who shut the door behind her without either a glance or a word for Francis; hoping by the completeness of her disregard of him, to bring home to him her disapproval of his conduct in encouraging his sister to flout her governess.

The catch of the door closed with a little click, and Francis was left to his problem.

*

The rest of that day was a kind of nightmare for them both. Bella might have fancied their secret would not last an hour after their parting in the drawing-room; but it was far more than an hour later, and Charles Barton had long been gone, when Francis sought her out. His look of miserable irresolution was not what she had expected to see.

'Francis! You have not been to father alone, without me?'

He shook his head. 'No. I have thought about it, Bella, and I cannot make up my mind what to do. I shall not go to father yet.' He paused a moment and then went on, 'I gave my word, on that first day, when I did not know him for what he is, not to betray him. Now that we have learnt that he is otherwise than we believed, I do not know if it would be honourable to betray him.'

She stared at him. 'But it is our duty.'

'Yet would it be honourable, after I have promised?'

'I did not promise not to betray him, Francis. I can go to father.'

He looked at her set face. 'I remember clearly how you told him he could trust us, even before I gave him my word.'

Now that he said it, she, too, remembered it and turned her head from him, hating to have been reminded of that moment. She did not argue with him when he said, 'They say that one should always sleep on an important decision. I shall wait until tomorrow and then do what I think best. After all,' he added, 'he's not going to run away from the Dower House. Whether they go to arrest him today or tomorrow, he will still be there, where he believes he is safe.'

The tears which Bella had not shed when she had first learnt the truth, came later; and it was after midnight before she had wept herself to sleep.

Francis, torn first one way and then the other, did not sleep all night; but by dawn he had made up his mind as to what it was right that he should do.

Before breakfast he said to Bella, 'It is better to err on the side of honour. I have decided I shall not betray him. But neither shall I help him any longer. After breakfast I shall go to the Dower House and tell him he must leave there.'

'I shall go with you. It is Saturday, so I should be able to contrive it.' She remembered then that it was what they had planned to do with the day: to spend as great a part of it as possible at the Dower House. Oh, how long ago yesterday morning seemed now!

'No! It is not fitting that you should be in the company of a common thief. I shall go alone, Bella.'

'I have been in his company for some part of almost every day for the past three weeks.' He could not deny the truth of the bitterly spoken assertion; and before he could find another argument to use against her, she said, 'I've been concerned with you in this matter from the beginning. I am going to be with you at its ending also.'

She did not say that her real object in wanting to accompany him was so that she could hear the truth from Seumas's own lips. For, though her reason told her it was the truth, she knew that there would always, all her life, be one small corner of her mind which would reject this truth and whisper that Seumas might have been misjudged, unless she had heard him admit his guilt himself.

16

Miss Proudfoot having given Bella permission to walk with her brother in the park, they set out soon after breakfast. All the way across the park to the Dower House they did not speak to each other once. They were both sunk in their bitter, painful thoughts; and of the two of them, it would have been hard to say which had been the more injured. Because the one is accounted a virtue, and the other is held to belong among the seven deadly sins, it does not follow that pride is less easily hurt than faith; or that, once wounded, pride suffers less than faith betrayed.

They did not speak, but halfway across the park Francis reached out and took Bella's hand, and without turning her head to look at him, she clasped his tightly in return. And so they walked, hand in hand; not so much for mutual comfort, as in a kind of pact, to set, as it might be, a seal on their determination, and to let their separate, individual angers strengthen, merge, and fuse as one.

As they came in through the back door and made their way along the narrow passage which separated the kitchen from the still-room, they could hear Seumas in the kitchen: the clatter, clatter of the pail going down the well, and Seumas's whistling. Then the slap as the empty pail met the water, followed by a little squeak at every turn of the winch, and the splash of water slopping over its sides back into the well, as the pail came up. The whistling changed to words:

Of all the girls that are so smart
There's none like pretty Sally;
She is the darling of my heart,
And she lives in our alley.

They entered the kitchen just as Seumas was setting the pail on the curb of the well and was about to unhook it from the chain. He heard them and turned, steadying himself with one hand on the curb.

'Good morning to you both. See what fine progress I'm making, and how independent I've become. I thought it would give you a surprise to find me keeping house for myself.' He seemed suddenly to realize that their silence, as they stood together in the doorway, was not due to surprise, for his cheerful smile died and he said in a puzzled tone, 'Is it anything wrong there is?'

Francis took three steps farther into the room, but Bella stayed where she was on the threshold. Seumas looked and sounded just the same as he had yesterday, she was thinking. Might it not, even now, turn out to be some terrible mistake, and might he not, after all, still be really Seumas Macdonald – their own Mr Macdonald?

Francis had no such doubts. 'James O'Leary,' he said, making it both a statement and an accusation.

The two of them stared at one another across the kitchen without further movement or word. Then, moments later, Seumas turned round slowly, took the pail off the hook, looked about him as though he had forgotten where he had placed his stick, found it propped against the well-curb, and supported himself carefully with it before lifting the pail down and beginning to walk towards the table. Water slopped on to the table top as he raised the pail and set it down. He once more turned then, bracing his back against the table's edge. Francis and Bella had neither of them moved again, but their relentless eyes had followed him across the kitchen, and were now fixed on him, waiting.

'Sure and I'm James O'Leary.'

'Wanted for theft and c-coin-cl-clipping and highway robbery.'

Hearing Francis, Bella suddenly realized that she had long completely forgotten that, when he was very much younger, Francis had sometimes stammered a little when he was very excited or agitated or angry. It was so many years since he had last done so, that she had not remembered about it.

'And a score of other things besides, I've no doubt.' Seumas's tone was casual.

This was not what Francis had been expecting. 'Then you do not deny it?'

'Faith! And why should I deny it, and you knowing it all?' His laugh was a little shaky: but he managed to laugh.

The laugh angered Francis, more than he was angered already. His face white and his hands clenched at his sides, he said, 'And you are not a J-Jacobite?'

Seumas shrugged his shoulders. 'Why should I be lying to you now? It is nothing to me who sits on the throne.'

Bella spoke for the first time. 'Oh, it was wicked of you, wicked, to say you were a Jacobite!'

'What would you have had me do, and you showing me the way I could be saving my life? Thief or traitor, a man's life is as sweet to him, and he'll be doing what he can to save it.'

'There was no need to lie to us. We would have helped you anyway.' Because of the liking she had grown to have for him, she believed it while she was saying it – but she did not believe it for very long after his reply had been spoken.

'Would you, Miss Bella? Would you, now?' Seumas asked softly.

For ten seconds or more they held each other's gaze, and then Bella's glance fell before his.

'You made it plain, the both of you, that you'd only be helping a Jacobite. So what would you expect me to do, and the militia only ten yards away?'

Francis, furious as he was, could yet be just. 'Even a common criminal has the right to try and save his life, I suppose. But where was the need for all ... for all those other l-lies you told us afterwards? Your Scottish name and that you were a Jacobite, perhaps. But not all the rest of it.'

His defence still taking a bantering tone, Seumas said, 'Only the half of my name was a lie, I'd have you know. For it's Seumas I am. Seumas O'Leary, fourth son of Patrick O'Leary, printer, of Dublin city. Seumas I was christened and Seumas I was to my father and mother, and Seumas I still am to my good friends, though I've not seen Ireland since I was fourteen.'

'B-But all the rest of it was lies: about seeing the Prince, and C-Culloden and everything?' Francis's voice was shaking badly by this time, and with anger as much as with anything else.

'It was, and it's sorry for it I am now. Though I only told you what you were wanting to hear.'

'How could you do it!' Bella's voice was shaking, too; but not so much with anger as with the hurt of it all.

'God forgive me, but I never could say a plain yes or a no. I always must be embroidering it, as one might say. Building up the fanciful situations so that I almost believe them myself, in time.' For one brief moment his voice sank to an almost pleading note. 'And was it not trying to stop it I was, and you not letting me?'

The scorn on Francis's face showed how little he credited this.

'And none of it, none of it at all, was true?' Bella, though she knew it to be hopeless, was nevertheless yet trying to salvage some small thing from the wreck of her admiration for the gallant stranger. 'Even about...' her voice faltered and dropped, 'even about ... your sweetheart?' That had been the thing which he had told her for herself alone: Francis had not shared in that knowledge. And now must it, too, be a lie?

He hesitated a moment, then said, 'It's not entirely untrue that was. I suppose you might say that I have a sweetheart, but it's not a farmer's daughter she is and her name's not Mary. She was a foundling from the gutter and she's known as Sukey. And it's little use at all she is at sewing, and she'd be sorely put to it to know how to bake a cake. But I never lied about her looks. It's the yellow hair like buttercups she has, and big grey eyes, and her red mouth is always laughing, as I said.' The reproach in Bella's eyes drove him to defiance. 'She's a darling girl, is Sukey, and the best little pickpocket on the diving lay. Och, many's the rich old skinflint we've made the lighter of his purse between us, Sukey and I.'

'A pickpocket!'

How could she have known he was striking out at her with the cruel truth only to hurt himself? Her reproachful looks quite cast out by scorn and anger, she exclaimed again, 'A pickpocket!'

Her contempt moved him to defend Sukey, not there to defend herself. 'Sure and she is! A pickpocket and none the worse for that. She's gay and she's good company and her heart's as big as St Paul's Cathedral. Sukey always has a welcome and a helping hand for a friend whose luck is at low ebb, as mine's been many a time. Faith! If it's a foundling born in the gutter you'd been, and never knowing who your parents were, maybe it's a pickpocket you'd be yourself.'

'I will not have you insult my s-sister!'

Seumas's mood changed instantly. Suddenly weary and deflated, he flung out one hand in a defeated gesture and said, 'Och, it's the fool I am to expect you to understand. I'm sorry, Miss Bella.'

Her face quite without any other expression than well-bred contempt, she stared at him for a few moments longer; then she looked towards her brother and said in a cold little voice, 'It's chilly in here, Francis, and damp. I am going into another room.' She turned her back on Seumas and slowly and with immense dignity went from the kitchen. It was intuitively and quite perfectly done. Bella, who always despaired of ever being able to achieve her mother's poise and sophistication, had conducted herself in a manner which would not have disgraced Lady Rimpole at her most self-possessed.

To Francis, his sister had merely behaved as she should. Any admiration he felt for her demeanour was because, though angry, she had not lost composure; but Seumas, both far more imaginative and far less self-centred than Francis, was not as much hurt by her studied contempt as by his own guess that she had left the room so that there should be no possible chance of his seeing her weep at his words.

Bella walked along the passage towards the hall, successfully fighting back her tears. This was no time for tears, she told herself – and anyway, why should she want to weep when she was so angry?

In this house of empty or unwelcoming rooms, her feet carried her without her intention to the only habitable place. On the threshold of the Chinese room she paused at finding herself there. She could not go into that room again, not now. It was as though someone were dead, she thought; which was, on reflection, a strange way to think of it. Yet perhaps not so strange after all; for had not someone died? Seumas Macdonald, the brave Jacobite Highlander, who had fought and suffered for his rightful king – he was as surely dead as though the bullet which had grazed his arm had passed instead through his heart. She shivered suddenly and moved away from the door to stand at the head of the passage, quite still, her hands clasped in front of her, looking along it in the direction of the kitchen, wondering what the two of them in there were saying now. The minutes passed. Once she stirred and took two hesitant paces back the way she had come, and then stopped and stood again.

In the kitchen neither of them spoke for a while after Bella had gone: each was waiting for the other. Finally Seumas moved himself into a less uncomfortable position against the table and shifted more of his weight off his right ankle. With a return to his bantering manner, eyebrows raised, he challenged, 'Well, and what will you be doing about it? Is it handing me over to the law you'll be?'

Francis answered him in a level voice. 'That is what I would like to do. It is what we both would like to do. It would be a satisfaction as well as a duty. But,' he went on stiffly, 'I gave you my word, when I thought you were a Jacobite, that I would not betray you. Whoever and whatever you are, I cannot go back on my word, and my promise holds.' With a momentary break in his very adult self-control, he added warmly and with spite, 'Unfortunately!'

'Sure and your gentlemanly punctiliousness does you credit, and it's grateful to you for it I should be.' Seumas made Francis a mocking little bow, then added with a flash of bitterness, 'And so I am, I suppose. Though a ha'p'orth of compassion weighs heavier than a hundred guineasworth of high principles, to my mind.'

After a furious moment, Francis pulled his purse from his pocket, tipped out into one hand all it held and stepped forward to the table. He dropped the money on the table-top as far from Seumas as possible and stepped away again. 'That's the money I had for the buttons I sold for you. You will no doubt find it useful when you are on your way. I regret that it is short by half a crown, but I spent half a crown of it on you and I . . . I am not at present able to refund it.'

Seumas glanced at the coins. 'Since you spent it on me,

there's surely no need for regrets. I'd not be taking it from you at all, but, as you say, I shall be needing it when I'm on my way.'

'It is only natural that I should regret buying anything, for whatever purpose, with money made from the sale of presumably stolen goods.' It was Francis at his most consequential, and Seumas laughed, genuinely amused.

'Och, if that's what you're after regretting, I can set your mind at rest. I bought the coat and the buttons, too.'

'With stolen money, no doubt!' Francis snapped back at him.

Seumas gave another chuckle. 'Sure and you have me there!'

'You had better take the money and fetch anything else of yours that you have in this house, and go.'

Seumas, startled and dismayed, echoed, 'Go? Now?'

'The sooner the better, and we shall be glad to be free of you. You can walk well enough now, so there's nothing to prevent your going.'

'At this very instant, are you meaning?'

'Yes.'

'Is it turning me out in broad daylight you are, and I with a price on my head?'

'Had it not been for us, at the best you would be out now' – he quoted, unable to keep the mockery entirely from his voice – 'in broad daylight, with a price on your head. At the worst, you would no doubt have been caught days ago. So what have you to whine about?'

Seumas looked at him steadily and then he laughed shortly. When he spoke, his voice, like his laugh, had a bitter edge. 'So it's making the best of both worlds you'd be? Saving your precious gentlemanly honour by not giving me up yourself, but making sure that I'm nabbed by sending me out at this moment to my death.'

'There's no certainty of that.'

'How far do you think I'd get along the road and I limping and a stranger, with village folk as curious as they are, and they remembering how I was hunted through the district, three weeks ago?' He paused, looking questioningly at Francis; while Francis looked back at him implacably.

'Och, come now, give me a chance. Let me wait here until dark, and be going then.'

'No.'

'Give me a chance and, however you feel about it now, it's loving yourself the better for it you'll be for ever after.'

Francis did not reply.

'Sure and it's the hard-hearted, vindictive one you are – and small blame to you for it. It's not too well I've been behaving, neither.'

'I presume you think that if you can keep me here talking for long enough, it will be evening and growing dark.'

Seumas grinned amusedly. 'It's the devil's own task I'd be having to do that at midsummer, with it twelve of the clock now and you in no mood for conversing.'

'Then go!'

Seumas made no move and for a while he said nothing; then he asked quietly, 'Is it hanged you want me to be?'

'Yes!' The answer came promptly: too promptly, without time for consideration of the question.

Seumas shrugged his shoulders. 'In that case there's no more to be said, and I might as well be going. If I were to talk from now until doomsday, instead of dusk, I'd be getting nowhere, I can see.' He began to drop the coins slowly, one by one, into his pocket. Looking at the money as he handled it, and not at Francis, he spoke, 'It's small use my saying thank you to you for what you have both done, and you in the humour you are at present. So it's only good-bye I'll be saying.' All the money in his pocket, leaning on the stick, he began to move towards the door. 'It's grateful I am, all the same. You may believe that or not,' he said as he passed Francis.

Francis said nothing, but watched him as he went, his brow furrowed with sudden indecision. When Seumas reached the door to the passage, he abruptly called out, 'O'Leary!'

Seumas stopped and turned, inquiringly.

Francis took a deep breath and said quickly. 'You may stay here until tonight. I'll come over and let you out when it's dark.'

Seumas smiled. 'It's more like your old self you are, this very minute. You'll not regret it, I'm telling you. But you'll not need to be putting yourself to the trouble of coming over here to-night. I can see myself off the premises.'

Francis did not bother to explain that he would have to unlock the park gates, which the gamekeeper would have locked at sunset; he only said curtly, 'I shall be here.'

'To make sur that I do not prig any of the knick-knacks, I presume.' Seumas laughed shortly and harshly. 'I deserve that, I suppose.'

He moved on along the passage and into the hall, the stick tap-tapping on the flag-stones. Seeing him come, Bella backed away uncertainly and awkwardly, to avoid his passing close to her, and she did not look at him as he turned in at the door of the Chinese room; nor did he glance at her.

Francis followed him slowly from the kitchen. When he reached Bella he said briefly, 'I have told him he may stay until tonight.' He sounded almost as though he expected her to blame him for it. She said nothing.

Francis went into the Chinese room. 'I shall be here tonight as soon as I can contrive to get away. Be ready, so that you can go at once and I do not have to wait for you.'

'I shall be ready. There's little enough packing of baggage I have to do for my journey, so why should I not be ready?' He added mockingly, 'For, after all, where could I be hiding about my person the chandelier or the tea-kettle stand or . . . or that ugly creature there that seems to find all this a good jest the way it's after grinning at us.' He pointed with the stick towards the Chinese lion, still peering out from the white sheet draped about its shoulders. The gesture brought the stick to Seumas's mind, for he said, no longer with mockery, but still lightly and as if indifferent to the answer, 'Unless it's lending me this stick you would be, until I can be cutting myself one from the woods. For it's not fast nor far I could go without it yet.'

'Lending!' exclaimed Francis. 'Giving, you mean. How would you return it, when you had done with it? Always supposing you mean to do so! No, I have helped you enough. You will leave it here.'

Seumas shrugged his shoulders. 'You are right, of course. It is much too fine a stick to be trusted to a prig, with its silver top and all.' He raised it to examine the knob, twisting it in his hands. 'A fine knob of silver, with a stag's head engraved on it. That will be your family crest, I'm thinking.'

Francis, in momentary exasperation, cried, 'Oh, take it with you, if you want it! What does it matter, so long as we are rid of you tonight!'

Seumas, still studying the silver knob, said, 'I'm thinking that it could matter quite a bit. When I'm nabbed – as I'm bound to be soon with all the district out after me, and with little enough blunt to be travelling with, and without a prancer to ride, or even a disguise to be making me feel safer – when I'm taken, it's wondering how I came by it, they'll all be.' He glanced up from the stick to grin mockingly at Francis. 'It would not look too well, would it now, if I were to be telling them I'd had it from respectable young Mr Rimpole, whose guest I'd been these three weeks? It's not only respectable young Mr Rimpole who would be having questions asked of him then, but his father as well, and himself a Justice of the Peace and all.'

They looked at each other, Seumas mocking and Francis puzzled by his words. Then slowly Francis grasped, as he thought, the point of what Seumas had said. At first incredulous, then furious, he cried, 'Are you threatening me? Are you t-trying to force me into helping you further? Into giving you money and a horse? You scoundrel! After all we have done for you!'

Seumas stared back at him with, to begin with, a similar incredulity; then, as he realized Francis's meaning, his anger was kindled and rose flaring and sparking on the instant.

'By heaven! Is it thinking that I'm after trying to extort money and more help from you by threats, you are? And you with your respectable, honourable, gentlemanly standards! If high principles can bring a cove to thinking such things of another without cause, it's glad I am that I have none. Oh, there's plenty I've done in my time which I should not, and it's not ashamed of it I am. But there are some things which even I would never dream of doing, and that is one of them. I've met mealy-mouthed cullies enough – fat, respected hypocrites whose respectability was no more than a sham – and if I've never stooped to threaten to unmask them for my own gain, do you think I'd be doing it now to someone who has been kind to me?'

Bella could not follow what they were quarrelling about. She heard their voices raised in anger about something that had escaped her, some point in what they had been saying which she must have missed. Bewildered and afraid, she slipped into the room and stood close to Francis, a little behind him, her wide eyes staring at Seumas, now, in his hot anger, more of a stranger than ever. She wanted to take Francis's hand for reassurance, but felt instinctively that he would resent it, and maybe even shake her off.

'No, it's no more than jeering at you I was, honourable Master Francis Rimpole, for your respectability; that fine respectability that yet lets you have such thoughts in your head as you have been uttering this moment gone. It's no more than about to refuse your kind offer I was, and to tell you that you'd best be keeping this for your own peace of mind.' He flung the stick down on the couch. 'Well, it's relieving you of my unwelcome company this very moment I'll be, and going down that road to the village with the daylight bright on me and showing me to the world. And when it's taken and nubbed I am, I hope you'll be glad of it, the pair of you.' His last words seemed to bring Bella back to his mind suddenly, just at the very moment when he became aware that she was in the room.

His swift rage died down as quickly as it had arisen, and he fell silent and regarded her. Then he said quietly and with what, in any other man than one who had proved himself so adept a deceiver, would have been unquestionably accepted as sincerity, 'It's truly sorry I am, Miss Bella, to have given you distress and heartache, and it's with great regard that I'll always be remembering you, for you have taught me something that I did not know. My father, he was a good and respectable man, and my mother, she was good and respectable too; and my brothers and sisters, young as they were, they were after being good and respectable, also.' His voice strengthened and he spoke less quietly. 'Och, it's a cold, hard thing their goodness was, and their respectability was even colder and harder, and I'd soon had my fill of them both, and they being forced on me, day after day. When I was fourteen I ran away from home, and I've never been good or respectable since. And until these last weeks I've never regretted what I left behind me in Dublin. But you have shown me something about respectability which I had forgotten – if, indeed, I was ever knowing it at all – that it's not only high-sounding principles and self-esteem it need be, but warmth and kindness and mirth can have a share in it as well, and those are three things I like well. But it's small use it is my regretting any part of respectability now, for I threw it all into the Liffey, ten years ago, and there's no getting it back. even if I wished to, which I do not.'

She heard him uncomprehendingly, and so, unmoved. Her sympathy was closed entirely against him; she was making no attempt to understand. It was just so many words – and, therefore, so many lies – uttered in that persuasive voice which now could never persuade her again.

He saw this, and with a sweeping gesture of one arm brushed away earnestness and once more altered his mood. 'But I'll not be wearying you with my talk any longer, and you both wanting to see the back of me.' He reached for his hat from the top of a shrouded tea-kettle stand, brushed off a speck or two of dust, clapped it on his head, and made for the door, talking all the while. 'Well, it's on my way I'll be now – wherever that way may be leading me – and you'll never be seeing me again in this life, though it's thankful I'll be to you both until my last day. And I'll never be breathing your names to a soul, so you can rest easy, for you've no need to be fearing on that score.' Borne along on the crest of his words, on his voyage out of their lives, from the doorway he bowed to them with a flourish. 'Your servant, ma'am. Your servant, sir. Try not to be thinking too hardly of me, and I possibly gone to my death.' With a last flashing smile and a careless wave of his hand, he turned and made off towards the front door, with just that right medley of jauntiness and gallantry which he considered fitting for the occasion, walking firmly and resolutely upon his still slightly aching right ankle.

Bella did not move, but Francis went to the door and looked along the hall after him. When Seumas was almost at the front door, and not before, Francis spoke in a cool, unhurried voice in which all note of triumph was so carefully controlled and hidden as to be glaringly obvious to the hearer, 'You will find that door is locked, and I have no key for it. The back door is open.'

His hand already stretched out to the door handle, Seumas stopped. He remained facing the door for a moment, then he turned and began to grin as he walked back towards Francis.

'Och, you had me finely there, and I making the grand, noble gesture and an exit worthy of Mr Garrick at Drury Lane!' He flung back his head and laughed.

Francis's triumph was instantly diminished by Seumas's unfeigned amusement. On being made to look foolish, he should have been either angered or abashed: he should not have been amused.

'How can you laugh?' Francis demanded furiously.

When his laughter was done, Seumas said, 'The back door is open, you say? Then it's that way to the road I'll be taking. It's through the front door that brave Mr Macdonald the hero came in, but the back door is good enough for Seumas O'Leary the thief. And so it should be, for that's the way of the world.'

Still jaunty, and swaggering a little, he made his way down the passage and opened the back door. There he turned his head and called over his shoulder to them both – for Bella was now beside Francis in the hall outside the Chinese room – 'It's truly good-bye it is this time. You'll not be seeing me again – unless I go to the nubbing-cheat at York and you come to see me swing!' With a last wave of his hand and a grin, he was gone, and they were left staring at a closed door at the end of a passage.

17

NEITHER of them spoke for quite a while; then Bella said hesitantly, 'Francis, he will never manage to get safely away, will he? Do you think it was truly keeping your promise to let him go like that, straight out through the gates into the lane, with perhaps people about?'

Francis took some of his resentment out on his sister. 'Must you be such a fool, Bella? You need not be anxious for him. He will come crawling back to that door within five minutes, begging me to let him stay until dark and to show him the way out then. Or rather, he'll come ruffling back and putting a good face on it. Have you forgotten that the gates are padlocked? There's no way he can get out to the lane except through the park and he does not know the way to any of the gates from this house.'

'He may go into the park and search until he finds the west gate.'

'Not he! He'll not risk prowling about the park at midday. He will be back in five minutes, you'll see.'

They waited five minutes and Seumas had not come; ten minutes or more, and there was still no sign of him.

'He must have made his way out into the lane,' said Bella.

'How could he? Fly, I suppose! There's no means of getting through the front gates, you know that.'

'He may be in the park, trying to find a way out,' persisted Bella.

'He is more likely to be skulking in the garden, feeling too much of a fool to show his face in here until we have gone.' After another short silence, he said irritably, 'Oh, I suppose we had better go and find him. Come on.'

From the back garden they made their way around the side of the house to the front. Even at the very top of the drive they could hear the sound of dogs barking excitedly in the lane.

'He's been caught!' exclaimed Bella; and they both began, on the instant, to run towards the gates. Well before they reached them they could see that they were still closed, linked together by a chain and a large padlock, just as when they had last seen them; yet there was no sign at all of Seumas. But still the dogs barked in the lane, out of sight.

Arriving rather breathless at the gates, Francis put his head through the bars and looked up and down the lane as far as he could.

'Och, be off with you, you noisy crew. Yapping fit to wake the dead, you are, silly barking-cheats.'

In front of the yew hedge to the right of the gate, just in sight if one craned one's neck, Seumas was sitting in the lane, attempting at the same time, both to frighten off three fierce-looking mongrels and to raise himself to his feet by gripping the lower branches of the yews which stood in a thick and ancient hedge on the outside of the tall railings on either side of the gates.

'They are Tuttle's dogs and not as fierce as they look,' Francis called to him.

Seumas, halfway to his feet, turned his head at the sound of Francis's voice, lost his balance and sank back on to the dusty lane, his face twisted with pain. He clasped his ankle and bent over it, the dogs still leaping and snarling about him. When he had recovered, a few seconds later, he looked towards Francis once more and said with a rueful smile to the head thrust through the bars, 'I've done it again. Is it not the fool of fools I am?'

Francis had a sudden most unmanly desire to burst into tears – tears of disappointment, self-pity, rage, and despair – followed by a desire, equally strong, to withdraw his head through the bars, ignoring all that lay on the other side of the gates, to take Bella firmly by the arm and lead her home. He controlled both desires with an effort, and was able, a few moments later, to ask resignedly, 'How did you get out?'

'I tried to climb over, and fell instead.'

'It would, I suppose, be asking too much of you to expect you to have fallen on this side.'

At that moment there was a whistling down the lane, as

though for a dog. The three mongrels pricked up their ears, but only one of them, a brindled bitch, showed any signs of being willing to answer the summons. Yet, in the end, none of them went, and soon they were once again barking and leaping about Seumas. The whistling came again, louder this time, and more prolonged.

'Someone will come for them, and find him,' said Bella.

'Try to drive the brutes off,' said Francis. 'Don't just sit there and do nothing.'

'What is it you think I have been doing these ten minutes and more?'

'We must open the gates, Francis, and bring him in.'

'How do you suggest we could do that?'

Undeterred by his sarcasm, she offered, 'Should I go home and find Mr Thompson's key?'

'How much time do you think we have to spare?'

'Perhaps we could break open the padlock –' She stopped when she saw his expression and said, 'No, I suppose we could not.... But there might be a file in one of the kitchen closets here, and then we could file through the chain.'

'Must you be so stupid, Bella? How long do you think that would take us? And anyway,' he added, 'what would happen when it was noticed that the chain had been filed through? Or are you proposing that we should weld it together again afterwards?' As the whistling started again imperiously and impatiently, he said, 'I shall have to climb over.'

'But what will you do when you have climbed over?'

'Get rid of the dogs before anyone comes for them, of course.'

'What if you are too late, of if Tuttle comes in any case to see why they were barking?'

He ran his hand through his hair despairingly. 'Oh lord! What else is there I can do?' His brow cleared a little. 'I know! You must run for all you are worth to the west gate, go through and across the lane to Tuttle's cottage and try to stop him from coming along the lane for the dogs. Talk to him, ask to see his wife, anything, so long as you can keep him away from here until I have O'Leary hidden somewhere.'

'Right! I'll do it! But I doubt if I can be there in time.'

'At least try, and do not waste time in arguing, for heaven's sake. I'm going over.' He started, rather doubtfully and with considerable difficulty, to climb the gate, which had not been designed for such a purpose.

'Do be careful, Francis,' Bella called over her shoulder.

'Oh, hurry up and go, and stop scolding at me. You have something of your own to do. Go and do it.'

Bella, her skirts held up in one hand, tore off up the drive.

Francis eventually reached the top of the gates – though the climb seemed to have taken an excessively long time – and cautiously got himself over the ornamental spikes at the top to find the descent on the other side even more awkward than the ascent had been; and he had in honesty to admit to himself that Seumas, with his hardly stout ankle, had had every excuse for falling. He made the last few feet of the descent to the accompaniment of a new almost continuous distant whistling and the excited leapings and barkings of the three dogs, who were, by this time, dividing their attention between him and Seumas; though they showed themselves less inclined to be threatening towards him, since he was not such a complete stranger to them.

As he finally dropped thankfully to the ground, they gave him their whole attention, rushing at him in one concerted onslaught. Too angry to care whether he was bitten or not, he grabbed at the brindled bitch who headed the attack and flung her away from him while kicking at the other two. 'Down, you brutes! Down!' This gave them a slight respect for him, and they retreated to the middle of the lane, from where they continued to bark and snarl, so that he was able to turn to Seumas, who had taken advantage of the respite from their attack to crawl the five or six feet to the gatepost and haul himself upright with the aid of the bars. Clinging on with one hand, he was endeavouring without success to take off his boot with the other.

'It's swelling . . . like rising dough . . . it is. The devil . . . take it. Cannot cut off . . . this good boot,' he gasped.

'I should think not!' Francis, remembering vividly and with repugnance the scene in the cobbler's shop, dropped to his knees and seized the boot. 'Hold fast to the gate while I pull.'

He dragged at the boot quickly and brutally, almost falling backwards into the lane as it came off. 'Thank heaven for that!' he said. He got to his feet as the dogs came at him again, swinging the boot at them and catching one of them on the nose, so that it retreated with a yelp, which made the other two more cautious.

Turning to see Seumas's sweat-streaked face, now a sickly green, and his hands, white-knuckled, still gripping the bars, Francis had a momentary qualm and said shortly and with constraint, 'I'm sorry. I never meant to hurt you.'

Seumas unclenched his teeth and managed a smile. 'Sure and I know that.'

Francis was suddenly aware, at the same instant as the brindled bitch and one of the other dogs – though the third had so far noticed nothing and was renewing the attack – that the whistling was coming closer. Bella must have failed in her mission; or she had not yet had time to reach the west gate.

'Oh, lord! Tuttle is coming. You must hide. But where?' Francis looked all about him. There was a ditch on the opposite side of the lane; but even had it afforded adequate cover – which it did not – the dogs would soon have drawn their master's attention to anyone hidden in it.

'Were it not for those cursed railings on the other side, it's creeping under the hedge and into the garden I could be. But then,' Seumas added, 'were it not for the railings, I'd not have fallen, for it's through the hedge I'd have come out.'

'The hedge! That's the only possible place. You must contrive somehow to stand between the hedge and the railings. You could then not be seen from this side, and it does not matter if you can be seen from the garden.

The hedge had grown through the railings long before, and been trimmed back neatly, flush with them, on the garden side, time after time; and even when Francis had dragged the stiff growth back through the railings, there was hardly space to stand a broomstick, let alone a man. While the whistling came nearer, alternationg with a bellowed, 'Here, you rapscallions!' Seumas forced a painful entry between railings and hedge, while Francis tried to hold back the thick, resilient green mass, without at the same time getting in his way; and the dogs, torn between their excitement over what was going on and the imminent approach of their master, barked as loudly as ever and ran up and down before a two-yard stretch of hedge and gate.

At last, somehow, it was achieved and Seumas was lodged, crushed between hedge and railings, about four feet in from the gatepost at which the hedge began.

Francis extricated himself from the hedge and looked anxiously to see if total concealment had been managed. It had. There was no sign of Seumas visible, the five-foot wide hedge looked as always, save for some broken branches and crushed young, bright green shoots near the gatepost, where Seumas had thrust his way in. Francis hastily swept these out of sight and then began to set himself to rights, straightening his coat and brushing yew leaves off his clothes.

'You cannot be seen from the lane. But you must keep completely still. Is all well with you?'

'It's only being pressed to death I am, and choked with mouthfuls of yew and it as poisonous as sixty snakes.'

Francis, vainly trying to clean his face and hands with his pocket handkerchief, and only spreading the dirt, snapped back, 'If you'd rather be choked with a rope, then come out!'

There was a faint but unmistakable chuckle from the depths of the hedge. 'Not I!'

'Hold your tongue!' hissed Francis suddenly.

The barking had ceased now, as had the whistling, and the bellowing voice came from only a few yards away. 'Drat you, you silly stinkabouts! You wait till I catch you. I'll yark you!'

One final useless flick at his breeches and one final glance in the direction of the invisible Seumas, and Francis stepped into the middle of the lane with some vague idea of diverting attention from the hedge by keeping away from it. Then he saw Seumas's boot, lying in front of the gates. At the very last moment he darted to it, snatched it up and, there being now no time to do anything else, he flung it over the gates without even aiming, and hoping it would land out of sight. It landed two yards beyond, right in the middle of the drive, a single boot, entirely out of place and very noticeable.

At the same moment Tuttle appeared around the curve of

the lane. The village woodman and carpenter, who often worked up at the Hall, he was a tall, burly man with a ruddy-complexioned, good-humoured face; though at the moment he was perplexed and mildly irritated by the behaviour of his dogs, who completely quiet at last, slunk apologetically towards their master, the brindled bitch first, wagging her tail ingratiatingly.

'You bellkites, you! How dare you not come when you're bid? Heel!' He grabbed at each dog and cuffed it. 'Heel, now! Or you'll get worse than that! What in the name of Old Scrat came over you all, you daft gabys?'

The dogs dropped meekly to heel, though not without longing glances at the hedge, and Tuttle caught sight of Francis. He touched his cap, surprised to see him there. 'Eh, now, Master Francis! Good day to you, sir.'

'Good morning, Tuttle.'

Tuttle took in Francis's dishevelled appearance, the dust on his clothes and face, his hair straggling out of its ribbon, and said knowingly, 'Thrown by your grey, were you, sir? Where's he got to? Bolted?'

Stiffly and crushingly, Francis replied, 'No, I was not.' Then, thinking better of it, as he remembered that any possible suspicion must be averted, he added slightly more expansively and with a degree more affability, 'I am taking a walk.'

Tuttle, reflecting that boys would be boys, whether they came from the Hall or from the cottage of one of Squire's tenants, grinned and said, 'Aye, it's a right fine day for a walk, and all.' He glanced at the dogs. 'Happen you might have noticed what ailed these old fools of mine? I've been whistling and whistling to them, but never a bit they heeded, and went on barking their daft heads off. You must have heard them as you came along, sir. At longwhiles I thought of that hangtrace old Widow Peel saw, that they say is still hereabouts, and I said to myself, "Happen t'dogs have got hold on him," I said, and I came to see for myself, like. Did you notice owt, sir? For I cannot think what came over the gowks.'

Francis, who had until that moment not made up his mind whether to deny all knowledge of the reason for the dogs' behaviour, or to invent an innocent explanation for it, saw the shrewd look in Tuttle's eyes as they rested on him, and decided on the latter course. As casually as he could manage, and with a fair imitation of boyish candour, he said, 'Well, as a matter of fact, it was really my fault, I suppose. I saw a . . . a pair of rats in the ditch, and was setting your dogs on them.'

'Rats, was it? That was a derrum and a deal of cess for two rats.'

'They were huge ones,' said Francis hastily. 'I have never seen any as large before. They were the size of . . . of rabbits, almost.'

'Eh, now, that's interesting, that is.' Tuttle looked about him for the bodies of these prodigious rats. 'Where are they, then? Did t'dogs eat them?'

Francis, by reason of his vulnerable position, forced to be cautious of everything and everyone, was by now in a state to be inclined to suspect every question of being a trap, and he decided, all in a minute, not to risk saying yes. 'Unfortunately, they got away,' he said with a wry smile which was meant as an apology for the lack of skill shown by both the dogs and himself.

'Got away, you say, sir?' exclaimed Tuttle incredulously. 'Got away from my dogs? Eh, now, I've never known Bitch Beauty here to lose a rat in all her life. Best ratter for miles around, she is, sir.' He looked down and saw how she had already slunk from heel and was crouching before his feet, hopefully. He bent and patted her. 'Aren't you, now, lass? Never lose a rat, do you?'

He looked up again, and Francis now felt quite certain of his suspicion. 'Whereabouts did they go to, then, sir, those rats?'

Francis, about to indicate the ditch, saw that one of the other dogs, a wary eye on his master, was wriggling forward inch by inch on his belly towards the hedge, irresistibly lured towards Seumas's hiding place, and in a single second changed his mind rather than risk being caught in a lie. 'They ran under the yew hedge. They probably have a hole in there.'

Tuttle turned towards the hedge, saw the disobedient dog, who stopped in his tracks and rolled his eyes upwards beseechingly. 'Still after them, are you, Spot?'

Reassured and encouraged by his master's jovial tone of

voice, Spot got to his feet and started barking and thrusting his head under the hedge, exactly where Seumas was hidden, five feet beyond him. Immediately the two other dogs joined him, and Tuttle, going up to the hedge himself, bent down and peered through the lower branches.

Francis was appalled and immediately regretted his choice of a home for the rats. But the choice had at least allayed Tuttle's suspicions that he was lying – he would hardly have gone to the trouble of investigating under the hedge himself, if he had not believed the rats might be there – that was one thing for which to be thankful, Francis decided.

Tuttle, even redder in the face than was normal for him, straightened up and said, 'No sign of them now, sir. But happen I'll bring t'dogs along later, after dinner, or this evening, and we'll rout about then, like. Squire'll not want two bilking great rats in Dower House garden. And, anygates, I'd be interested, like, to see them, if they are as big as you say.'

'That's a good notion,' said Francis heartily. 'I hope you catch them. Beauty certainly deserves a catch. I must have distracted her just now, if you say she usually never loses one.'

Tuttle laughed. 'Happen you did just that, sir. She's not used to hunting with the gentry, like.'

They both laughed at that, Tuttle with mirth at his own joke, and Francis with relief that it was turning out so well after all; and then Tuttle suddenly stopped laughing, pointed and said, 'Eh, now, what's that, then?'

Francis, following the pointing finger with a sinking sensation at his stomach, said, 'Why, a boot! I wonder whose it is, and how it came there.'

Tuttle inspected the boot through the bars of the gate. 'It's a good boot and new, too, I'd say. A pity there's nowt but the one. A pair of those would be a right good find for any man. Happen it might belong to George Rigby?'

Francis could think of no reason why the head gardener should leave one of his boots lying in the drive while, presumably, walking off in the other, so he felt regretfully obliged to reject this helpful suggestion. 'I doubt it. I cannot think whose it can be, unless someone put it there as a joke. If I remember, and have a few minutes to spare, I might go into the garden sometime and take a look at it.' He tried to dismiss casually the dangerous subject of the mysterious boot, and succeeded so well in appearing bored, that Tuttle thought that Master Francis had had enough of his company and said, 'Well, now, I'll be off to my dinner and leave you to your walk, sir, and thank you.' He touched his cap, called the reluctant dogs and made off along the lane in the direction of the west gate of the park, almost opposite which stood his cottage and one other, thinking as he went that Master Francis was certainly behaving unexpectedly of late: first talking so affably to Mrs Cotter and always buying jugs of ale and food to eat, and now ratting with the village dogs, and the young gentleman so nunty as a rule. He shook his head as he walked on, the two dogs at his heels and Beauty at his side. He was, for all he had a certain shrewdness, a simple man who disliked anything untoward – Beauty missing those rats, for instance; and Squire's son not being himself.

Francis waited to make absolutely sure that Tuttle was not coming back, then he spoke into the hedge. 'He's gone.'

'I'm not sorry to hear it.' Seumas's voice came to him muffled by layers of greenery.

'I have no notion of how I am to get you back into the house – or when. At the pace you will be able to go, it would be impossible to get you as far as the west gate unseen.' The first danger over, Francis's anger was beginning to reassert itself. He added viciously, 'I only wish that I could leave you where you are!'

There was no answer to this; and after a few minutes' thought, Francis snapped, 'Have you no practical suggestions?'

'If I had a horse, it's riding to your west gate in fine style I could be.'

'Well, you have no horse!' said Francis tartly. 'I asked you for practical suggestions, not foolish observations.' In a flash, he saw that Seumas's observation had not been so foolish and impractical after all. 'If you will remain where you are for a little longer, I'll go and fetch Sultan, and he can carry you. That way we shall make better speed and, with luck, we may get back to the Dower House without being seen. You will have to wait where you are until I return, I should be here again within a half-hour.' Without waiting for Seumas to reply to this, Francis set off at a jog trot up the lane. Where Tuttle's cottage and the one beside it came into sight, he slowed down to a dignified and unhurried walk, in case anyone should be watching, and wonder at his haste. Just inside the park gates he found Bella, agitated and still hot and crimson-cheeked from her run.

'Oh, Francis, what happened? I never saw Tuttle, though I could hear his whistling for a time. I waited and waited, and then he came back with the dogs. He must have gone from the cottage before I arrived here.'

Briefly, Francis told her what had happened. 'I am going to the stables for Sultan,' he added. 'I shall never get O'Leary to the Dower House, or past the cottages, without.'

'Do you want me to come with you?'

'No. You will only hold me back. I shall have to run fast, there's no time to waste. It will be the best opportunity for trying to get him safely past, while they are eating their dinner. You had better come on after me and go in to dinner yourself. There's no point in our both being late. I shall manage very well alone.' He ran off across the park, but turned his head a few yards on to shout to her, 'Leave the gates wide open, it will save time.'

She looked after him hesitantly, and then, having opened the gates as bidden, walked slowly back, not to the Hall, but to the Dower House.

Just half an hour later, Francis, on Sultan, trotted down the lane from the west gate and dismounted outside the gates of the Dower House.

'O'Leary?' There was no reply. Francis called more loudly, and that time there was a faint response which sounded like, 'Is it back you are?'

'Who else do you think it is? You will have to make your way out now.'

With a difficulty almost as great as that with which he had been hidden, Seumas was liberated from behind the hedge, looking rather the worse for his ordeal. His white face and his hands were scratched and bleeding, his ankle was shockingly swollen, and even clinging to the bars of one of the gates, he could hardly stand.

'For heaven's sake hurry and get in the saddle,' urged Francis irritably. 'This is no time to swoon. I could not pick you up unaided. I warn you, if you fall, I shall leave you lying here to be found by the next person who comes along.'

Eventually, Seumas was in the saddle and clinging to Sultan's neck; and with Francis running at his head, Sultan was urged into a trot.

'Whatever happens, hold on and do not fall off. If you fall off, we are lost,' warned Francis.

Seumas, a little recovered, said, 'I'll not fall. It's clinging like ivy to the prancer I'll be.'

With no one in sight, they got safely past the cottage which stood beside Tuttle's; but from Tuttle's open door, where two of the dogs lay on the threshold, Beauty saw them and got to her feet, barking. Tuttle bellowed to her from inside, but she ran into the lane, still barking and setting on the other two dogs to barking as well. At any second Tuttle might leave his dinner and come out to see what was the matter. With only twenty yards to go to the west gate, Francis gasped, 'Hold on for all you're worth!' and slapped Sultan on the quarters as hard as he could. Sultan, startled into violent speed, took the last twenty yards at a gallop with Seumas swaying dangerously in the saddle, turned through force of habit into the park, and was past the gates and out of sight with his rider only a second or so before Tuttle came to his doorway. Tuttle was in time to see Francis strolling along the road alone.

'Eh, it's you again, sir, is it?' he called. 'I thought it must be a stranger, like, they made such a noise. Happen the old fools think you're come to take them ratting again.'

Francis managed an amiable smile. 'Not again today, Tuttle. Another morning, perhaps.' He raised a hand in affable farewell and walked casually through the gates, shutting them quickly after him, to keep out the dogs, and wondering whether he would find Seumas on the grass and Sultan halfway to his stable.

As it happened, Seumas, badly bruised from his fall and shaken agonizingly by the gallop, on finding himself in the comparative safety of the park, had had the sense to pull on the reins and bring the pony to a standstill before he was thrown.

Thankfully, Francis saw them, still together, a little way off and hastened to catch them up. He grabbed at Sultan's bridle and ran with him towards the Dower House, not even stopping to look about him to see if there were anyone else in sight to observe their progress.

Bella was waiting for them near the back door of the Dower House, nervously plucking leaves off a gooseberry bush, shredding them between her fingers and dropping them bit by bit on the path at her feet, her despondent eyes watching the wicket gate.

Francis led Sultan as far as the back door. There, while he was manoeuvring the pony into a position which would leave Seumas with the least possible amount of walking to do, Seumas's swollen ankle was unfortunately squeezed between Sultan and the door-post. Seumas succeeded in getting out of the saddle unaided, but the pain of his ankle was by this time so acute that he mismanaged the descent and came down heavily on the wrong foot.

'Take Sultan out of the way,' Francis ordered Bella. He helped Seumas across the threshold, and then Seumas said, 'Let me . . . be resting . . . here a moment . . . before we go on.'

They paused, and then, very slowly, Seumas's knees gave under him and he collapsed silently and gracefully in a heap on the flagstones, just inside the back door.

'Oh, heavens!' exclaimed Francis, exasperated almost beyond his endurance. 'He might have waited two minutes longer!' He looked helplessly at Seumas for a moment and then grumbled, 'Tie Sultan up and come and help me, Bella. However do you think I can manage alone?'

Between them they turned Seumas over on to his back, and taking an arm each, dragged him along the passage to the hall and so into the Chinese room.

'Fetch a pail of water.'

When Bella – having left a trail of spilt water all the way from the kitchen table – returned with the pail which Seumas himself had filled, Seumas was neatly stretched out on the floor beside the couch and Francis had covered him with one of the blankets. Bella set down the pail and Francis splashed handfuls of water over his face. When his eyelashes began to flicker and his head to move a little from side to side, Francis said, 'He'll do now. We can leave him. We must go, because I shall have to wash and change my clothes before dinner, and we are late enough already.' He pulled a cushion off the couch and thrust it under Seumas's head, got up from his knees, and pushed Bella towards the door, urging her irritably to hurry.

Once out of the house and through the wicket gate, Francis swung Bella up on to Sultan's back unceremoniously, and then mounted himself. 'Why on earth did you wait?' he complained.

'I thought I might be of help to you.'

'Well, you were not.'

'I helped you drag him along the passage.'

'Surely you do not think I could not have managed to do that alone?'

Bella did not answer; and after a moment or two Francis said, 'Since you did wait, you might as well try to make yourself useful by thinking of a reason for my being late for dinner and covered in dust.'

For the rest of the way home, Bella tried miserably to think of a mentionable prank of which her usually well-behaved and sedate brother might be accused.

18

THAT afternoon, when dinner was over, Francis was standing at the schoolroom window staring out moodily and sullenly, while Bella, sitting at the table, stared equally moodily, though less sullenly, at its top, scarred by penknives, stained by ink and carved with the initials of three generations of young Rimpoles.

After they had been silent for a very long while, she looked up and said to his back, 'Francis, what are we going to do about ... him?' She could not yet bring herself to speak of him as O'Leary, and he was no longer Mr Macdonald. Privately and to herself, in a kind of compromise, she was beginning to think of him familiarly as Seumas, since that alone was still as much his name as it had been before.

Francis glanced over his shoulder at her briefly. 'How should I know? It is time you suggested something helpful instead of always letting me do the thinking for you.' He gave his attention again to the window for a moment or two, and then suddenly turned around completely to stand facing her. 'And why ask me, anyway? It is your fault that it ever happened. If you had not been so convinced that he was a Jacobite, on that first day in the park, I'd not have accepted him as one.'

Bella burst out indignantly, 'That's not fair! You were as much taken in as I was.'

'It was you who were taken in, not I. And it was you who persuaded me. It is the stupid kind of thing a girl would do, especially a girl who is as big a fool as you!'

She stormed back at him, 'If I am only a girl, and if I am as big a fool as you say, then you are an even bigger fool to have believed me! And you are a liar, anyway, because I never needed to persuade you.'

'Annabel! Francis! What a way to speak to one another!' Miss Proudfoot, her approach quite unheard by them, so noisy had been their dispute, was standing in the doorway, an expression of shocked displeasure on her face.

Their anger chilled instantly into guilty, horrified silence – just how much had she heard? – and two minds raced frantically through the possible reasons which might be invented for their quarrel. But fortunately Miss Proudfoot was too concerned with the enormity of their accusations to care why they had been made.

The normal melancholy of her glance increased by her present disapprobation, she advanced into the room, having shut the door behind her firmly and noiselessly, somehow making even that simple, ordinary action into a gesture of disapproval. 'Francis, you will immediately beg your sister's pardon for calling her a fool. And you, Annabel, will express your regret and shame to your brother for calling him a liar.'

They apologized to each other with bad grace. Miss Proudfoot settled herself in her chair and called them both to her. For the next fifteen minutes she gave them both a sharp scolding on their ill-mannered and unfitting conduct, while they stood before her, side by side, unwilling and unloving confederates, blushing, ashamed, and supremely uncomfortable, the very picture of the guilt they both felt – though they felt it for quite another reason than the one to which Miss Proudfoot ascribed it.

After that they were made to sit, one at each end of the table, in absolute silence, under her deprecatory eye, and read in improving books for the next hour. By the end of that time, Francis was in a cold, hopeless rage, and Bella was utterly miserable and ready to weep.

Thoroughly out of charity with each other, they did not speak to one another for the rest of Saturday, and they hardly exchanged a single word all the next day. Certainly neither mentioned the subject which was continually in both their minds; until at last, on the Sunday evening, near her bedtime, instead of avoiding him as she had been doing all day – as indeed he, also, had been avoiding her – Bella, managing to corner Francis alone, asked in a tone which he chose to consider accusing and therefore immediately resented, 'What are you going to do about food for . . . for the Dower House?'

Looking at her with near dislike for having opened the forbidden subject again, he said aggressively, 'What do you expect me to do?'

'He will have to be fed.'

'He can starve for all I care. I gave my word not to betray him, but I said nothing about feeding him.'

'If we do not give him food, it will amount to betraying him. He will become so hungry that he will have to come out of the house to find something to eat, and then he will be caught.'

This seemed very likely, and Francis had already thought of it and decided that they would have to continue to feed Seumas: but he did not relish having his sister point it out to him.

'You need not think that I am going over there with food for him tonight, because I am not! I'll see him in Halifax first!' Calming down, he said, 'I'll take him something after lessons tomorrow.' With grim satisfaction he observed, 'He should be very hungry by then.' To this, after a moment's consideration, he added with feeling, 'I hope that he is not only hungry, but that, as well, he believes we are going to let him starve.'

In spite of his words, at midday on Monday Francis arrived at the Dower House with a loaf and some cheese. He found Seumas sitting on the couch with one foot up, watching the doorway warily, half-poised to rise quickly should there be need. As Francis came in, their eyes met briefly and then they both looked away abruptly, Francis with deliberate and unconcealed distaste. He placed the food on the chair which stood beside the couch and which served Seumas as a table, ignoring Seumas's mild, 'Thank you.' Glancing at the pail of water, he saw that it was half empty and with irritation picked it up without a word and took it to the kitchen. When he had brought it back full and set it down, again ignoring Seumas's word of thanks, he looked around to see what else needed to be done. Noticing his watch on the chair, he pointedly took it up and put it into his pocket. He ended his inspection with his eyes on Suemas's still very swollen foot, and asked sharply and with complete absence of sympathy, 'How is your ankle?'

'About as it was three weeks ago, I'm afraid.' At Francis's

frown, Seumas added, 'I'll be practising walking every moment that I can, and soon I'll be walking finely again, and then it's away out of your lives I'll be and no longer a millstone around your necks.'

Francis received this assurance ungraciously. 'I indeed hope so!'

Suddenly remembering the boot in the middle of the drive and hoping that it was still there, he left the room without any explanation and went to find it. It was still there and none the worse for its two days' outing. He carried it into the Chinese room and dropped it to the floor beside the couch.

'I'd been wondering what had become of that.'

'I threw it over the gate,' said Francis shortly.

'It's glad I am that it's safe and sound. It would have been a pity had it been lost, and it so new and all.'

Francis, goaded by what he chose to regard as complacency, snapped back, 'It would certainly have been a pity. My sister had to sell her gold chain to pay for those boots.'

He was turning away to go when Seumas said, 'I have the money you gave me for the buttons. Should I be –'

Francis did not wait for him to finish. 'I'd not accept,' he broke in sharply and with finality.

He was in the doorway, going out of the room, when Seumas spoke again, and he paused there reluctantly and, even more reluctantly, turned his head to listen.

'Is it any use my saying I'm sorry for' – Seumas gestured towards his swollen foot – 'this, and for . . . everything else?' The rueful smile, the slightly raised eyebrows, the warm, rich voice, now muted in contrite appeal, gave him an engaging air that was only half deliberately contrived: but it failed.

Francis said stiffly, 'No use at all. I cannot think why you should expect to be believed.' With more feeling, he added, 'And you cannot possibly be more sorry about . . .' his voice became a sneer as he quoted, '. . . everything else . . . than I am!' He slammed the door behind him so that the noise echoed hollowly through the empty hall.

Francis continued to bring food and draw water for Seumas each day, but he spent as little time at the Dower House as possible, and he hardly spoke to Seumas when he was there. He provided sufficient food and of no worse a quality than before; but he drew the line at laying out money on ale, or even small-beer, when there was water to be had in the Dower House for nothing – or rather, he drew the line, not at laying out money on ale, but at asking credit of Mrs Cotter for ale, since he was now obliged to have all his purchases charged to him, the account to be paid when he received July's spending-money in about a week's time.

His attitude towards Seumas was now more that of a gaoler than a host – and an unwilling gaoler at that. For the first day or two Seumas had tried to bring about more cordial relations between them; but on meeting with no response he gave up trying, not because he doubted his ability to win Francis over eventually – in his twenty-four years he had talked into contented and co-operative acquiescence many others, older, more experienced, far more stubborn than Francis – but because his conscience told him that on this occasion he did not deserve to succeed.

After the Wednesday night of that week, Francis awoke very early in the morning, soon after two o'clock; and in the way that, at the moment of first coming out of sleep, one's chief waking worry returns immediately and unsummoned to take possession of one's mind, he instantly thought of Seumas. Almost at once, and with a shocking clarity, one particular conclusion about Seumas – hitherto unconsidered – struck him, and he was wide awake forthwith, far beyond the possibility of further sleep. It was an inference which seemed to him so likely, that he wondered why it had not occurred to him before. Considering it then, he remained sleepless until it was time to get up, twisting and turning it in his mind and reflecting wretchedly that his conduct in sheltering Seumas, already deplorable enough, would be far more heinous if his supposition were correct.

On that Thursday he gave Seumas food and water in silence, as usual; but as he was going, he managed to bring himself to ask, stiffly and contemptuously and as if without any real interest, 'So much pother as they have made over you – the militia called out just to catch a coin-clipper and a thief. Was it not rather excessive?'

Seumas got his unspoken meaning at once. 'Excessive for an ordinary thief, perhaps, but not for a grand, important thief like myself, who robbed a noble duke.' He gave his quick smile, amused, but with a faint trace of mockery. 'You can be letting your conscience rest: I've murdered no one.' The smile broadened to a grin and the mockery strengthened. 'I've not killed a man in all my life – which, I'll take my oath on it, is more than I could be saying if I were the Jacobite soldier you wanted me to be.'

Francis flushed. He had not reckoned upon his fear being read quite so clearly or so swiftly; and Seumas's denials of guilt in this particular respect, when – or if – they came, he had expected to be earnest protestations of virtue and innocence, and appeals to be believed, not a cool, amused, and scornful reassurance to his questioner. Taken aback and unable to respond forthwith with equanimity, he kept silent. Yet he did not like to go, leaving his dignity unretrieved, and without another word to assert his superior moral position, so he paused, hiding his temporary uncertainty behind an inflexible stare.

Seumas was still smiling. 'Perhaps you'd care to be hearing about it? Or would it shock your respectable ears too much?' When Francis did not answer immediately, Seumas went on, 'It came to me one day in the spring – in April it was – that it's a great while I'd been in London, and I was growing a little tired of London town and wanting to see something of the countryside maybe, and it all turning green and smelling like the flowers at that very moment. And I do not mean Hampstead or Highgate, or indeed anywhere within a day's ride of the city, but somewhere farther off than that, where I might be seeing a little of the world, as you might say.' He paused a moment to smile challengingly at Francis before going on to remark deliberately, 'Besides, I was wanted just then for being concerned in the diminishing way – coin-clipping, that is, in case you do not know – and I had no mind to be lying at ground for a month or two in a dirty London back alley and the summer coming on. I was after telling this to Charley, a friend of mine who's a bridle-cull, when we were at Jack Thorne's, drinking a glass of diddle together, and he laughed and said that if ever I was thinking of going into Yorkshire, I was to tell him in good time, for he had a package he had long been wanting to send to an acquaintance in York, who was after being on the same lay as himself, and he with no one whom he could trust going in that direction to be carrying it for him. Well, York seemed to me as good a place as any for me to be heading for, and I'd never seen those parts; so, two days later, I made a farewell supper in Jack Thorne's diddle-shop for my good friends and told them I'd be with them once again when the summer was over and London would be calling me back, and it's on the road for the North I was in the morning, with Charley's package in my saddle-bag. I'll not be telling you anything of the journey, for you'll not be caring to hear, save only that I enjoyed it and it's not unprofitable it was. In time I rode into Yorkshire, and in York city I found this Joseph Benton and gave him Charley's package. To be making short work of a long story, Joseph Benton took to me – though I not as much to him, but that's another matter entirely – and, as I'd once been on the bridle-lay myself for a while, we were after doing the one or two little jobs together successfully. Joseph, he was good at it, I'll say that for him. But he was the ambitious one, and no mistake. He wanted to be robbing the Duke of Shale, the Lord Lieutenant himself, who never goes out without diamond buckles and buttons and rings and all the other gew-gaws, worth the ransom of a king; while his Duchess has a pair of earrings and a necklace of diamonds, each one as big as a pigeon's egg – or so it was said. At first I spoke against it, though I'm usually not one to hold back. But I like to be sure of a pal when there's a big risk, and I'd not known Joseph Benton long enough to be sure of him. However, as I was after telling you, I'm not one to shirk danger, so we stopped his Grace's carriage one night when he was on his way home from a ball with the Duchess and a little army of servants – twelve of them there were, and only the pair of us. Och, there were diamonds there, right enough, and sparkling in the starlight, and his snuffbox and his small-sword all gold and stuck with rubies, and himself drunk and snoring. And it's sure enough as big as pigeon's eggs they were, the diamonds the Duchess was wearing. Joseph held a pistol to the poor lady's head and threatened to be blowing it off if anyone moved, and before you could have counted twenty, I had stripped himself of the lot, right down to his pomander and his toothpick case, and left him without a meg, while Joseph took care of the necklace and the earrings. We left them there, the bunch of them, making a great to-do, and rode away. And in the morning we divided the swag. I was all for keeping my share and disposing of it in London when I was there again, and I was after advising Joseph to do the same. But he said he'd not care to be trusting the London fencing-culls, and he a northerner. The York fence to whom he usually sold, refused him a fair price for his Grace's trinkets – and sure it was understandable, seeing it's family heirlooms they were, with great S's engraved on them, and his Grace's coat of arms and all. Not to mention a big reward offered, and good descriptions of every missing item, and poor, unflattering descriptions of Joseph and myself, sent to all the magistrates and justices and constables in the county. And himself in a fine rage over it and fit to rouse all Yorkshire for a treasure hunt.'

Francis, fascinated in spite of himself, listened with appalled interest, and Seumas went on. 'And so we were hiding ourselves and being very cautious for a time. But Joseph, he could not wait to be getting rid of the swag and having some gelt in his hands. It's talking him out of it I was, so long as I had the breath left for talking, but what does the fool do one day when I'm not there to be stopping him, but go and try to sell his Grace's watch – and that not even to his friend, but to another fence who's been after bearing a grudge against him for years and waiting for a chance like this.' Seumas shrugged his shoulders. 'As you might be expecting, in no time at all poor Joseph was nabbed and locked away in York gaol.'

Seumas stopped, and Francis said, coldly and deliberately, 'And then, I presume, you ran away and left him to hang for you both?'

'Och, no! You are doing me an injustice. Was it not after risking my life I was, with bribes and all the rest of it, trying to get him out of gaol before the Assizes? And not doing too badly, neither, for a stranger in a strange town. And then what must Mr Judas Joseph be doing but buying himself transportation instead of the rope with my name and a description of me – good and accurate this time. So what could I be doing after that but forgetting him and trying to save myself as well as I could? My friends are all in London, and York is full of Joseph's friends, and none of them caring enough for Seumas O'Leary to be hiding him away. So I gave my share of the swag to the old woman in whose house I'd been lodging, telling her that if I'd not been back for it by the time a month was past, she was to be saying that she had found it – under the floor-boards in my room, maybe, or whatever other spot there was in the house that would not already have been searched by the law – and be claiming the reward for it. Then I took to my horse with all his Grace's hounds after me and hot on the scent, and I a bare five minutes ahead of them and not knowing how to be shaking them off. It's not so badly I did, though, for I'd reached Guisborough before I was nabbed, two days later. They set out there and then to carry me back to York to join Joseph in the gaol. There were six of them, and you may be thinking that would have left me without much hope. But there's time enough in a half-day's riding to get acquainted with six men, and on a two day's journey one has to be putting up somewhere for the night. By the time we came to the wayside inn where they had made up their minds to stop, it's not on too bad terms we were. Och, it's a marvellous thing what food and drink will do for a man, and he having had a tiring day. It's in a more kindly mood they put him at once, and with less suspicion in his heart. Faith! It's after talking my throat dry for hours on end and telling them jokes I was, and making the whole time as though I had no thought in my head of giving them the slip, so that we spent a very comfortable evening together, laughing and drinking until it was time to turn in. I was put into a small room under the roof, and they taking good care, two of them at a time, to sit up and watch me all night. I gave no trouble and made as though I was sleeping, until it came to what I judged to be the right time of the night and the right pair of watchdogs, and then I pretended to wake and we set to chatting. From chatting we passed to grumbling that there was no drink, and the landlord having long gone to his bed, I dared one of them to go and find us some ale. Away he wont, creeping down the stairs, and no one could have been more surprised than the other, when I gagged him with the pillow-case and tied him to the chair with his own cravat. And then, because the one who'd gone for the ale had locked us in together and taken the key, I had to be leaving by a window hardly large enough for a cat, and he well fed. I slid down a roof, dropped to the ground, and so away I was in the dark, and my horse left behind in the stable. Two days later there was a band of militiamen out searching for me – that must have been his Grace's doing – and they with their muskets and I not knowing the district at all and not liking to risk making for the moors and not daring to stay near the farms and villages. And so it went on for five whole days – and the rest you're after knowing already.'

Seumas paused a moment. Then he said, 'So that's why it's been the militia and a good price on my head, and not merely a village constable and a lousy thief-taker or two.' He gave a laugh. 'Sure and that's what comes of flying too high and milling a noble Duke. It's a little like that old Greek I am, whatever his name was – my father would be after telling you, it's the knowledgeable man he was – who made himself the fine pair of wings and stuck them on with wax and then flew too near the sun. You can be guessing for yourself what happened to him.' He grinned broadly as he relived the episode in his mind. 'Sure it's not unlike the sun himself was, neither, with his face glowing in the moonlight, what with the drink he had taken and his rage, and I thinking that at any moment he was going to have an apoplexy.' He began to chuckle with amusement at the recollection; and then, catching sight of Francis's expression, the laugh hardened a little and he said, 'But no doubt you're thinking, respectable young Mr Rimpole, that it's a shocking tale that I've been telling you, and at this very instant you're hoping I'll be nabbed again before too long – and this time, for good.'

Francis stared at him for a few moments longer, then he said in as steady and cold a voice as he could manage, 'My own feelings do not enter into the matter. What I have undertaken to do, I shall endeavour with my best to carry out.' He went, shutting the door behind him as if on something beneath contempt; and Seumas was left alone to the disconcerting realization that he did not know whether he wanted to laugh at Francis's pompousness or to weep for his pride.

'Och,' he muttered to himself with sudden irritability, 'why should I be knowing exactly how his heart is aching, and be feeling for him, and he so different from myself?'

19

THE following day, as Francis approached the wicket gate to the back garden of the Dower House, he saw that it was ajar. His first shocked reaction was to suppose that one of the gardeners was working there; then he remembered how, some three weeks previously, soon after they had first hidden Seumas there, he had deliberately got into conversation with Rigby and led the talk round to the subject of the Dower House. He had asked Rigby if he would be likely to be working there himself, or to be sending one of the other men, during the month, and had been relieved to have the answer, 'There'll be nowt done at t'Dower House for five or six weeks yet, Master Francis. There's a mickle of work to be done at t'Hall, where there's folk to see it, like. Dower House is empty. Dower House can bide for a bit.'

Francis's second thought was that it might be Bella, but this was dismissed instantly. Bella had not been near the Dower House since the fateful Saturday, almost a week before, and she had, he knew, no intention of going there again, until it was empty of Seumas. Besides, Bella would have taken care to fasten the gate, not draw attention to her presence there by leaving it open.

His heart in his throat, he dismounted and tethered Sultan to the gate-post, then, having first prudently hidden the food he had brought for Seumas under a shrub near the gate, he advanced quietly and cautiously along the garden path, looking warily to either side for signs of danger.

The sudden sound of an excited youthful voice – too strong and shrill to belong to one of the gardener-lads – led him, still stepping cautiously, in the right direction, to find two small village boys, their mouths stuffed with ripe fruit, hastily filling their caps with raspberries.

Francis's instant of relief was immediately succeeded by

anger at the risk to Seumas that their presence offered. Taking them completely by surprise, he strode forward between two rows of currant bushes shouting, 'What are you doing here? How dare you come and steal the fruit!'

With cries of dismay and fright they leapt up, clutching their full caps, and tore for the pathway. Francis grabbed at them both, missed the first, who was too quick for him, but managed to catch the second by leaning precariously over a red currant bush to reach him. The child screamed in terror and howled an appeal for rescue to his somewhat larger companion, who never paid the slightest heed, being too bent on saving his own skin.

'You are wicked little thieves! And if you so much as set one foot in this garden again, the Squire will . . . He will have you transported!'

Struggling to free himself, with every movement spilling raspberries on to the ground from his cap, the child wailed out rash promises of future good behaviour.

'I'll let you go on this occasion, but make sure that you warn anyone else who might be thinking of coming here, that there will be no mercy for anyone caught in this garden. Do you understand?' He gave the child a shake to emphasize his threats.

Repeated wails and promises assured Francis that another fruit-picking invasion was unlikely for some weeks – or, at least, until the earliest of the plums were ripe – and he let go of the small boy, who fled down the path after his friend, and so into the park, both of them making for the west gate, by which they had sneaked in a half-hour before. Their precipitate speed, as they passed through the wicket gate, startled Sultan into prancing and whinnying and straining on the reins, so that Francis was obliged to calm him and make sure that he was still securely tethered before he was able to retrieve Seumas's dinner from under the bush where he had hidden it.

Indoors, Francis found Seumas walking about the Chinese room with help from the stick, exercising his now improving ankle. Still unnerved from the shock which the two children had given him, he snapped, 'I hope you have kept away from the window, if you have been moving around.'

'Now, have I not always kept away from the window?' asked Seumas mildly. 'For what would I be wanting to show myself to all the passers by, and I needing to hide myself from them?'

'Well, you had best take even greater care from today. I have this moment caught two of the village brats in the garden.'

Seumas stiffened and became instantly wary. 'What were they doing here?'

'Stealing raspberries.'

Seumas, into whose mind had come a picture of ardent young reward-hunters, relaxed and chuckled. 'Is that all? I thought from your long face that it's after me they were.'

Francis, annoyed, said, 'You take it too lightly. Apart from the danger to us of anyone's coming into the garden for any purpose whatsoever, they were stealing.'

Seumas looked amused. 'The poor little devils like raspberries, maybe, and have none of their own. Sure and you wouldn't begrudge them one or two raspberries, and they just going to waste or the birds?'

'Whether the fruit is picked or left for the birds makes no difference. It is better that it should be wasted than that it should be stolen.' With fine scorn, Francis added, 'But, of course, you would not agree with me.'

Seumas, instead of being abashed, as Francis had hoped and intended, actually laughed. 'You're right! I'd not agree with you.' Suddenly he stopped laughing and said quietly, 'Some people are after having all they want and more, while others have so very little – or nothing. And it's hard, you know, when one sees others having the things one needs or wants for oneself, and they making little use or none at all of them.'

Defensively – though he could not have said why he felt the necessity for being defensive – Francis retorted, 'Theft is never justified.

Seumas regarded him thoughtfully. 'Do you not think so?' he asked after a while; adding conversationally a moment or two later, 'Have you never stolen anything yourself?'

'Of course not!' The indignant denial was out before Francis had given himself time to consider the question. Then he flushed and corrected himself, 'Well, that is ...' He hesitated;

then he said, his voice sharpening with dislike, 'That is, not until I had to steal on your behalf.'

'And it's sorry I am for that. But you need not be troubling your conscience about it, for, under the circumstances, it's as though I'd done the stealing myself, not you,' Seumas said airily. He then studied Francis with interest. 'So you've never stolen anything at all, barring the things you took for me?'

'I told you, no!'

'Then it's lucky you've been, never to have needed to,' remarked Seumas drily. Then, seeing Francis about to protest, he said quickly, 'Och, I'm not pretending that I've ever needed to steal. I did it from choice. I was born one of the lucky ones, too. Not as lucky as yourself, maybe, but lucky enough for all that. My father never had a fortune to spend, yet he had enough. And it was plenty for all of us to be living our respectable lives on. But I chose differently and I've no excuse for it, nor do I pretend to have one. Yet there's stealing and stealing, you know. There's stealing because you are hungry and haven't a penny and need what you steal if you're to go on living, and there's – Och, well, there's my sort of stealing, so help me! My father, he was always fond of reading in the books he printed – I dare say he still is – and sometimes he would read to us from them. He read to us from the plays of William Shakespeare now and then, for it's after liking poetry he was. I remember well one bit he read us once – you will be knowing it, maybe? – about how some are after being born great and others have greatness thrust upon them. Sure, it's that way with stealing, too. Some are born thieves – and that's like myself – and some have thieving thrust upon them because of their circumstances, because it's poor and hungry they are.' He paused for a moment, and then went on, 'You'll not be knowing what it's like to be either poor or hungry, will you now? Living in the country in a big house with a sound roof over your head to keep the weather out, with a larder full to bursting, and turning up your gentlemanly nose at the smell of a farmyard midden, you'll not be knowing what it's like, the way the poor are after living in the towns. Och, London is a fine place, with its big churches where the respectable folk go on Sundays, all dressed up in their best, and its big shops where a man can be buying anything at all that he pleases – if he has the blunt – and the big houses where the rich gentry coves live, and the fine, broad streets where they drive in their carriages. But no farther than a man could be throwing a stone, and he standing at their back gates, are those other streets, too narrow for a carriage, where the refuse lies until it rots and the unwanted babies lie until they die, and a man, picking his way through the stench and the filth, has to be turning his head aside for fear that his soft heart will be after urging him to take up a sickly, crying brat and give it a chance to live. To live! It might be better if it died, I'm thinking! To live – on stale bread and small-beer in a house with a leaking roof and walls which let the wind through, a score or more of folk to each room, and the cellars full as well with whole families who lie on the floor in the darkness with their pigs and their donkeys when the rush lights are burnt out. To live – to fight with the rats for a crust and with a mangy cur for a dry bone. The only lullaby a child that cannot sleep for hunger is after getting in a home such as that, is a mouthful of gin to send it to sleep for an hour or two – or for ever. And unless it's right beside him it is, that he might be getting a rotten beam or a tile on his head, a man does not even look up when he hears a house like that fall down. It's after happening too often to be worth the heeding, you see. And then, when the house is down, the beggars hurry in to dig among the rubble and strip the corpses of their rags. And when the beggars have done, then the homeless creep in, to live among the stinking ruins. Do you think it's easy to grow up honest in the back alleys of a town? Faith! It's few of the poor who can afford to be honest, I'm telling you.' He stopped abruptly and flung out one hand impatiently. 'But for what am I ranting on like this, wasting my time talking to deaf ears, and you not understanding a word I've been saying? Maybe you'll be understanding one day, when you are older and have seen more of life. But I doubt it. I think you're after being the sort that never understands.'

20

EARLIER that week a letter had arrived for Sir John from his brother-in-law, Adam Bradshaw, a well-to-do Bristol merchant, informing him that as he had shortly to drive to York on business, he proposed to set out a few days early, so that he might first travel a few miles farther north and remain a day or two at Thorsby, if it suited the convenience of the Rimpoles, with whom, so his long and rather wordy letter assured them, he was anticipating a most happy reunion and many hours of discourse such as had been mutually enjoyed by them on previous similar and delightful occasions.

Upon having this piece of news read out to her by her husband, in no very enthusiastic voice, Lady Rimpole's first comment was, 'I wonder what useless and expensive gift he will have found to bring us this time.'

'And I wonder what subject he will have found to talk to death,' said Sir John resignedly.

'Such tedious company, but so well meaning and so kindly,' sighed Lady Rimpole.

'I marvel, whenever I meet him, my love, how your sister Maria bears with him.'

Lady Rimpole laughed. 'Oh, you flatter Maria! She has never been anything but an amiable goose. Of the three of us, Elizabeth and I had all the wit. I have always considered Maria and Bradshaw excellently suited.'

A few moments later, she was saying, 'I must not fail to have that hideous Chinese pottery animal brought over from the Dower House for Bradshaw's visit. It would not do to hurt the poor man's feelings. He was so proud of having obtained it for us, two years ago.'

'That dog, or lion, or whatever it is, must be the most costly and the most useless of all the gifts which he has made to us,' remarked Sir John with distaste.

'Not entirely useless,' said Lady Rimpole fairly. 'Your stepmother was very pleased to have it for her new Chinese room.'

'And I wish it might remain there!'

'It shall go back there immediately Bradshaw has taken his leave, I promise you. But it must be in the drawing-room so long as he is with us,' declared Lady Rimpole firmly.

An indirect result of this exchange – at which, naturally, neither Francis nor Bella was present – was that relations between Keighley and Fowler, never very cordial, were temporarily worsened.

On the Monday of the following week, soon after breakfast, on her way to the schoolroom for the morning's instruction, Bella unnoticed by either of them, overheard the start of an altercation between them. Keighley, heavily and ponderously walking towards the larger drawing-room, was suddenly confronted by little Fowler, who sprang out through a doorway and set himself directly in the butler's way.

'Mr Keighley, I must have a word with you. I wish to make a complaint about that new young footman, Edward Bright.'

'Not now, if you please, Mr Fowler. I have affairs to see to.'

Keighley made it sound, thought Bella, as though he were Mr Pelham the Prime Minister, with affairs of state requiring his attention.

The little valet bridled. 'Mr Keighley, I will not be put off in this manner. I must and I will speak with you immediately.'

Fowler was always amusing when he got into one of his states of fussation, and the situation was promising, so Bella dawdled in the passage to hear more of it, taking only very slow and short steps, in order to make her journey to the schoolroom last as long as possible: because, of course, it would be unthinkable, according to Miss Proudfoot, to eavesdrop on a servants' quarrel.

Keighley became a little more natural and rather more Yorkshire – but no less ponderous. 'There's no manner of use your fashing yourself. I cannot spare the time for complaints this morning. Happen I'll be free for ten minutes or so after dinner

– if ten minutes will be long enough for your complaints about my footmen,' he added with weighty sarcasm.

Fowler's voice rose shrilly. 'Mr Keighley, I insist on being heard here and now. I will not tolerate –'

Keighley lifted a broad hand, palm outwards, to silence him. 'You'll have to tolerate, Mr Fowler. I am more than usually busy this morning,' he stated importantly, with a return to his grand manner. 'As well as all my customary duties, I have to make time to go over to the Dower House for her ladyship.'

At the mention of the Dower House, Bella gave up all pretence of movement and stopped dead, to hear Keighley go on to say, 'I have to fetch that earthenware lion – or so her ladyship called it, and no doubt she knows best. But what I call it is a nasty, ugly, heathen idol.'

Fowler, sidetracked for a moment from the shortcomings of the new footman by this display of ignorance, said with a superior air, 'That lion, Mr Keighley, is not a heathen idol, but a piece of virtu. It is Chinese, and quite in the latest fashion, let me tell you.'

'If that's the latest fashion in China, the good Lord be praised that I'm an Englishman!'

Fowler tittered. 'Not in China, Mr Keighley. The latest fashion in London. But, of course, how could you know!'

Keighley, not a whit abashed at having his ignorance shown up, said broadly, 'Eh, if that ugly brute be London fashion, give me honest Yorkshire fashion, that's all I can say.' Seeing Fowler opening his mouth and about to speak again, he said crushingly and with an air of finality, 'If you please, Mr Fowler, reserve your arguing for below stairs. Let us not conduct ourselves in an unseemly manner where we can disturb The Family. Now, if you will pardon me and let me pass, I will be about my many duties. It's not all of us who have time to waste on making complaints.' Irresistibly he went on his way, brushing the angry and indignant little valet out of his path.

Bella, appalled, stood still for long moments after they were gone, her mind presenting her with a picture of Keighley, followed by one or more of the footmen, unlocking the door of the Dower House and treading ponderously along the hall to the Chinese room; while Seumas, all unsuspecting and believing it to be Francis, waited, unaware of his fate, to be caught. Something had to be done – and at once – to warn him. But what? Francis was by then already at the vicarage, and Miss Proudfoot was awaiting her in the school-room.

Bella's first idea was to send one of the servants to Francis, telling him to come home immediately, so that she could explain matters and he could hurry to the Dower House and hide Seumas. Then she thought of writing Francis a note, to save time, so that he could go straight to the Dower House from the village, without first returning to the Hall to see her. But neither course seemed very safe or very feasible; and they would both, in any case, take too long, so that perhaps Francis would reach the Dower House after Keighley was already there.

There was only one thing to do, she decided at last. She must go and warn Seumas and hide him herself. But how could she, when she was supposed to be having an Italian lesson with Miss Proudfoot? She must somehow – somehow – avoid the morning's lesson and go to the Dower House. If she were left alone for long enough – an hour would be sufficient: no more was necessary – she could be over there and back again, leaving Seumas hidden on the upper floor, where Keighley would be unlikely to look if he were merely fetching the Chinese monster, and no one need even know of her temporary absence. That was the best and only way to do it, she was convinced.

She tried first to achieve her object legitimately and with permission. Mastering her agitation as well as she could, she walked into the schoolroom with an eager, winning smile, to be instantly greeted by Miss Proudfoot – before even a single word of appeal had been spoken – with, 'Ah, come along, dear, sit down. You are being exceedingly slow this morning. Let us not waste any more time. Today I wish us to study a short poem by Petrarch. First I shall read it to you, while you listen carefully and try to understand as much as possible. Then I shall want you to read it to me. Afterwards we shall translate it together and discuss it.'

With as much persuasiveness as she could manage – though it had been a little damped by the delay, the eager spark of persuasion had by no means been quenched – Bella said, 'Oh,

Miss Proudfoot, it is such a beautiful morning and it might be raining this afternoon. Please could I walk in the park this morning, ma'am, while it is fine, and have lessons this afternoon instead?'

Miss Proudfoot was quite naturally astonished by this unprecedented request. 'Of course you may not, Annabel! Whatever put such a notion into your head? We can walk in the garden or in the park this afternoon. Lessons must come first, as always.'

'But supposing it rains this afternoon?'

'I very much doubt if it will rain at all today. And if it should, why then, dear, you will have to take the disappointment with resignation – it will be good for you to have to do so – and stay indoors. After all, it has rained before in the afternoon and not been accounted a tragedy.'

'Please, ma'am, let me miss lessons this morning.'

But all Bella's powers of inducement were unavailing. 'No, Annabel. Sit down and pay attention. I cannot think what has come over you.'

'Please, please, ma'am. Only for today. I'll never ask you again, I promise.' Bella was no longer trying to be winning or persuasive; she had reached the stage of desperate entreaty.

'I have said no, Annabel, so let me hear no more of this nonsense. Sit down, if you please, this instant.'

Both inducement and appeal had failed. Almost in tears at her lack of success, Bella sat down and Miss Proudfoot opened her book at the place which she had marked with a piece of grey ribbon and began to read.

> Rotta è l'alta Colonna e 'l verde Lauro
> che facean ombra al mio stanco pensero;
> perdut'ho quel che ritrovar non spero
> dal borea all'austro, o dal mar indo al mauro.
> Tolto m'hai, Morte, il mio doppio tesauro,
> che mi fea viver lieto e gire altero;
> e ristorar nol può terra nè impero,
> nè gemma oriental nè forza d'auro.

Bella never heard a single word. Her mind was running rapidly on other means of contriving to be alone for an hour. If she were disobedient, or rude to Miss Proudfoot, perhaps she would be sent to her room, she thought. But then, she would probably be locked in, and that would defeat her ends. Yet there was always the window.... She was soon deep in a scheme for tying the bedclothes together and climbing out of the window. Her bedroom was on the west side of the house and looked out over the garden and the park. She might be noticed from the stables, which were also on that side of the house, or by one of the gardeners, as she climbed down: yet it was worth an attempt, she decided. But supposing she fell and broke her leg – or sprained her ankle, like Seumas? Then there would be no one to warn him. She determined, however, to risk the climb, but was startled out of her thoughts at this point by the sound of Miss Proudfoot's bony fingers rapping sharply on the table top.

'Annabel, I have asked you twice if you know what is meant by Boreas. Wake up, child.'

'Boreas?' Bella could not see what Boreas had to do with it, and looked mystified, although she knew perfectly well that he was the North Wind.

'Annabel, I do not think that you have been listening to a single word that I have read to you. You are acting most oddly this morning.'

Bella, about to stage a scene of misbehaviour which, she hoped, would result in her being sent to her room, was, at the last moment, inspired by Miss Proudfoot's words to change her tactics. She pulled as long a face as possible and said in a suffering sort of a voice, 'I'm sorry if I'm acting oddly, ma'am, but I do not feel very well this morning.'

'In what way do you not feel well, dear?'

Bella pressed a hand to what she hoped would pass for an aching brow. 'My head hurts, Miss Proudfoot.'

Miss Proudfoot, a trifle dubious about this previously unmentioned headache, said encouragingly, 'In that case, dear, it is better for you to sit quietly in here, reading Petrarch, than to be walking around the garden in the bright sunshine, as you asked to be allowed to do.'

'Perhaps if I might lie down in my room for a little while, I would feel less unwell,' suggested Bella.

'I think that you would do far better to concentrate on the

lesson, and you will probably find that you will have forgotten your headache after a while. Read the poem to me now, Annabel, and do not neglect to take pains with your pronunciation, especially the diphthong *au* – a good rounded sound, remember – *Lau*ro, *au*stro.' She handed the book to Bella.

Things were not turning out as Bella had hoped. More decisive symptoms were going to be necessary. In a small voice she read, ' "Rotta è l'alta Colonna e'l verde Lauro . . ." ' Then she laid down the book on the table. 'Ma'am, I think that perhaps I am going to be sick.'

Miss Proudfoot, by now thoroughly suspicious of this very sudden indisposition, eyed Bella's healthy colour sternly. 'That, no doubt, will be the result of overeating yesterday. I told you that you were eating too much and too fast at dinner-time. Now you see how greed brings its own well deserved punishment. Pray continue with the reading.'

Miss Proudfoot seemed determined to be sceptical, Bella thought miserably. She wondered frantically how she could convince her of the genuineness of her illness. A swoon would convince her immediately: but Bella doubted her ability to feign a swoon successfully. If only Miss Proudfoot would leave her alone for a minute, or even go to the bookcase to fetch a book, or turn away to look out of the window, Bella thought that she might put her finger down her throat and truly make herself sick. Then, surely, she would be allowed to go to her room?

But Miss Proudfoot showed no sign of granting her an opportunity for this ruse. It seemed impossible to achieve her object: yet she had to do something about hiding Seumas. If she did not, then Keighley would discover him, he would be taken and hanged, she and Francis would be found out, and Sir John's reputation would be ruined and the honour of the Rimpole's lost for ever, when it was known all over the North Riding that his children had harboured a thief in his own house. It was an appalling predicament and she was the only one who could prevent a nightmare from becoming actuality.

'Oh, Miss Proudfoot!' she wailed. 'I do feel so ill. Let me go and lie down.'

What her over-acting had been unable to bring about, her very real distress – whatever its cause – achieved, and Miss Proudfoot was moved to consider that, although it was most unlikely, maybe Annabel really was feeling ill – she might perhaps be sickening for some disease – and it would be best to be on the safe side, while, at the same time, not giving way to possible malingering. She laid a hand on Bella's forehead, found it cool enough, and said briskly but not unkindly, 'Now, Annabel dear, do not make a childish fuss over a trifling indisposition. I am sure there is no need for you to lie down. Sit there quietly and close your eyes, and I will go and fetch my smelling-bottle. If you keep very quiet and sit still for a few minutes, I am sure that you will feel better directly.' She brought a cushion from the window seat and put it behind Bella's head, patted her shoulder, saying, 'I shall not be long,' and went out of the room.

She would be gone no more than two minutes, Bella reckoned. But that would be time enough to make herself convincingly sick. Her mouth wide open and her finger already aiming for her throat, the daunting thought came to her that if she were sent to bed ill, either Miss Proudfoot or Old Nurse might well take it into her head that she was too ill to be left alone, and come and sit, eagle-eyed, beside the bed. She took her finger out of her mouth, utterly dismayed at the idea. In less than one minute from then Miss Proudfoot would be back and her opportunity – perhaps her only opportunity – for action would be lost. The honour of the family and the life of a man depended on her. No matter what happened to her afterwards, she must reach the Dower House before Keighley.

Desperate situations call for desperate measures, as Francis had found not so many days before. She got up, ran to the door, opened it cautiously and peeped out. Miss Proudfoot was not in sight. Bella slipped through the door, not even pausing to close it behind her, and lifting her skirts, ran for the stairs and down them and along to the side door and out. Through the garden to the park she fled, in plain sight of anyone who might be looking. Now that she was safely away from the house, she abandoned all caution. If she stopped to make sure that there was no one about to notice her, she feared she was likely

to be seen and pursued and prevented: so she went recklessly on.

She ran most of the way across the park. There was no one – as far as she could see – ahead of her, so she felt reasonably certain that Keighley and anyone else whom he was likely to take with him, had not yet left the Hall; for they, too, would have walked across the park and used the wicket gate to the back garden of the Dower House as being the shortest route.

As she ran, she looked behind over her shoulder every so often; but there was no one coming after her: neither anyone sent to bring her back – which meant that there was a good chance that she had not been seen and might, therefore, when the inevitable hour of reckoning came, be able to keep her destination a secret – nor Keighley on his way to fetch the Chinese monster.

She reached the wicket gate panting and almost sobbing with exhaustion, and with a stitch in her side. In spite of her imperative haste, she instinctively – as on all previous surreptitious visits to the Dower House – fastened the gate after her, before racing along the path to the back door to open it cautiously. It was always just possible, though most unlikely, that the servants had reached the house far ahead of her. But all was quiet inside. She stumbled along the passage to the hall, flung open the door of the Chinese room and stood there, half bent over and gasping, one hand pressing on the stabbing in her side and the other clutching at the door-post for support; now that she had reached her goal, quite unable to deliver her warning.

21

SEUMAS, who had spent the last two hours resolutely practising walking until his ankle had begun to burn and throb threateningly, was resting on the couch, bored and dispirited and starting to read, for the third time, *Pamela, or Virtue Rewarded* – for Francis, who no longer troubled to provide for his entertainment, had neither taken the book away nor replaced it with another, after its first reading.

Hearing Bella's approach along the passage, Seumas had presumed it to be Francis, and had braced himself for the invariable awkwardness of their daily confrontation; at the same time surprised to find either that Francis was, apparently, early, or that the tedious morning should have slipped by to midday so rapidly. He would have turned to consult the red and gold lacquered long-case clock beside the fireplace, which he had found under a dust-sheet and wound up and set to ticking for company, but he remembered that it was still covered with its dust-sheet, its face discreetly veiled; so that one had to go to it and peep behind the folds, if one wished to know the time between hours.

Looking up as the door burst open, he was astonished to see, instead of Francis with his by now habitual expression of disdainful disapproval, Bella, in obvious distress, clinging, half doubled up, to the door-post, and plainly trying to tell him something. Yet, though her mouth kept opening and shutting, no recognizable words came out, but only painful gasps and inarticulate sounds.

'Miss Bella!' He threw aside the book, swung his leg off the couch and, forgetting his ankle, stood up so quickly that it gave way under him agonizingly. Righting himself with a grimace of pain, he snatched up the stick and hurried to her. He had at first thought that she was ill, about to be taken by some fit or seizure, but then he realized that she was merely winded.

'Faith! Is it running a league you've been? Come and sit

down now, and you'll be recovered in a trice.' He helped her to the nearer of the claw-footed chairs and she collapsed on to it, clinging to its back.

'That's the way. Hold fast now while I'm fetching you a drink.'

He filled his cup from the water pail and brought it to her. He had hoped, after their last meeting, that he would never be called upon to face her again; just as she had determined never again to set eyes on him. But now, in the circumstances of their present meeting, all this was, on both sides, temporarily forgotten, and to Seumas she was only a little girl whom he liked and who needed his help; while to her he was someone in danger who had at all costs to to be saved – and for his own sake quite as much as for the Rimpoles.

He knelt down by the chair and held the cup for her, as her own hands were shaking too much to prevent the water from spilling. At first she had insufficient breath to allow her to drink; but after a while she managed first a few sips and then a gulp or two; while Seumas kept up a flow of encouraging and cheerful nonsense.

With the pain of the stitch in her side subsiding, and her breath coming with less difficulty, Bella, a little fortified by the reviving coolness of the water, took thought again for her mission. Suddenly thrusting away the cup and Seumas's hands which held it, she blurted out. 'You must hide. They are ... coming ... here.'

'Who?'

'Keighley ... the butler. Maybe others.'

'When? Now?'

She nodded. 'Any moment. This morning ... he said.'

'Have they discovered about me?'

She shook her head with a vigour that made her gasp for breath again. 'No. But they will ... if we ... do not make haste.'

He pulled himself to his feet, leaning heavily on the chair upon which she still sat. He looked about him at the room with its signs of obvious occupation. 'Are they sure to come in here?'

'Yes. They are coming to fetch the lion.' She gestured,

without looking, towards where the dust-sheet-robed monster stood, grinning eternally at its surroundings.

He did not look at it either – couch and chairs and pail of water were enough to occupy his eyes – as he stood uncertainly for a moment, unable even to begin to remember what the room had looked like on his first night there.

'We must hurry,' Bella said urgently, her fear sounding plainly in her voice.

He turned to her at once, his quick smile ready. 'It's set to rights in no time at all the room will be, if you'll only be reminding me of how everything should look.'

Bella did not tell him that she hardly knew herself. She got to her feet and together they tried to remove all evidence of the room's occupation. She carried pail and cup and kitchen crockery out to the kitchen and hid them all in a closet, and then made sure that the lid was on the well and that nothing else in the kitchen appeared disturbed – on the chance that one of the servants might go in there – before hurrying back to the Chinese room, where Seumas was covering the pair of claw-footed chairs with their sheet. They piled rug, blankets, cushions, book, and spare candles, and anything else that they could find out of its rightful place, on to the couch; then between them – Seumas balancing his weight on one foot only – with difficulty they turned the couch round and pushed it up against the main pile of shrouded furniture, so that its back was outwards, and spread its dust-sheet over it.

'Where would be the best place for me to be hiding myself? Is there a cellar?'

Bella shook her head. Once again out of breath after the exertion of furniture moving, she said in gasps, 'We should need ... a light for ... going down into the cellar. We could not risk ... your slipping in the dark.' Her breath began to come more easily. 'Besides, it may be locked. You must go upstairs and hide in a bedroom.'

'What if they go upstairs?'

'They will not need to go upstairs if they have come only to fetch the monster.'

'Is it sure you are that it's only the monster they're coming for? Supposing they want ... well, the couch, maybe?'

'I heard Keighley speak only of the monster. And if they should take any of the furniture from here, it would be nothing out of this room. My mother detests the Chinese fashion, for all it is the latest thing in London. I have heard her say so.'

'After four weeks of having that animal grinning at the thought of the savoury meal I'd be making it if it got its teeth into me, I'm thinking that your mother is a lady of good taste, and it's glad I am to know that we agree.'

They looked to see that they had left nothing lying on the floor; Seumas picked up his stick which had rolled half under a dust-sheeted chair, and Bella rubbed out, with the toe of her shoe, a betraying footmark made by one of them on some damp morning or other. They gave a careful glance around the room and Seumas exclaimed, 'Faith! See what we're after forgetting!' He pointed to the four-foot tall torchère, standing like a cloak-draped little person with a mushroom-shaped head, on the edge of the central heap of furniture, upon which he had – appropriately enough – set the kitchen candlestick. He limped over to it and carried it to the couch, intending to put it under the sheet with the other things.

Bella, growing fearful again, said, 'Oh, do hurry! Hurry, please!'

Rather than keep her waiting while he laid down the stick in order to have two hands for dragging up the dust-sheet, he took a chance on the kitchen candlestick's not being noticed so far from its own quarters, and leant over the back of the couch to lay it down on top of the sheet, and then limped quickly back to Bella, who was giving one final worried and rather wild look around the room: but nothing else untoward was noticeable in the diminished light afforded by the curtains' being still drawn three-quarters over the window.

'It's none too ill we've done in the time, I'm thinking,' said Seumas cheerfully, after a glance at her face. 'Is it, now?'

Bella, relieved by his confident tone, relaxed a little. 'I'll help you upstairs and then I'll have to leave you, since I am not meant to be here at all. I am supposed to be having lessons, and Miss Proudfoot will be searching for me.'

'It's truly certain you are that I'll be safest upstairs?'

'As certain as I can be. But if you should hear them coming upstairs, you could hide in a closet.'

He grinned at her. 'And if they should open the closet, I can always be groaning at them as though I were the banshee.'

Bella gave a nervous little giggle at the idea; and then, suddenly apprehensive, said, 'You would not pretend to be Lady Alice unless there was real need, would you? There might be one of them who was brave enough to investigate instead of running away. You will take care?'

'However great the temptation, I shall resist it, Miss Bella.' He accompanied the words with a mock heroic gesture; and then added with reassuring seriousness, 'I'll be taking care. You can trust me to do that.'

They started together towards the door, which was ajar, though not wide open; both of them, though still anxious, feeling now quite hopeful about the outcome of the morning's alarms. They were halfway to the door when they heard voices from the hall and they stopped instantly, Bella grasping Seumas's arm to hold him back, though he had gone still and stiff at the very same moment as she.

They looked at one another in dismay. Bella had become all in a moment quite white, her mouth was open and her eyes starting from her head.

'They've come. What can we do?' she whispered, suddenly dry-throated.

'We must hide in here.'

'But where?' She looked about her helplessly, on an instant bereft of all her initiative and most of her intelligence. To have succeeded in so much, only to fail at the last moment! It was cruel.

'Close the door, lad. Where were you raised? On the moor? Doors were made to be closed.' This was Keighley's voice, and it was followed by the sound of the front door being closed, none too gently.

'Now, lad, there's no need for a show of temper because I have to correct you. More of that, and you'll get a clout.'

They heard a mumbled and apologetic, 'No offence meant, Mr Keighley. It's a heavy old door, and I used more strength than I needed, like,' from the new footman Edward, followed by a sceptical laugh from someone else, and, instantly after, Keighley's sharp, 'And that goes for you, too, Tom, lad. You've been in service long enough to know better.' Then, more affably, 'You can save your strength, Edward, for carrying the peaso-vairtoo.' After a brief pause, he added, 'On thinking it over, happen you'd best leave the door open, as you'll be carrying something when you go out, and needing both hands to be doing it with.'

Bella was standing, staring at the door, twisting her fingers in front of her, quite unable to move. Seumas grabbed at her arm and turned her around. 'Under the table with you!'

To relieve the tedium of his lonely days, he had, at various times, looked under all the dust sheets in the Chinese room to see what the furniture hidden beneath them was like. He now pushed Bella towards a small card table, draped to the floor, which stood on its own behind the much larger central pile of furniture. He forced her to her knees because she seemed incapable of acting for herself. 'Get under there.'

Keighley's voice came closer and grew louder. He was taking his time about things – in spite of all the many duties he had mentioned to Fowler – and holding forth importantly for the benefit of Edward. 'You've not been here before, lad, have you? This is the Dower House, where the widow of the late baronet usually comes to live when her son inherits and his wife becomes mistress up at the Hall. It's only an old house, but none the worse for that, and the last Lady Rimpole – Squire's stepmother, that was, who died not eighteen months ago – she had it made as brave as you please just before she died, though she did not live long to enjoy it, poor lady.'

Bella, halfway under the table and beginning to recover her wits, realized that it was too small for both of them to hide beneath. She withdrew her head and looked up at Seumas. 'What of you?'

'Behind the curtains. Hurry!' She was right under the table when his hand reached in and gripped her arm so tightly that it hurt, and his voice came to her in an urgent whisper, 'Bella! Promise me one thing!'

Her assent in that vital moment was instant and unqualified. 'Yes. What?'

'If they find me, you stay still and not be coming out and showing yourself. There's no need at all for you and Francis to be involved. I'll be saying that I broke into the house.'

'But –'

'Hold your tongue. They're here. And you promised, remember!'

He pulled the dust sheet down all round the carved, outcurving legs of the table, gave a last glance to see that she was completely concealed, and limped across the room to the window. He was only just behind the heavy velvet folds of the curtains and they were yet trembling from the disturbance, when the door was pushed wide open and Keighley entered, followed by the two footmen, Thomas bored and Edward gaping about him at the rather peculiar beauties of the Chinese room; at the wallpaper which covered the dark old wooden panels and was painted in every colour with profusely-flowering trees growing from little hillocks, a pheasant on every branch, mallards, and lotuses on streams between their trunks, and every available upper space filled with a bird on the wing or a huge butterfly; at the lacquered fretwork ornamentation about the door frame, which was hung with tiny gilded bells; and at the carved and gilded chimney-piece with its twining vines, three-tiered umbrellas and palms in pots, which surrounded a mirror painted with the picture of a slant-eyed woman playing a lute, the whole erection being topped by a pagoda roof.

'Zookerins!' he exclaimed. 'I thought I'd seen summat at t'Hall, but this fair beats everything.'

Keighley was pleased that he should be impressed, and he smiled at him approvingly; but Thomas, who had been in service at the Hall for almost three years, was inclined to affect scorn of his new colleague's ingenuousness.

'That's nowt,' he declared. 'You should see what's under those sheets. T'old lady main lanced out, didn't she, Mr Keighley?' He went straight on, presuming Keighley's agreement. 'Not that you can see much in this murk. Let's have a little more light.' He went over to the window and began to draw back the curtain behind which Seumas was standing.

Keighley, however, decided that Thomas had been allowed

enough licence and was taking too much on himself in his desire to impress Edward, and was now in need of a bit of a set down. 'Now then, lad, you let those curtains be. They're none of your concern. If Mrs Keighley has seen fit to leave them like that, she has her own good reasons for it. Let too much light in, and you'll have things fading.'

'There's nowt much could fade under all those covers,' said Thomas rebelliously. But he let go of the curtains and started instead to lift up the corners of one dust-sheet after another to see underneath, saying, 'Here, Ned, here's something to tell them about at home,' and, 'See this? I'll bet you a whole George you've never seen t'like of it before.'

'Dowager Lady was a great one for getting her own way when she set her mind on owt,' said Keighley, half reminiscently and half wishing to impress. 'All this fine furniture here, she had made for her in London.'

This was not strictly true, though Thomas did not contradict him, partly out of deference and partly because he, too, was anxious to impress Edward. But he remembered well enough how the Dowager, recollecting a previous vogue for the Chinese style, current in the days of her youth, had come to the Hall and stood watching, hawk-eyed, leaning on her cane, while store-rooms, lofts, and servants' attics were ransacked in search of furniture of three or four decades earlier, discarded as outmoded; and satisfied at last that there was no corner left unsearched, had returned to the Dower House with her booty: a writing desk, a tray, several vases, and no fewer than three japanned cabinets – one of them the very one which he was at that moment disclosing to Edward's wondering gaze, with a 'What do you think of this then, Ned?'

'Aye, poor lady,' Keighley continued, shaking his head, 'she had this room all furnished as she wanted it and then she never lived above a few weeks to enjoy it.'

'Cut off in her prime, like!' said Edward with fitting gloom.

Keighley, remembering the formidable old lady, as straight-backed and as sharp-tongued in the last week of her life as she had been in her first week as a bride at the Hall, more than thirty years before, said, 'Aye, that she was.'

But Thomas laughed. 'Eh, you are daft, Ned! In her prime! She was sixty, if she was a day, was Dowager.' He continued moving aside dust-sheets and exhibiting portions of hidden treasures, like a conjurer displaying his tricks.

The two footmen had worked their way around to the back of the outskirts of the main heap of piled up furniture and were approaching Bella's table, when Keighley, having indulged them as long as he saw fit, said, 'Come now, lads, we're not over here to be idle. There's work to be done.' He made his way towards the Chinese lion and gestured to it regally.

They both followed him reluctantly; and then young Edward gave a yell of surprise and pointed, 'Save us! Mr Keighley, what's that, then?'

'That, lad, is what we've come to fetch.'

'Lors! Isn't it horrid?'

Thomas gave a guffaw. 'Flayed by it, Ned?'

'But what is it, Mr Keighley?' asked Edward, unable to take his eyes from it. 'Is it a dog or a cat or a dragon, or what?'

'Now, I ask you, did you ever see a dog or a cat that looked like that?' exclaimed Thomas in scorn. 'What a sackless zany you are, Ned! Of course it's a dragon. A dragon like St George is killing in t'coloured glass window in church.'

'Now then, Tom lad, there's no need to show your ignorance and mislead young Edward. St George's dragon, indeed! That's no dragon. It's a peaso-vairtoo, that's what it is. A Chinese peaso-vairtoo and worth a lot more brass than you or I will ever have, as well as being the very latest fashion in London.'

'Zookerins! Do you mean that everyone in London has one of those in t'drawing-room, like?' Edward was still staring at it.

'Nay, not everyone. Only the gentry. And not even all the gentry, neither, I'll be bound. Only those that have the brass and the good taste that Squire and her ladyship have.' On this suitable note of praise for their master and mistress, Keighley hastily ended, before he was asked any questions to which Fowler had not supplied the answers. 'Now then, back to work, lads. Off with the dust-sheet, and one of you at hinder end and t'other at front, and lift it up. And slow and careful, mind.'

Thomas sighed audibly, Edward squared his narrow shoulders, spat on his hands, and tried to look strong enough to pick up the monster single-handed; then, seeing Thomas roll up his sleeves, he did likewise.

22

FRANCIS, whose lessons had ended nearly an hour earlier than usual because Dr Mortlake had received an urgent summons to visit an ailing parishioner, arrived at the wicket gate of the Dower House at around the time that Keighley was correcting Thomas for misinforming Edward as to the species to which the monster belonged. Having tethered Sultan, he carried a pie and a piece of cheese in a napkin along the garden path and entered through the back door at just about that moment when Keighley was saying, 'Off with the dust-sheet.'

On reaching the hall, he caught sight of the open front door and instantly presumed that Seumas had opened it, forgetting that, without a key, he could not have done so. Annoyed by this piece of rash folly, he made hurriedly for the Chinese room, hearing no tell-tale voices from there because by then the two footmen were rolling up their sleeves for action and no one was saying anything.

Francis began to speak irritably even before he reached the room. 'What in the world are you about, opening the front door? Are you –' On the threshold he stopped, appalled. 'Keighley! What are you doing here?' His eyes flickered rapidly around the room and saw no sign of Seumas. That could mean that he was safely hidden or was gone – or that he was lying bound on the floor, momentarily out of sight, waiting until such time as the village constable arrived to fetch him away.

'Eh, now, Master Francis, I'm sorry if we surprised you. We have come to fetch the peaso-vairtoo for her ladyship.' Keighley had known Francis since he had been a few hours old and in his cradle, and Francis was always far less aloof and more forthcoming with those among the upper-servants whom he had known all his life than he was with any outsider; and though Keighley would never have presumed to say it out loud, the look he gave Francis said plainly enough, 'That's what I'm doing here. But what are you doing here yourself?'

With a most admirable attempt at self-control, Francis said, 'I thought that you were thieves or trespassers.'

Keighley said cheerfully, 'Nay, no thieves nor trespassers here, Master Francis. Only us, carrying out her ladyship's orders.'

No trespassers. So Seumas, wherever he was, had not been caught. Francis's relief was profound; but, even so, things were very far from safe.

One does not have to justify one's actions to a servant; but when one has a guilty conscience, one imagines that one has to explain one's behaviour to everyone, lest it should be misconstrued – or rather, lest it should be rightly interpreted. Hoping that they had not noticed from which end of the hall he had approached the Chinese room, Francis said, 'I saw that the front door was open and thought someone had broken in.' He held himself rigidly upright in the doorway, one hand clenched into a fist at his side, and one clutching the napkin of food behind him; for otherwise, he was sure, his legs would have given way under him from the shock.

As soon as he had spoken, he realized that probably even the new footman – and most certainly the other two – must know that one could not see the front door of the Dower House from either the park or the road. That is always the way with lies: one tells one and then one has to tell more to bear it out. 'I found some of the village children in the garden the other day, stealing the fruit, so I thought I had better make sure that they were not here today.' Once again, having spoken, he was, too late, aware of the discrepancies in his story: one could see the front door only from the front garden, and all the fruit bushes were at the back. But he was not going to amplify or to try to explain any further. Let them make what they liked of it.

'Stealing fruit, were they, little wizzles? If they start that road, they'll be climbing trees and breaking windows in no time at all. I'll tell George Rigby to have one of his lads come down here now and then to take a look around, like, more often.'

Hastily, Francis said, 'That would be unnecessary and the

waste of a man's time. The boys will not come here again, I'm convinced. I put a proper scare on them with talk of transportation.'

Keighley nodded approvingly. 'Aye, I'm glad of that. The little good-for-nowts, they deserve a right good welting. I suppose you do not know whose bairns they were, Master Francis?'

Francis shook his head. 'No, I don't.' Greatly relieved though he might be, that all seemed well so far; he knew the danger was not nearly past, and that all would, in fact, not be well until they were gone from the house. He made a push to get rid of them. 'What was it you said that you had come to fetch?'

'The peaso-vairtoo.' Keighley indicated it.

'Oh ... that. Yes.' Francis was completely mystified by Keighley's name for it, but he had not time to waste on puzzling over it. The sooner they were out of the house with it, the better, and he was determined to see them safely off and on their way himself.

Hoping he sounded casual, he said, 'Well, now that I know you are not thieves, I must not hinder you.' He made as if to go, and then, as though at a sudden whim, stopped and said with what he trusted would pass for boyish enthusiasm, 'How are you going to carry it? I should imagine that it is pretty heavy, as well as breakable.'

'Aye, it is. But it'll be difficult only as far as the front door, Master Francis. After that it'll be easy and safe enough on the handcart.'

'The handcart?'

'Aye. Did you not see it as you came in? It's standing outside the door.'

Oh, these lies! These wretched lies which involved one more deeply every minute! 'Why, yes, of course I did. But I was thinking too much of the boys stealing the fruit, and then, when I saw the door open, of thieves, to take particular notice of it.' Then, both to change the subject before Keighley should start marvelling at his apparent blindness, and to return to the point, he looked expectantly at the monster and said, 'I must admit I shall be interested to see how you manage. I'd not like to have to get a safe, carrying grip on that creature, with all those spikes and knobs in the way.'

Keighley took the hint. 'Come on, lads. As I said, one of you at hinder end and t'other at front.'

Thomas whisked the dust-sheet off, so that the monster was now completely exposed in all its hideous glory. 'You can have t'front end, Ned, so that it'll be you that's nearest the teeth.' He stationed himself behind the monster and reached down to take hold of its back legs. 'Hod on, now!'

Edward bent forward, searching gingerly for the best grip, and then exclaimed 'Eh, save us! Look at this in its jowl! However did it get there? I thought you said, Mr Keighley, that no one had been in here for weeks past.'

'You're right, lad. No one has. What have you found?'

Edward straightened up, holding out to the others with an awed expression, a pink rosebud, freshly picked and unwilted.

'In its mouth?' asked Keighley incredulously.

Francis, stepping closer to look, was appalled. How would he ever be able to explain that away? Had he been standing anywhere near the monster, he could have pretended that it was he who had put the rose in its mouth. But he could not possibly have done so from where he had been, by the doorway. It was, he saw at once, one of the pink roses from the rosebush that scrambled about the back door – he ought to recognize them, he had seen them almost every day for the last four weeks – and he was impotently furious at this latest piece of inconsiderateness on the part of Seumas. To stand at the back door and risk being seen by trespassers in the back garden, merely in order to pick roses to decorate the monster! And, above all, to do it on the very day when the servants had come to fetch the monster away! It was insupportable.

'It's t'ghost,' said Thomas in a small, scared voice. 'It's t'White Lady that put it there.'

'If one of you two lads is playing a trick, he'll be sorry for it,' threatened Keighley.

But they were both too genuinely surprised and alarmed for him to suspect them for more than a moment.

'It's t'White Lady all right,' said Thomas in a tone which would well have been suited to announcing the end of the world.

Bella, under the table and surrounded by folds of dust-sheet, as though in a dark little tent, could not see out any more than she herself could be seen, and she was totally unable to guess what had happened. She was sure of only one thing: whatever it was, it sounded serious – and that probably meant serious for Francis and Seumas and herself – and moreover, judging by his present silence, Francis seemed unable to cope with the situation.

Seumas, on the other hand, knew exactly what had happened, and he cursed the sudden impulse that had led him, soon after dawn, when coming back from the privy in the yard and stopping a moment in the doorway, looking out through the trees of the garden at the rising sun, and wondering how long it would be before he was away from that place and safe again, to pick one of the pink rosebuds, still wet with dew, which were beginning to scent the cool early morning air. And he cursed still more the impulse which had made him, on returning to the Chinese room with the rose in his hands and catching sight of the monster with its everlasting grin, to say aloud to it, 'Can you not be looking a little more friendly at me? Is it my fault you're not rid of me yet? I never wanted to fall off the gate, though you may pretend you think I did.' And then to go to it, saying, 'A gift might be sweetening your grin, maybe? Here's one, then. You can be adorning yourself with it or eating it, whichever you please!' and to put the rose between its jaws. And, above all, he cursed his carelessness in utterly forgetting what he had done, when he and Bella had put the room to rights. It was that very same kind of carelessness, he told himself, which, sooner or later, sent a man to the nubbing-cheat – in his case, he reflected wryly, the way things were going, it might well be sooner, rather than later.

'It's t'White Lady,' repeated Thomas, who seemed copletely to have lost his nerve on believing himself confronted with the supernatural.

'Nay, that's daft,' said Keighley. 'Ghosts don't pick roses.'

Francis, desperately trying to retrieve the situation, said, 'It is one of the roses from the bush climbing beside the back door, I believe. I see no reason why it should not have been picked by the ghost.'

Thomas was glad to find support against Keighley's scepticism. 'That's what I say, Master Francis. It's t'White Lady's home, why should she not pick her own roses?'

'Happen it's an omen of death, do you think?' asked Edward, his eyes wide and round and starting out of his head. 'Do you reckon that Squire is going to die?'

Keighley was outraged. 'What a daft, gaumless thing to say, Edward, and in front of Master Francis. You keep such thoughts to yourself.'

Francis, seeing that he had two of them already on his side, was encouraged to a further effort. 'I sincerely hope it betokens nothing of the sort,' he said as earnestly as though he were indeed considering the possibility. 'I would say, myself, that it probably has no specific significance. But,' he went on to lie valiantly, 'I have read a great deal about ghosts, and it seems that they do frequently manifest themselves in some physical manner, such as by picking flowers or by ... or ... or some such thing, as well as by showing themselves and moaning and clanking chains and ... and doing all the more customary things which ghosts do.' He was improvising wildly and trying to sound as authoritative on the subject as possible; and he could only hope that he would be able to keep it up for long enough to convince Keighley that the rose had not been picked by human hands.

He seemed to be achieving a partial success. Keighley, impressed in spite of himself by Francis's support of the footmen's credulity, said, 'Eh, well, I don't know what to think, Master Francis. You're the scholar and have read all about it and I'm only ignorant of such things, and happen you may be right. But it seems odd to me that the White Lady should suddenly start to pick flowers when she's never done owt of the kind before, not in all her born days.' He looked at the rose, still in Edward's hand, and repeated, 'I don't know what to think.'

They all stared in silence at the rose, Keighley puzzled and doubtful, the two footmen quite convinced, and Francis frantically racking his brains for some specious argument which would finally resolve the question and settle Keighley's doubts. And then, into the silence, the long-case clock against the wall beside the fireplace struck twelve. The strokes were slightly muffled by its dust-sheet, but they were otherwise perfectly clear.

To Seumas, it might as well have been the striking of midnight heralding the morning of the day upon which he was to be hanged. Francis had been doing his best over the rose, he reflected, but surely not even Francis could manage to persuade them that the banshee had wound up the clock and set it going?

From under the table, cut off from a sight of everything that was going on, Bella had been able only vaguely to make out what all the talk of roses and Lady Alice was about. But the fatal significance of the striking of the clock was apparent to her at once; as it was, also, to Francis, who, even in that moment while he condemned Seumas's rashness and folly in winding up the clock, had the honesty to admit to himself that Seumas had an excuse, since he had taken back his watch so promptly on Seumas's fall from favour.

Keighley, no longer in the slightest degree doubtful, said, 'The White Lady never set that clock going. And no one from the Hall did, neither. I know for a fact that no one from the Hall has been in here for at least three weeks. Nay, there's been someone in this house who had no right to be here.'

'Trespassers or thieves?' suggested Edward, glancing apprehensively around the room, unknown natural dangers appearing to him for the moment to be almost as fearful as supernatural ones.

'You're right, lad. Trespassers for sure, and happen thieves, also.'

With a scorn which sounded a little shaky, Francis said, 'Why should trespassers or thieves set clocks going?'

'So that they could find out what hour it was?' suggested Edward.

'Nonsense!' Francis snapped at him. 'It was one of the servants, or Mr Thompson, and not an outsider at all.'

'I'll take my oath it wasn't one of us, Master Francis,' said Keighley. 'And it wasn't Mr Thompson, neither, because I mentioned to him this morning that I was coming here and he said to me that he's not been here himself for a month at least, he's been that busy. "And, Keighley," he said to me, "while you're over there, look in the dining-room to make sure there's been no more birds' nests in the chimney." Because in the spring he found a jackdaw's nest fallen down the chimney into the hearth in the dining-room. No, Master Francis, it's an outsider, that I know.'

Thomas, his spirits quite recovered now that the supernatural had been discounted, suggested eagerly, 'Happen it was that London criminal t'militiamen were after?'

Francis would have enjoyed throttling him for the suggestion; but Keighley said, 'Happen you're right there, lad.'

'Why should he remain in the district?' demanded Francis. 'With the militia after him, he would make his way somewhere else as fast as he could.'

'Widow Peel saw him taking eggs from her hencoop, not two weeks ago, Master Francis, sir,' Edward reminded him.

'She says that she saw him!' Francis found it infuriating not to be able to refute the untrue tale without betraying his own personal knowledge of where Seumas really was on that particular night. 'Besides, how could any outsider come in here without a key?'

'He could break open a window, Master Francis,' said Keighley.

'Have you found a broken window?'

'We've not looked yet, Master Francis.'

'Are we going to search t'house?' asked Thomas eagerly.

'Aye. That we are.'

'Very well, search!' said Francis. 'But I wager we shall find nothing.'

With some idea of getting them out of that room, since it would be likely to provide them with the greatest number of clues, Francis gestured the two footmen to the door and made as if to shepherd them out. If only, he thought, he had the luck to be the one to find where Seumas was hidden, he could then prevent the others from discovering him. But his plan was foiled at the very outset by Keighley.

'By your leave, Master Francis, we'll all keep together. Happen there's still someone in the house – after all, the rose is still wick – and happen he'll be armed, so we'd best stay together all the while, and take good care.'

'I have my clasp knife!' Edward produced it proudly from a pocket.

'Good lad.'

'With my two fists, we'll not be needing your knife, Ned.'

Keighley set out his plan of action. 'Now, we'll start in here, Master Francis and lads, and search the whole room thoroughly. All the dust-sheets off, look under the furniture and behind the curtains. Then we'll move on to the dining-room and do the same there, and so on until we've finished this floor. Then we'll go upstairs.' Moving his position and looking about him, he noticed the kitchen candlestick lying on the covered couch. 'Eh, what's that, then? Candlestick, is it? Pass it to me, Tom. It'll make a handy weapon.'

Thomas gave him the heavy iron candlestick and, grasping it like a club, Keighley said, 'Now, are we ready?'

Both footmen spoke at once, 'Aye, Mr Keighley.'

'Master Francis?'

Francis made one final effort. 'We are wasting our time. You'd do far better to take the monster to the Hall, which is what you came here to do, and forget all this nonsense about thieves and trespassers.'

'Happen you'll be proved wrong before we're done, Master Francis,' said Keighley, who was beginning to have had enough of Francis's lack of co-operation and attitude of superior scorn. Any other boy of his age, he thought, gentry or not, would have been thoroughly enthusiastic at the prospect of an exciting hunt through an empty house for possible villains. He tightened his grip on the candlestick. 'Now then, all together. We'll look behind the curtains first, so that we can draw them back and give ourselves more light.'

Before they could move in their concerted action, from beyond the central pile of furniture there came the sound of a chair or table legs scraping on the floor. They all looked in the direction of the noise, three of them startled and wary and expectant, and Francis with miserable apprehension. He wondered whether Seumas, with his lame ankle, was about to attempt a dash for the door; and if so, whether he himself, without appearing to do so, could try to help him in some way. Perhaps he could, as if by accident in the eagerness of the pursuit, trip up the two footmen? Keighley was undoubtedly the best armed, but, being older and heavier, could move less fast. Or perhaps Seumas, unable to rely on his ankle, would not risk a run for freedom, but instead, cornered, would endeavour to fight his way out. Or even, perhaps, knowing he had no chance of escape, being Seumas, he would manage to come out smiling and with a jest and give himself up without a struggle. While the different possibilities flashed through Francis's mind, the dust-sheeted little table on the far side of the large pile of furniture wobbled and danced on its legs, and then toppled over on to its side. The mass of dust-sheet heaved and billowed, and, largely concealed from the watchers by the pile of furniture which separated them from her, Bella crawled out and then stood up in full view at last, her hair falling about her face and her cheeks scarlet with the exertion and with nervousness.

'Miss Bella!'

'Bella!'

Francis's astonishment equalled that of the others and therefore successfully cleared him of any possible suspicion of collusion with his sister.

With as much dignity as the circumstances left her, and with as much casual self-possession as she could manage, Bella shook out her crumpled skirts and came round the pile of furniture towards the others. 'Good morning, Keighley.' She was trying to give herself time both to invent an acceptable reason for her presence in the Dower House and to discover the exact connection between the monster and a rose, before the explanations had to begin.

'Good morning, Miss Bella.' There was a moment or two of silence and then Keighley asked the obvious question which Francis had not dared to ask – though he knew the others were waiting for him to do so – lest Bella had not yet thought up an answer. 'What in the world are you doing here, Miss Bella?'

The delay, though brief, had been long enough. 'I overheard your telling Fowler that you would be coming here this morning to fetch the monster, so I thought it would be fun to hide beside it and to growl when you came near to pick it up. But it ... it ... I found it was not practicable, so I hid under a table instead.' She managed the explanation with tolerable calmness; and then, remembering, she hastened to add, 'While I was waiting for you, I amused myself by winding up the clock.'

'And it was you who put the rose in the monster's mouth, where we found it?' prompted Francis.

'Yes, of course.' So that was what it had all been about, she thought.

'Of all the stupid things to do, Bella! How did you prevail upon Miss Proudfoot to let you come here alone, and during lesson time?'

'I did not prevail upon her. I ran away when she was out of the room.'

'Well, all I can say is that you'll be in trouble when you go back again. And so you deserve to be. I've never heard of such a childish and hare-brained scheme.'

In his relief, and trying at the same time to be helpful, Francis was a little over-acting the disapproving brother, and Keighley said, 'Nay, then, Master Francis, there's no need for you, too, to be so hard on her. There're enough others who'll be that, when they hear of this morning's goings-on.'

'Anyhow, Keighley, I was right about it's all being nonsense, that there was an outsider hidden in the house.'

It was the wrong thing to have said. Keighley, suddenly conscious of an unexplained fact, looked puzzled and said, 'Aye, Miss Bella, how did you manage to get in here?'

Francis held his breath.

After a hesitation that was not nearly as long as it might have been, and certainly not as long as it seemed to her, Bella answered, 'Through the front door, with a key.'

'But where did you find a key?'

Bella drew herself up and looked him straight in the eyes. 'I'm sorry, Keighley, but I cannot tell you. That is my secret.' So that he should ask no more, she added, 'And I'm sorry if I startled you. Francis is right. It was a silly trick to play.'

Keighley was very fond of her, and always had been, so he was sorry to think that she would be in trouble with Miss Proudfoot. He allowed himself to relax momentarily the stiff unnaturalness of his formal manner of speech and say to her, broadly and naturally, as though she had not been one of The

Family. 'Eh, it's nowt to be worrying over, Miss Bella. There's no harm done. You fair capped us all, you did.'

She smiled gratefully, then looked past him to the two footmen. 'I'm sorry if I startled you, too.'

Edward grinned bashfully. 'No offence taken, miss.'

Thomas said gallantly, 'It made a brave change from everyday, Miss Annabel.'

Francis, eager to get everyone out of the house as soon as possible, broke in, 'We have wasted quite enough time. You had better go straight home as quickly as you can, Bella. I will follow you in a few minutes. Now that I am here, I want to see the monster taken out. Go along, Bella. Out of the front door as fast as you can.' The last injunction was lest she should betray them by making as usual for the unlocked back door.

But she moved over to stand beside him. 'One might as well be hanged for a sheep as a lamb, as old Robert is always saying. I shall stay and watch the monster moved, too.'

Keighley was once again marshalling his forces. 'Now, then, as we said before: one at the back and t'other at front and carefully does it. Remember, it's breakable.'

'Bella, must you be such a fool and make it worse for yourself?' asked Francis loudly. Under his breath he added, 'I'll stay until they are out of the house.' Then, in an even lower whisper, 'Where is he?'

'No, I'll not go. I am staying with you.' She dropped her voice. 'I do not think that I could walk at this moment, if I were to try. My legs could not carry me. Behind the curtain.'

They stood side by side and watched the monster raised, both footmen straining and pulling faces and making as though it were much heavier than it really was, and trying to impress Mr Keighley as well as the young lady and gentleman with their strength and all the hard work they were called upon to do. Having raised it, they began to walk with it, slowly and carefully, Edward stepping backwards, clasping the ugly, grinning head to him and protesting about not being able to see where he was going, and Thomas chaffing him under his breath the whole time, while Keighley stalked from side to side, directing operations.

Under any other circumstances, Francis and Bella would

have found it delightfully funny; but though Francis managed to grin and even make a few, loud, disrespectful comments about the monster, Bella stood stiffly, as though watching a funeral procession, holding her hands clasped tightly before her and with her teeth clenched together in an effort to prevent from being apparent to the servants, the fit of shivering that had come upon her as a reaction to her ordeal.

Francis, noticing, said loudly, 'Bella, you are half-witted to have come here without your cloak. You will catch cold in that thin dress in this damp, old, empty house.' He took off his coat and flung it around her shoulders, hissing in her ear as he did so, 'We have succeeded until now. Do not spoil things at the last minute. For heaven's sake, remember that you are supposed to have risked nothing worse than a whipping. Try not to look as though you were about to face all the tortures of the Spanish Inquisition.'

After that, she managed a fixed little smile.

The monster having been safely carried into the hall, Keighley folded the dust-sheet neatly and laid it down to await the monster's return, gave a last look around the Chinese room to make sure that he was leaving all as it should be, and saw Francis's napkin of food, which he had, a few minutes before, laid down on the back of the couch, hoping to leave it behind unnoticed. Keighley picked it up and handed it to Francis who snatched it from him nervously, with a muttered word of thanks, and thrust it at Bella saying, 'Here, you can carry this.' Adding in a whisper, 'Under the coat.'

Bella clasped Seumas's dinner to her under Francis's coat as bidden; and when Keighley had closed the door of the Chinese room, walking with him, they followed the monster in its progress along the hall. At the front door, as the monster and its bearers were being directed by Keighley down the four steps to the handcart, Francis dawdled behind and tugged at his coat-sleeve. Bella turned round. He held out his hand to her, wordlessly. She looked mystified. He frowned and gestured that she should give him something. At last it was clear to her, and she covertly gave him the napkin of food and moved to block the doorway, standing with his coat skirts spread on either side of her, while he ran back to the Chinese room, opened the door,

dropped the parcel in and said, 'We are all going now. Wait where you are for a few minutes longer. Food by the door.' He closed the door and ran back to Bella in time to see the monster being laid on a piece of sacking which had been spread on the cart to receive it.

Keighley locked the front door, watched closely by Francis. Francis's apparent bullying of his sister had increased Keighley's sympathy for her. He thought how forlorn she looked, standing there with her hair dishevelled, dust smudges on her face and her brother's coat draped about her. He smiled at her. 'How would you like to ride back to the Hall on the cart with the peaso-vairtoo, Miss Bella?'

Genuinely thankful – just how thankful, he could not possibly have guessed – Bella was lifted on to the handcart, and sitting on the sacking with her arms clasped around the monster's uncomfortable neck, she was pulled by Thomas and pushed by Edward – with Keighley as an escorting outrider – back to the Hall in style; while Francis, delayed a little by having to fetch Sultan, followed a short way behind.

23

THE cortege arrived at the Hall to find that Bella was being searched for all over the house and garden by a distracted Miss Proudfoot, a tearful Old Nurse, and most of the servants; for Miss Proudfoot, although she had been almost certain that Bella was up to some unusual mischief, had yet had an uneasy feeling that perhaps she might, after all, have been taken ill, and at that very moment be lying senseless or groaning out her life in some distant corner of the garden or farthest attic room; and the longer Bella's absence had lasted, the stronger this feeling had become, until her fears and those of Old Nurse – who, after the first half-hour, had become so truly distressed that she had even ceased declaring that at any moment the excitement would cause her to have a spasm – had communicated themselves to almost all the servants, and set the household in an uproar.

Relieved though she now might be to see her alive and well, Miss Proudfoot pounced upon Bella, displaying only vexation. 'Where have you been, Annabel, you bad child?'

Bella told her the same tale that she had told to Keighley, but omitted all mention of how she had managed to enter the Dower House; and it did not occur to Miss Proudfoot to inquire about this. Her relief turned to anger. 'You deceitful disobedient, wicked girl! Pretending that you felt unwell in order that you might go and play a childish trick on the servants!' She boxed Bella's ears very hard and sent her to wait in her room, while she herself hurried off to inform Lady Rimpole – who, Sir John being away from home that day, was the only one of the household who had been entirely unaffected by Miss Proudfoot's agitation – that her daughter had been found safe and well; then, in an apologetic manner, as though she felt herself to be to blame for Bella's bad behaviour, she acquainted her with the details of Bella's escapade. To the governess's surprise, Lady Rimpole laughed instead of being shocked.

'Oh, Lady Rimpole,' Miss Proudfoot protested, 'Annabel has been a very wicked girl.'

'She has indeed,' said Lady Rimpole, seemingly quite unperturbed by the fact. 'Well, Miss Proudfoot, you will know best how to deal with her. I leave the matter entirely to you. I have, as you know, a perfect trust in your good sense.' With a charming smile of dismissal, Lady Rimpole returned to her book, that one of the Abbé Prévost's romances which had the most lately come into her hands, *Mémoires d'un honnête homme*, published only the year before, and which she was finding vastly entertaining.

Miss Proudfoot had made up her mind that, for her own good, Bella must be whipped; but Bella was saved from this – quite unintentionally – by Old Nurse, who, furious because of the scare which Bella's disappearance had given her, took it upon herself to tell Miss Proudfoot that, in her opinion, Miss Bella should be soundly whipped. Miss Proudfoot, resenting being told her duty by a servant, said coldly, 'I have already decided upon Miss Annabel's punishment, thank you, Old Nurse,' and immediately abandoned all idea of a whipping, lest it should be thought that she was taking Old Nurse's advice. And so Bella, after a long scolding from Miss Proudfoot, was locked in her room for the rest of the day and given neither dinner nor supper. For the whole of the next day, also, she had to remain in her room, with only bread and water for the three meals of the day.

Old Nurse, threatening even more emphatically than usual to have a spasm, muttered all around the servants' hall, grumbling about Miss Proudfoot's leniency and Bella's shocking conduct; but Keighley stood up for Bella, demanding, 'And why should Miss Bella not get up to mischief now and again? We're nowt the worse for it, and she owned up as boldly as any lad would have done. If she weren't gentry, I'd say she was a right bonny little wench, our Miss Bella.'

Old Nurse, greatly affronted, said sharply, 'But she is gentry Mr Keighley, and don't you forget it. And gentry don't go about behaving like hoydens, not if they've been brought up as they should.'

Bella spent most of that first afternoon and evening of her imprisonment in feeling sorry for herself; mainly because, having successfully outwitted everyone and saved Seumas, she should have been feeling supremely triumphant – but was not. Had Seumas still been Mr Macdonald the Jacobite, she would hardly have been able to contain her joy and pride at having been privileged to save him from his enemies, instead of feeling guilty – as she did – at having helped a criminal once more to evade justice; and had Seumas still been Mr Macdonald, her punishment would have seemed a glorious martyrdom, instead of only a fraction of the penalty her immense wrong-doing really merited.

By breakfast time the next morning, when a silent and disapproving Old Nurse brought her two slices of dry bread and a jug of water and slapped the tray down beside her without a glance at her and marched out of the room again, she was extremely hungry and very ready to welcome even such an unappetizing meal as that. Munching her dry bread thankfully, she thought of Seumas, whom they had once left without food for almost three days, and she began to feel a certain measure of sympathy for him.

From feeling sympathetically to feeling charitably was, for Bella, only a short step; and having nothing better to do with her time, she set herself, partly out of good nature and partly, it must be admitted, from a desire to make her own and Francis's conduct in aiding him seem less culpable, to enumerate, not Seumas's virtues – for a thief, a coin-clipper, a highwayman, and heaven only knew what else besides, could not be admitted to have any virtues – but at least his good points.

And he had a few, she found. For instance, the day before, in the midst of his dangerous predicament – far, far greater than hers – he had given thought to her and Francis and insisted that if he were caught, she was to try and save herself; he had always seemed grateful enough for what they had done for him; he had never demanded or threatened; he had never stolen anything of theirs; when unmasked for what he was, he had made no attempt to deny the truth; and so on. By the time a still disapproving Old Nurse brought her her dinner, she had discovered a number of good points in Seumas's favour, and was beginning to think that, with so much to be said for him, it was a pity that, having been saved from the gallows, he could not be made to give up his wicked ways and start to live an honest and useful life.

She would not have been Bella had she allowed her regrets to stop there. Almost at once she was wishing that, even as she and Francis were answerable for saving Seumas from being hanged, so they might be answerable for converting him to honest ways and for persuading him to cease from misspending that life which they had saved. Not very long after that, she was lost in a gratifying daydream in which she saw herself and Francis, a few years hence, being thanked – with all his old charm, now no longer misapplied – by a happy, hardworking, and honest Seumas, for having been the ones to set his feet on the path of righteousness.

For once it was not someone else's interruption that brought her back to reality. This time it was she herself, who broke into her own daydream to condemn it as impractical. Between the pleasing picture of a reformed and smiling Seumas, and the hunted – yet, even so, smiling – criminal hiding in the Dower House, there stretched, she was forced to acknowledge, a wide gap: only the smile remained constant and unaltered. Yet, given Seumas's good points and a real determination on their part, it would surely not be beyond the powers of Francis and herself to find some way of making an honest citizen of him; so that never again would his life be in danger at the hangman's hands – or other people's property be in danger at his.

By the time Old Nurse brought her supper, Bella was happily engaged in thinking up suitable trades and employments in which Seumas's better qualities could be utilized, and by means of which he could earn an honest living.

The next morning she awoke still eager and filled with zeal for her latest ambition. Her imprisonment ended that day after breakfast, and on being released she lost no time in seeking out Francis and telling him of her new notion.

Francis received it with a complete lack of enthusiasm. 'It would take someone far older and cleverer than you, to reform O'Leary. Besides, I do not expect he wants to be reformed, and any attempt would be likely only to make him stubborn. No, let him go as soon as he can walk. We shall be well rid of him, whether he goes back to stealing or not. And, what's more,' he added, 'we shall be very fortunate if we can indeed be rid of him without further trouble and without being found out.'

To any other arguments put forward by Bella in favour of an attempt at reformation, Francis was equally crushing; until at last, thoroughly discouraged, she said, 'Oh, very well, then. If you say that it is useless and that we should not make the attempt, let us think no more of it. But if we had been able to persuade him to live honestly, and if we had found him some respectable occupation, it would have meant that things had, in the end, prospered, after all. And think how agreeable it would have been if we could have thought that, in spite of . . . in spite of all that happened, some good had come to the scores of lies we have had to tell and of the other bad things we have had to do. We should not need to feel so . . . so ashamed about it all, and so wicked.'

After considering the face-saving and conscience-salving aspect of her plan, Francis found himself more in sympathy with it. 'Well,' he said slowly and still rather dubiously, 'I suppose there would be no harm in our trying. Even if he does reject the suggestion, we can hardly make worse fools of ourselves than we have done already. Besides,' he added cynically, 'even though in an honest life the profits are less high, it must be far less uncomfortable to be honest than to be always wondering if one is about to be caught and hanged or transported, so maybe he might be ready to give honesty a trial, especially after this latest fright he has had.'

Bella was delighted. 'You must tell him when you see him tomorrow, that we are trying to find him honest work, and that by the time his ankle is quite healed, we hope to have found something to suit him. And try to impress upon him, Francis, how pleasant it will be for him not to have to feel afraid every time he sees a parish constable, or a night watchman going on his rounds.'

But this Francis refused to do. 'No, we must find him the work first, and then we can tell him about it. We should try to take him by surprise. It would be absurd to tell him of our plan and then leave him alone in the Dower House for hours and hours on end, to think the matter over and realize exactly how much more profitable and less wearisome dishonesty is. Of course, he knows that already, but there's no need to give him a chance to be doubly sure of it.'

This agreed to, there remained only to think of an occupation for Seumas. It was Bella who made most of the suggestions, and Francis who rejected most of the ones she made. Her first idea was that Seumas should be a shopkeeper.

'He would make a good shopkeeper, I think, Francis. He would always be cheerful and polite to his customers, and I'm sure that he would be very skilful at persuading them all to buy a great many things which they did not really want. He would be prosperous in no time.'

'I am convinced he would,' said Francis drily. He went on to demolish the suggestion for practical reasons. 'In order to be a shopkeeper, one has to have a shop, and that means owning or renting premises. And then one has to have things to sell, and that means making them – like a cobbler or a saddler and so on – or, I suppose, buying them from someone else and reselling them. Anyway, whatever he sold, it would need money to set him up as a shopkeeper, and where could we find the money for that?'

'What of his being an innkeeper? How does one become an innkeeper?'

'I have no notion. But I do remember hearing father say that far too many innkeepers are leagued with the smugglers. Making him an innkeeper would amount to putting him in the way of dishonest company again.'

'What of a thief-taker? I once asked father about thief-takers, and he told me that very often they are men who have been criminals themselves, and so, because they know so much about the ways of criminals, they are able to give great help to the magistrates. Oh, Francis, it would be the very thing for him!'

But Francis, for some reason which he could not have named, felt immediately certain that Seumas would not consent to become a thief-maker. 'It might well do, if he would agree to it. But I rather think that he would not,' he said doubtfully.

'Perhaps he would like to be a soldier, and go and fight against the French?'

'He'd probably consider the risks too high for the profit. After all, I hardly imagine he has been in the habit of risking his life for as little as a soldier's pay.'

And so it went on, for all that day and the next, with Francis showing no great enthusiasm, yet not being entirely discouraging; and Bella remaining stoutly hopeful.

On the following day, which was a Friday, a distraction was provided for Francis by the arrival from Middleham in Wensleydale, beside the River Ure – where, since the days of the monks of Coverham and Jervaulx, so many fine horses had been bred – of the horse promised to him by his father earlier in the year. It was a handsome, three-year-old black gelding named, appropriately enough, Raven.

Francis spent most of the day trying out Raven's paces in the park; and, so great were his admiration for Raven's points and his appreciation of Raven's capabilities, that what should have been for him a day of undiluted delight, was yet not entirely spoilt by his knowledge that, because of his deceitful and dishonourable behaviour, he deserved no gifts at all from his father, let alone one so perfect as Raven.

24

THE next day the expected visitor arrived in his large travelling coach, attended by several servants. Adam Bradshaw bore a great many loving messages from his wife to her sister and her brother-in-law, and, as always, gifts from himself for his host and the family: a little brooch with a rose-cut diamond and pearls set in silver for Bella; a pair of handsome duelling pistols for Francis; a gold and ebony handled umbrella for Lady Rimpole, to protect her from the Yorkshire climate; and a German flute for Sir John, who, unlike most gentlemen of his standing, had no taste or aptitude whatsoever for music.

The presenting of his gifts always gave Mr Bradshaw great pleasure, however the recipients might feel about the matter; and on this occasion he insisted upon Lady Rimpole's spending twenty minutes walking with him up and down the terrace – followed by Mahomet, grinning broadly and carrying his mistress's fan – while he demonstrated to her the umbrella's practical advantages against the sun, thereby proving its usefulness in all weathers.

Of them all, Bella was reckoned to be the only one to have come off really well, since her brooch was dainty and pretty and not unsuitable for a young girl; and Francis was not too disappointed in his pistols, which were certainly very fine ones – though he would rather have had something more practical, like a fowling-piece. However, on the whole the gifts were a great deal better and less useless than those which Adam Bradshaw usually chose; and even Sir John's flute was admitted to be nothing as bad as the Chinese monster, which its donor was delighted to find in the place of honour in the larger drawing-room, all by itself on a Persian rug between the two tall windows – a spot from which a beautiful little marble-topped table, a favourite piece of Lady Rimpole, had been removed to make room for it – and flanked by a pair of carved and gilded torchères upon each of which a three branched silver candlestick was set, so that its grin might be illuminated to the best advantage.

Adam Bradshaw, portly, loud voiced, and, nearly always smiling, was an immensely generous and kindly man – overwhelmingly so, sometimes. His father, a Bristol merchant and shipowner, had made a fortune in the slave trade, in which most profitable and lucrative business Adam Bradshaw was still engaged. Sir William Heston of Devonshire, extravagant and over-fond of gambling, had married off his youngest daughter Maria to a man very far beneath her in rank, for the sake of the enormous settlement which he had made; and Maria herself, who, for three weeks before the wedding had continuously wept and protested in vain against being sacrificed to pay her father's gambling debts and to repair the family fortune, had never, for one moment, since the day of her marriage, had cause to regret it. For, whatever the more intelligent Lady Rimpole and Lady Norton might say about his tediousness and his lack of amusing conversation, their sister had the kindest and most devoted of husbands.

On the day after their guest's arrival, the whole family dined together, at his express wish. He talked almost without pause throughout the whole of the meal, praising every dish as it left the table and complimenting his hostess a dozen times on her cook, as well as upon her becoming gown and the way her children had grown since he had last seen them, two years before; and, indeed, extolling everything he could possibly find to commend, and all with the utmost sincerity.

He spoke tediously and at great length about the difficulties of finding enough sailors for those of his ships making the long triangular run – from England to Africa, thence directly to the Colonies, and from the Colonies back to England – asking if Sir John knew of any likely young Yorkshiremen who would care to try their luck at sea. He did not think to mention that one of the reasons why it was not easy to obtain good seamen for the slaving run, was that a ship often had to sail, for six months or even longer, up and down the unhealthy, torrid West African coast, from one port to another, waiting for the traders to round up and deliver the cargo. A further reason was that the stinking, fever-ridden cargo itself – almost a quarter of which always failed to reach North America or the West Indies alive – was a dangerous source of infection to those sailors who manned the ships which carried it.

Sir John, in reply, said that he did not think he knew of any young Yorkshiremen with seagoing ambitions, and then managed, very adroitly, to steer the conversation – temporarily – towards a more interesting topic.

Francis, very bored, had been paying little attention for the last ten minutes; but Bella was fired by the thought of all those sailors needed in Bristol to help in the slave trade. Would that not be the very thing for Seumas? Truly the very thing, this time. An honest career at sea on board a slaving ship was the perfect solution to the problem. She tried, in her excitement, to catch Francis's eye, but he was not looking in her direction, so she had to wait patiently until dinner would be over and she could tell him her wonderful idea. Surely this time he would not be able to find fault with her suggestion? The only practical difficulty was how to get Seumas all the way to Bristol and on to one of those ships where he was so badly needed.

Before the meal was over, however, even that difficulty seemed to have been partly solved, for their uncle, beaming kindly at Francis, asked him, 'It is to be Eton at last, after Christmas, is it not?'

'Yes, sir, in the new year.'

'Not long now! Not long now! Well, we must see what we can do in the way of a little extra spending-money for the great occasion. I dare say a few extra guineas would not come amiss. Or if there is any other thing you think that you would like to have to take with you, you must not hesitate to let me know.'

'Thank you very much, sir.'

Lady Rimpole laughed. 'You must not spoil him!'

'Nonsense! One is only young once. Eh, nephew Francis?'

'Yes, sir.'

'Well, then! Remember: anything you want....'

'Thank you, sir.'

Adam Bradshaw now beamed at his sister-in-law. 'Maria is still waiting for the children's promised visit to Bristol, you know. She bade me most particularly to see that they come to us soon and stay a month or more. She insists that it shall be this summer, as Francis will have far less time for visits when he is at Eton and away from home for so many months of the year.' He paused briefly to give emphasis to his next words. 'That is what Maria says. And now this is what I would like to make so bold as to suggest: if you and my nephew and niece are agreeable, why should I not make my return journey start at Thorsby instead of York? In other words, when I have finished my business in York in around four days' time, what do you say to my coming back here to fetch Francis and Bella and taking them home with me?'

Sir John reflected that if his brother-in-law did indeed do this, it would save him, later in the year, from having to send the children to Bristol in his own travelling coach with a number of his own servants; and Lady Rimpole reflected that if Francis and Bella were in their uncle's charge, then Miss Proudfoot would not need to go to Bristol with Bella, but might have the rare indulgence of a much deserved holiday; and so they both agreed to the suggestion.

Adam Bradshaw was pleased. He beamed at Bella. 'And what have you to say to it, my dear?'

Bella beamed back at her uncle. 'I should like it above all things, sir.' It could not be working out better for them. They would somehow – somehow – contrive to take Seumas down to Bristol with them, and there in Bristol would be a new and honest life awaiting him.

'And you, young man?'

Francis, quickly calculating that in four days' time they should certainly have managed to get rid of Seumas, whose ankle was now almost healed, said, 'I should like it very much, thank you, sir.'

Adam Bradshaw beamed round the table at everyone in turn. 'Then that is settled. Capital! Capital!'

At the first opportunity after dinner, Bella told Francis of her proposal for Seumas's future career. After a few moments of looking dubiously for any possible impediments, Francis admitted that it seemed to be a good notion – always supposing that Seumas agreed to it.

'Of course he will agree to it!' said Bella, willing him to do so by a premature acceptance of his co-operation. 'Only think how interesting it will be for him to see all those foreign countries where the slaves come from, and America, and the plantations and everything.' She ended on a less confident and more pleading note. 'Oh, he must agree, Francis. He must. It would be so satisfactory if this whole sorry affair might end happily, and I fear that this may be our only opportunity of trying to bring it about.'

'I'll tell him of it tomorrow. But do not count on it too much, Bella, will you?'

'I'll go with you myself and help you to persuade him.'

Francis looked at her thoughtfully. 'That's not a bad notion. Indeed, you can tell him about it. He is far more likely to listen to you than to me.'

Adam Bradshaw drove off early on Monday morning, booming farewells and promises to be back within four days through the window of his coach; and soon after midday both Bella and Francis arrived at the Dower House. When Seumas, who had decided that morning that his ankle would be sound enough for him to set off the following day or the day after that, saw the two of them enter the Chinese room, he presumed that they had come together to tell him it was time that he was gone.

He came towards them from the window where he had been standing, looking out at the garden from the concealment of the curtains. He smiled. 'Is it to tell me to go that you've come? For I was reckoning, myself, on saying good-bye today or tomorrow.' He looked at Bella. 'I'm glad that you've come too, Miss Bella. It gives me a chance of saying thank you for all you did to save me the other day. Is it not the quick-witted one you are! I've never seen anything like it in all my days. I only wish there was some way I could be showing my gratitude, something which I could be doing for you in return. But, then, there's not, so you'll have to be believing it when I say that I'm grateful.'

Bella seized upon the advantage he had unwittingly offered her. 'There is something which you could do for me.'

'There is? You name it, Miss Bella, and I'll be doing it.'

'I am not sure that you would want to do this thing, even if I were to ask you.' Instinctively and quite unknowingly, she was handling the matter in the manner in which women have always handled the business of getting their own way – by enmeshing a man in his own declarations.

He flung out one hand in a wide, sweeping gesture. 'Sure and there's nothing I would not do for you, after all you have done for me.'

She hesitated. She could, in that moment, she knew, have easily tricked him into a blind promise which he would afterwards have been forced to keep – or to break. But she was still young enough for that to seem to her a hardly fair way of doing it. Instead, she said, 'We have been thinking, my brother and I, that perhaps all this trouble that came upon you after you robbed the Duke, might perhaps have convinced you that it is better to live an honest life – even if it means working a little harder.' She paused, considering how to go on.

After a moment he said, 'Is it wanting me to reform you are? Is that what you're trying to tell me?'

'Yes.'

'Och, it's no use, Miss Bella. How could I be honest? It's born bad I was, and that's the truth of it.'

'Nonsense,' said Bella sternly, in a quite unconscious imitation of Miss Proudfoot. 'No one is ever so bad that he cannot try to be better.' After a few seconds she went on, more like herself. 'You said that you would do anything I asked of you.'

'Sure and I did. And I would, too. I'd even try to be honest for your sake, if it would please you. But it would be no use at all. I know no trade and I have no money. It's back at stealing in a week I'd be.'

'But we have found honest work for you. In about six days' time we go to Bristol on a visit to our aunt Bradshaw. I am sure we can contrive to take you with us. Our uncle Bradshaw is a merchant engaged in the slave trade. He is in need of sailors, and he does not care if they have never been to sea before. In Bristol there will be honest work for you on one of our uncle's ships. Will you come with us?'

Seumas was taken aback. To go to sea! It was the last thing he wanted. Or rather, almost the last thing. For, of course, the very last thing of all that he wanted, was to go to the gallows.

His hesitation unnerved Bella. She had to speak again; and now she could no longer keep the eagerness from her voice. 'Will you? You would find it interesting, I am sure. You would see any number of foreign lands.'

'From the deck of a slaver?'

'Yes, indeed. Our uncle is very prosperous, he has several ships. You could always be sure of work on one or another of them, I am certain.'

Seumas, who had rejected respectability ten years before, and had since lived by theft and trickery, yet had a moment of compunction at the thought of trafficking in human beings. Perhaps it was because he had, on occasions during the earlier part of those ten years, been himself cold and afraid and hungry, had lived in a stinking, overcrowded room, rat-infested, and filthy. Perhaps it was because he had known men and women who had broken the law and been transported – under conditions, he imagined, very similar to those under which the slaves from Africa were shipped. Whatever the reason, he had his moment of compunction, where Bella and Francis and kindly Adam Bradshaw had none. It was very brief and it had no more than a few seconds' duration before he brushed it aside: after all, they were only heathen blacks and hardly counted as people. And if this opportunity could be turned to his convenience....

It would be a way of passing the time – a safe way – for the next few months, until things had blown over in London. And if they could indeed contrive to get him away from Yorkshire and safely to Bristol – and he saw no reason why they should not, they were excellent contrivers, as he had learnt – then it might be worth the hardship and the discomfort of being a sailor for a while. Besides, he reflected, he owed it to them to let them believe they had achieved their object. He owed them so much for what they had given – and for what he had taken from them. And what other way could he be paying them back? It need be no more than the one trip: they would never know.

He looked at Bella, now openly eager, no longer even attempting to conceal how much his answer meant to her; and then at Francis, standing in the background, letting Bella win him over for them. Francis's own eagerness was carefully hidden behind a mask of cold and faintly contemptuous indifference. Secretly, in his mind, Seumas smiled to himself. The boy was expecting him to refuse, he knew it.

Perhaps it was that – the desire to astonish Francis – as much as his wish not to disappoint Bella, which, combined with the knowledge that he owed it to them, finally decided the matter for him.

'I'll do it,' he said, and had the satisfaction of seeing a flash of surprise on Francis's face.

Bella was frankly delighted. She smiled at him almost as she had been used to smile at him in the earlier days, when he was still Mr Macdonald, the Jacobite Highlander. 'I'm so glad. I'm sure you will make a very good sailor.'

25

THEY laid their plans very carefully and went over them again and again to make sure that nothing had been forgotten; and by the time that Adam Bradshaw, his business in York concluded, had returned to Thorsby, they believed their plans were as foolproof as possible. It appeared as though it would be easier – much easier – than they had dared to hope. Everything seemed to be working to their advantage. At first they had feared that Miss Proudfoot would be coming with them to Bristol, but she was going instead, as the guest of Lady Rimpole, to take the waters at Harrogate and enjoy the society in that increasingly popular spa for a month; and it was to be Old Nurse who would accompany Bella instead, and Old Nurse always dozed in a carriage, she said the jolting motion and the clip-clop of the horses' hooves lulled her to sleep – though Bella could not think why, since the jolting seemed to her enough to keep anyone wide awake. With Old Nurse asleep, there would be none of the servants from the Hall present to betray the fact that, far from having been a temporary under-gardener there – which is how they were going to explain Seumas to their uncle – they had never seen him before; and if, at the critical moment when Seumas joined their party, Old Nurse should not yet have fallen asleep, Bella had undertaken to keep her in conversation while Francis presented Seumas to their uncle, whose own servants offered no difficulty: Seumas would be a stranger to them even if the story about his having been a gardener at the Hall were true.

Seumas himself had assured them that, on the day of the start of their journey, he would leave the Dower House looking as though no one had been living in it for the past six weeks, and get himself safely over the gates before dawn – it was necessary for him to do this, because of the gamekeeper's habit of always locking the park gates for the night. Francis had been a little worried about the climb, but Seumas had promised not to fall again. 'I'll be in no hurry. I'll have all the night to be doing it in, if I wish,' he had said; adding with a grin, 'And this time there'll be no pride coming before a fall. I'll be alone and no one with me to be raising my bit of temper. It will all be bowman this time, you'll see.' So Francis had to be content with this.

The problem of how they were to be sure that their uncle's party would be able to accommodate an extra man, had been soon solved by Francis's idea of asking permission to take Raven with him. What more natural than that he would not wish to be parted from his new horse for a month, so soon after acquiring him? Nothing was thought of it when he said that he would like to take Raven, so that he might ride beside the coach whenever he wanted to.

Everything, indeed, seemed hopeful and more than hopeful. The one thing which they could see no way of contriving, was the bolting of the back door of the Dower House. This could not be done unless Francis went over there with the front door key during the night before the journey, bolted the back door and let Seumas out through the front door, locking it after them and then returning the key to the office. It was felt that this would be an unnecessary risk to run, as well as giving Francis even more responsibility than he already had; so they decided to take a chance on leaving the door unbolted. It might possibly be discovered when the monster was returned to its exile a day or two later; if not, it would certainly be noticed the next time Mrs Keighley and her cleaning-girls went to the Dower House. But, with luck, having entered through the front door, it would be a little while before one of the maids went out through the back door, and, on finding it open, she might well think that one of the others had unbolted it already.

Francis had given Seumas careful instructions as to how to reach, by cutting across the fields and avoiding the village, the place where he was to wait for them; and he had impressed upon him the need for being there by dawn and for keeping out of sight of any passers-by until the coach arrived. The spot had been chosen with this point in mind, as it provided a sheltering group of trees for a hiding place.

The Sunday night before the great day came, everything seemed ready to succeed. A little luck, the unwitting co-operation of uncle Bradshaw, and all would be well.

Seumas was the first to have to make a move. Long before Monday's dawn, while it was still dark, he was up and out of the Dower House by the back door, leaving behind him everything looking, he believed, as though long untenanted. He and Francis had worked hard at it the afternoon before, and he felt reasonably certain that he had left no signs which would betray them.

He was long over the gates and already walking across the fields to the meeting place by the earliest pre-dawn light; and the sky was all gold and green in the east when he reached the road and the stile and the clump of trees which Francis had so carefully described to him. He sat down on the stile and ate the breakfast he had brought with him. He had a long wait until the coach came in sight, and more than once during that time he told himself he was being a fool. He could be hiding himself in some strange town for three or four months, quite as well as he could be hiding himself at sea. So why be putting himself to the misery of being a sailor for that period – or maybe for longer, if the voyage were slow? But each time he came back to the same conclusion: he owed it to Francis and Bella. So he waited.

The coach, after many farewells, set out along the drive from the Hall and turned into the road with Adam Bradshaw settled comfortably in one corner, Old Nurse in another, a small basket holding her fan, her smelling-bottle, and a flask of reviving cordial, clasped between her hands on her lap, and Bella, tense and nervous beside Old Nurse and opposite her uncle; with Francis on Raven riding alongside the coach, in advance of the two servants who came after it.

By the time they passed the spot where the lane branched off to the right of the road, to run past the Dower House and Tuttle's cottage and the west gate of the park, Old Nurse was nodding. Two minutes later, and she was already dozing. Bella relaxed a little.

A mile or two on Francis brought Raven close to the coach

door and tapped on the window glass with his whip. With a smile at her uncle and a quick glance at Old Nurse, now seemingly fast asleep, Bella tried to let down the window. Her hands shook a little and her movements were clumsy. Her uncle promptly came to her aid.

Francis bent his head to the open window. 'I have just seen one of your favourite sights, Bella. Two wild swans.' This meant that Seumas was in view by the stile.

'Oh, Francis! I do hope they are going to our lake.' This meant that Old Nurse was asleep and Bella could be the one to make their uncle stop the coach. Had Old Nurse been awake, Bella was to have said, 'Which way were they flying?'

Pretending to wish to look for herself, Bella stood up in the swaying coach. Steadying herself by clinging to the window-frame, she craned her head out of the window to watch the non-existent swans. She could not see far enough along the road to where Seumas was waiting for them, but when Francis raised his whip to the level of his shoulder and then lowered it – the signal for her to speak – she said, 'Oh, sir, there is O' – O'Connor by the stile. He worked for us in the spring when one of the gardeners was sick. I talked to him once or twice. He is a most interesting and superior man. He told me his father had been a sailor and that he had a mind to go to sea himself. Do you think there might be work for him on one of your ships? Do stop the coach and speak to him. Oh, please, uncle, do!'

'Wants to go to sea, does he? Does he, indeed? Well, I'll speak to him if it pleases you, my dear.' He beamed at her, genuinely happy at being able to do for someone else something that was asked of him, and called to the coachman to stop the horses.

Meanwhile, Francis had reined in beside the stile. 'Good morning, O'Connor.'

'Good morning to you, sir.'

They were both speaking loudly in the hope of being overheard by the others when the coach stopped, as it did at that moment, some ten yards on.

'What are you doing out here this morning?'

'Och, just admiring the view, Master Francis. I finished my

work with Farmer Tranter yesterday, so today I'm idle, as you see.'

Bella moved from the coach window, so that her uncle could look out. She eyed Old Nurse apprehensively, but the stopping of the coach had not awakened her.

Francis walked Raven over to the coach, beckoning to Seumasr to follow him. Seumas swept off his hat and bowed in the direction of the coach. He was looking remarkably respectable in an old green coat and breeches of Sir John's, which Francis had rashly obtained for him from his father's clothes press the day before, reckoning that the repeated scenes which Fowler would inevitably make when he discovered they were missing, would surely have spent themselves by the time he and Bella were home again, a month later. Seumas's hair was neatly powdered with flour and tied back with one of Francis's black ribbons, and a clean white cravat – also belonging to Francis – was around his neck.

Bella turned away from Old Nurse and put her head out of the window to look at Seumas.

'Good day, Miss Bella. I hope I see you well, ma'am?'

Bella gave him a bright, nervous little smile. 'Good morning, O'Connor.'

'And a very good day to you, sir.'

'Good morning – O'Connor is it? You are Irish, are you, my man?'

'I am. James O'Connor, at your service, sir.' He bowed again.

He was acting it very well, Francis and Bella thought, glad that he was managing to sound and appear such a convincing labouring man; yet, at the same time, uneasily remembering, in spite of their fervent wish to forget it, the last part he had played equally well.

'Miss Bella tells me that your father was a sailor, and that you would like to go to sea, too.'

'I would indeed, sir. It would be just the life to suit me. Himself was always after telling me such tales of foreign parts that it's forever dreaming I was of being able to see those places for myself one day. But after the good Lord had taken him I was never able to leave my poor widowed mother, you'll understand, sir. Bless her soul, she died last month, so now it's free to travel the world I am, if I like.' The widowed mother was an improvisation which Francis and Bella had not heard before – a typical Seumas-touch – but it sounded all right.

'I am sorry to hear that. I am sure that you must miss her greatly. Are you working at present?'

'Not since yesterday, sir. Until yesterday I was helping Farmer Tranter with the sheepshearing, but it came to an end, so today I'm free. It's walking to Northallerton I'll be soon, and seeing what work they have there for a willing man.'

'Hm.' Adam Bradshaw looked Seumas up and down and made his decision: the pleading and the persuasion which Bella had prepared for that moment were not needed. 'I come from Bristol. I have ships going to and from Africa and the Colonies. If you truly wish to go to sea, I think that I could help you to achieve your praiseworthy ambition.'

Seumas looked suitably astonished and pleased and grateful. 'Now, if that isn't a gift from the good Lord Himself! Here was I sitting on the stile and wondering about my future, and you coming along the road in your carriage like an angel from heaven. Sure and I'd like to go to sea. Can I be following you to Bristol then, sir, and asking for a place on one of your ships?'

'It's a long way to walk, my man. I wonder if we could take you with us.' Adam Bradshaw frowned a little, trying to calculate the number of riding horses and the amount of room required for the coachman and the baggage.

This was Francis's cue. 'He could ride Raven, sir, and I could come in with you and Bella. I should not mind.'

'A capital notion!' Adam Bradshaw looked at Seumas. 'Well, you heard Master Francis's suggestion. What do you say to it?'

'Sure and is it not the kindest thing! Thank you, Master Francis, sir.'

'Have you anything you want to fetch from your home, or any affairs to be settled?'

'Och, no, sir. Not a single thing. All I have is what I stand up in and what's in my pockets at this very minute. It's on my way to Northallerton I was, as I was after telling your honour.'

'You are leaving no debts behind you?' asked Mr Bradshaw shrewdly.

'Only the ones which I could never be paying, sir,' Seumas replied promptly. 'The ones where people have done me kindnesses and I've never been in a position to be repaying them, the more's the pity.'

'That sort of debt, O'Connor, we nearly always have to leave behind us, unfortunately.'

'That's the truth of it, sir.'

Francis, with what amounted to considerable self-sacrifice, gave Raven up to Seumas with a few rather fussy instructions. 'You will need to length the stirrups a little. He is a trifle fresh as it is so early in the day. Do you think you can manage him?' and so on.

Eventually the coach started, and once again they were on their way to Bristol, their plan safely accomplished. Bella leant back against the green upholstery and glanced at Francis, opposite. They smiled at one another, but more in heartfelt relief than in triumph.

Old Nurse suddenly opened her eyes. 'Did we stop?'

'Only for a moment, Old Nurse. Nothing is the matter. You can go to sleep again,' Francis made haste to reassure her.

'I heard a strange voice. Who –'

Bella quickly leant sideways towards her. 'Take care, you are dropping your basket.' It had indeed slipped a little way down her lap while she slept, but it was nothing to cause concern, and she still had the handle firmly clasped in her hands. 'You must not lose it, Old Nurse.' Bella smiled at her and urged soothingly, 'Go to sleep again, and you will wake up and find yourself in Bristol.'

'That I shall not! I know how far it is to the West Country, even if you do not – for all the lessons you have with Miss Proudfoot. And don't you think I'll not be glad to get there, away from this barbarous place – because I shall!' She closed her eyes again; and though both Francis and Bella glanced apprehensively in her direction when their uncle spoke to them a minute or two later, she must have fallen asleep again immediately, for she gave no sign of hearing him and she never stirred.

'He seems a well-spoken, upstanding sort of young man, this O'Connor.'

'Oh, yes, sir, he is!' declared Bella over emphatically.

But uncle Bradshaw was not given time to wonder at her fervent tone, for Francis hastily broke in, 'Rigby – our head gardener, he is, you know, sir – thought highly of him, I understand.' Unlike Bella's, his tone of voice was a blend of just the right amounts of casual interest, indifference, and courteous agreement; and their uncle, well pleased, nodded, beamed at them both, and took a pinch of snuff.

26

AFTER an acceptably uneventual and – in spite of the bad condition of the roads here and there – not too uncomfortable journey, taken at no great speed, during which their uncle had pointed out to them any places or sights of particular interest which they had passed, Francis and Bella, arriving at Bristol, temporarily lost sight of Seumas, who was handed over to Adam Bradshaw's chief clerk, who managed his office and warehouses for him, and was well-known to the masters of all his ships.

In the Bradshaw's fine new house in fashionable Queen's Square, they were given a warm and delighted welcome by their aunt and received with flattering respect and admiration by their three cousins, the eldest of whom was only seven and very impressed by Francis, who seemed to little William Bradshaw to be quite grown-up.

Though they could certainly not forget him – he was still too much their responsibility for that – they were able to think much less often about Seumas in the days that followed, days that were busy for them with a variety of interests. Bristol proved full of delights and wonders. They were taken to view, in turn, the cathedral and the church of St Mary Redcliffe, the handsome, recently opened Corn Exchange and the new Library in King Street. They went to look at one of the coalfields which were so valuable to the industries of Bristol – to the brass and iron works, the sugar refineries and the glasshouses from where bottles were exported all over the world – and they stood wondering at its winding gear and strange machinery and the little, scattered cottages where the rough, wild-mannered miners lived. They inspected, at close quarters, one of the smoking cones of the glass works, and saw a ship being repaired in dry dock, and they visited the little playhouse outside the city, which provided entertainment both for those who lived in Bristol and the visitors to the springs at Hotwells. Conducted by the master himself, who patiently answered all their questions, they explored every inch of one of their uncle's ships, then in port.

But best of all they loved to linger by the river, crowded with craft of every kind, and the long quay where the vessels unloaded. They would have been happy to spend whole days there, watching every sort of commodity from distant lands – in bales and casks and sacks and chests – heaved off the ships and piled on to the waiting sleds, to be dragged away by strings of two or three horses.

About a fortnight after their arrival in Bristol, having returned to Queen's Square after a morning spent driving out with Maria Bradshaw through a mile or so of green fields to the spa at Hotwells, with its Pump Room, where the season was now at its height, Francis and Bella were alone together in their uncle's library, whiling away the half-hour or so that remained until dinner-time. Francis was systematically working his way along the bookshelves, looking for something to read, and Bella was sitting at the table, pen and ink beside her, and, before her, an almost blank sheet of paper upon which she was endeavouring to reply to the long letter they had received three days before from Miss Proudfoot, in which she had described, in great detail – on a single page, closely and minutely written, so that it would not be charged as a double letter by the Post Office – all the delights and interests of Harrogate, which, they had decided unanimously, could not hold a candle to Bristol, and exhorting them to behave themselves fittingly and do her credit while among strangers, promising them another letter before they returned home and bidding them be sure and answer this one.

Francis had ungallantly left it to Bella to do the answering, saying, 'If Haughtyhoof is going to write again, that will make two letters which we shall have to answer. You can answer the first, and I'll answer the second.'

When Bella had protested that, as the elder, and the better letter-writer of the two, he should be the one to write first, he had pointed out to her his generosity in giving her the chance of being the one to tell Miss Proudfoot all about Bristol and what they were doing there. 'When I come to write the second letter,' he had said, 'there will be nothing new left to tell her, and you know how difficult it is to write a letter all about nothing. You should consider yourself very fortunate.'

Privately, Bella doubted if a second letter would ever be written by them – though another was bound to come for them from Miss Proudfoot if she had promised it – but she did not say so to Francis, since he would be sure, she knew, to deny it indignantly. So it was that this particular day found her sitting at the library table with a martyred expression, staring at a piece of paper on which she had so far merely inscribed their uncle's address and a salutation, when one of the maid-servants put her head around the door and said, 'If you please, miss, there's a young man downstairs who says his name is O'Connor and that he used to be in service at your home and he wants to know if you and Master Francis can spare him a moment as his ship sails tomorrow.' She looked dubiously from Bella to Francis and then back again.

When Bella hesitated, Francis began, 'I don't think that it's necessary –'

But Bella interrupted him. 'No, Francis, we must. It is our duty to wish him well in his new life.' To the maid she said, 'Show him up here, if you please.'

'Very good, miss.'

The maid once gone, Francis said bitterly, 'I might have known we had not seen the last of him.'

'Why should we have seen the last of him, so long as he, too, was still in Bristol and not yet gone to sea?' asked Bella reasonably.

'If he is hoping for money or a parting gift, he will be disappointed.'

Bella's attitude was more charitable than her brother's. 'Oh, I expect that he has really only come to tell us that he sails tomorrow.'

Seumas, ushered up the backstairs, shown into the library and left there by the maid, looked very neat and spruce in his new seaman's petticoat breeches and a new cocked hat which he seemed to have managed to acquire since they had seen him last.

At his entrance, neither Bella nor Francis moved, save that Francis merely turned his back on the bookshelves to face Seumas instead, while Bella sat motionless at the table, still holding the pen. For a few moments after the maid had gone, they all looked at each other in silence, Francis hostile, Bella uncertain, and Seumas trying to gauge their temper.

In the end it was Seumas who spoke first. He smiled, eyebrows raised a little quizzically. 'Seeing that the ship I'm on sails with the tide tomorrow and we're never likely to meet again, I thought you'd not be minding if I came to say good-bye and to thank the pair of you.'

Francis, remembering too much, said nothing to this; and after a moment, Bella replied for them both, 'I am glad that we have been able to help you, and I am sure you will not regret your decision to lead an honest life.' It was a little speech worthy of Francis; but Bella, who sincerely was glad and did feel sure, had not meant it to sound stiff and unfeeling.

'Och,' said Seumas easily, 'you've no cause for worrying. I doubt if there's much mischief I could be getting up to at sea.'

'That's just as well,' remarked Francis drily; and Seumas, who had been looking at Bella, gave him a quick glance of amusement. Then, seeing Francis move purposefully towards the bell, he said, 'You've no need to bring anyone all the way up again so soon. I can be finding my own way out.' He added, 'And not be putting any of your uncle's property into my pockets as I go, neither.' He smiled at them both, half amused and half almost wistful. 'There's no more to be said and you'll obviously be glad to see the last of me, the pair of you, so I'll just be saying good-bye and thank you once again – and it's with all my heart that I'm saying it.' He made Francis a bow. 'Good-bye to you, and thank you for doing what you did for me, and all without a jot of fellow-feeling. I hope you'll be after forgetting me soon, for your own peace of mind.' He turned to Bella, and the very slight air of mockery that had been in his attitude towards Francis faded and his voice sank. 'As for you, Miss Bella, I hope you'll be remembering me sometimes, and with kindness, and I far away in the middle of the oceans of the world. For I'll never be forgetting you, Miss Bella.

No matter how cold life may become, it's like a warm fire to my heart the thought of you will always be.'

That it was flowery and spoken in his lovely, persuasive brogue, did not mean that it was insincere. Being Seumas, it was natural to him to express deep sincerity as well as shallow sentiment in such a manner. Yet to Bella it was a false-sounding, pretty speech. Had he said something simpler, she would have responded instantly and with all her heart; but he had deceived her with grand phrases too often, and now here was the grandest of all she had yet heard from him. She met his eyes steadily and calmly; and if there was no warmth in the look she gave him, then there was no reproach, either – which in itself was a hurt to him. Then she glanced down at her hardly started letter.

'Good-bye . . . O'Leary.'

He waited only a moment after she had spoken, then he shrugged his shoulders very slightly and smiled, half in amusement and half in a kind of pain. He bowed once more, 'Miss Rimpole, Mr Rimpole, your servant, ma'am, sir.' Then the door had opened and closed again behind him.

Francis broke the long silence which followed. 'Thank heaven that's the end of it. It seems to have been going on for years, not weeks. If only none of it had happened to us!'

Bella did not hear his heartfelt cry – the very last he was to allow himself to give concerning the matter. She was staring at the closed door. Seumas was gone. She would never see him again; never again hear that warm, rich voice, or watch that gay smile come and go so rapidly. He was gone. Tomorrow he would sail from England, maybe never to return – perhaps he would be killed in an accident in some land far away, perhaps he would be lost at sea, perhaps he would sicken of some strange, unknown disease, and die – and she had never taken his hand in friendship, never wished him good fortune. She suddenly jumped up, throwing down her pen and almost spilling the ink as she stumbled against the table, and ran to the door, flung it open and made for the stairs, her skirts held high.

'Seumas! Seumas!'

But she had left it too late. Long before she had set her foot on the first step, he was out of the house. And by the time she had reached the ground floor, he had turned out of the square and was striding towards the quay.

Very slowly she climbed the stairs and returned to the library. 'He was gone,' she said in an empty little voice. 'I was too late.'

'So I should hope! Really, Bella, what a way to behave, taking on like that and making such a commotion!' His outburst against her seemed to relieve his mood. He pulled a book from its place. 'This one will answer, I think. I can but try it, anyway.' He brought it to the table and sat down.

Bella went slowly to the window. It was too late. She knew she would not see him there, walking away out of their lives; but she went to the window just the same.

Francis opened the book with a show of interest. But Seumas still lodged in his mind, also. With a self-enheartening cheerfulness he said, 'Do you know, Bella, it could have been disastrous and was not.' He opened the book and looked at the title-page. 'It was a kind of nightmare, but it's over and done with now, and we can forget it.' He turned to the first page of text. 'It might have been so much worse, might it not? We might have been found out. Do you know, Bella, we were very lucky.' Oblivious of the fact that Bella did not even hear him, and was certainly not watching him, he made a point of settling himself comfortably in his chair – to show that his mind was equally comfortable – and began to read, seeing only one word in every five.

Bella stood at the window with her back to him. She was staring down into the square, but making no effort to look at what was going on out there. Yet had she been trying to look, she would have been able to see nothing, because of her tears.

27

THE days went by to the end of the year. The months had brought Francis and Bella other things to think about than Seumas. Their stay in Bristol had stretched almost to the end of August; and they had, after all, written twice to Miss Proudfoot, and had received no less than three letters from her. After their return home there had been the good news of the Prince's escape to France in the later days of September, which had brought joy and relief to them both. And then there had been the excitement, for Francis, of making ready to leave for Eton; and early in the New Year, the final setting off and the complete change in his way of life brought by this belated but much longed-for happening.

But, before that, near the end of October, there had been the return to Hazlett Hall of Mr Marivel, safe and sound. He had, it seemed, in good time thought better of his loyalty to the house of Stuart; and though remaining with the Prince's victorious army – so long as it was victorious – had somehow successfully contrived to avoid being engaged in any actual fighting, while waiting unobtrusively to see which way the wind would blow. As soon as reverses began to beset the Stuart cause, well before the battle of Culloden, he had slipped quietly away and ridden for England to throw himself upon the mercy of King George. King George had been pleased to be merciful, and so Mr Marivel was home again – though cut dead, it is true, by all his former acquaintance in the district. However, this situation was not to last for many months, and they were soon to overlook the mistaken politics – or the fairweather loyalty, according to their personal leanings – of a rich and hospitable young man and to forgive him. But meanwhile, he was home, having adroitly kept, not only his head on his shoulders, but possession of his fortune and his estate.

His return under such circumstances had shaken Francis and

shocked him deeply; but it had at least served to make Seumas's offence less flagrant by comparison. Standards of conduct no one would dream of expecting from a common Irish thief, one took for granted in an English gentleman. His admiration for William Marivel having been known by those close to him, Francis had come in for a number of self-satisfied and rather cruel witticisms from his father, and a good deal of teasing, lightly administered, but none the less sharply barbed for that, from his mother; as well as a sententious comment apiece from Miss Proudfoot and Dr Mortlake. Bella alone had said nothing. Realizing what he must be feeling, she had not known the right words to say and had been able only to offer mute sympathy – which had done him little good, as it had meant that he had had to be grateful to her for her tactful silence, instead of being able to relieve his feelings by snapping at her for some ill-chosen remark.

But the preparations for his departure from home, and then the departure itself, had served to restore him; and by the end of his first half at Eton, Mr Marivel had been replaced in his estimation by one of the Upper School prepostors, a dashing and rather elegant youth who had been gracious enough to notice and praise Francis's skill at fives.

As far as Seumas was concerned, by then Francis was able to persuade himself that he was well on the way to forgetting the whole disgraceful and embarrassing episode. And when Bella remembered it, it tended to seem more remote, less painful, sharp, wounding edges mossed over with the kindly accretions of time. And, such is the resilience of youth, the careful efforts which they had at first made to forget, were now no longer necessary: they forgot, for long periods, with no conscious effort at all.

In early June of the following year, little over twelve months from the day of their first meetings with Seumas in the park, a few days after Francis, his first half at Eton completed, had arrived home for the Whitsuntide holidays, a small package addressed to Bella was brought to the Hall one morning by a pedlar who had had it from the landlord of an inn at York, who had himself had it from a passenger travelling on the stage from London. The innkeeper had kept it by him for a week or two, waiting until someone whom he knew should be going in the direction of Thorsby; and when Lister, the pedlar, who was well known to him, had turned up one day on his way farther north, he had given it to him.

On his arrival at the Hall, several days later, Mrs Keighley had paid Lister for his pains, and then, while Keighley regaled him with a glass of beer and the local news, and the other servants gathered round, ready to spend their pence on his wares, Mrs Keighley went to find Bella, to give her the package.

Bella was surprised. She could not think of anyone who would be likely to send her a package, and by such a strange, roundabout way, which seemed to imply that it had come from a considerable distance. Smiling with kindly understanding of the thrill an unexpected gift can bring. Mrs Keighley left Bella alone to open her package.

Within the wrapping was a small wooden box, inside the box, iridescent and lustrous and carefully protected by a soft piece of cloth, was a necklace of shells – small, delicately-pointed, pinkish whorls, striped finely with deep gold. She took it from its box, and as it uncoiled, the light trickled along its length, like water.

Below the necklace, folded small, was a letter, a single sheet of paper, neatly written. It was headed simply, 'Bristol' and dated May 2, 1747:

My dear Miss Bella,
The Pride of Severn having lately docked at Bristol, I am back from my first and most interesting long Voyage to Foreign Parts, and I take the Liberty of sending to you this little Necklace from the Colonies. I hope that it may partly fill the place of the Gold Chain which I understand you once sold to Raise Funds for me. You need not hesitate to accept it, for it was purchased from my wages, honestly earned as a Seaman. I hope it may give you a little Pleasure. I trust you and y[r] Brother are in Good Health, as I am.

In Gratitude I inscribe myself
Y[r] most humble servant,
Seumas O'Leary

Bella's eyes were shining by the time she had finished reading the letter. Clasping to her both letter and necklace, she jumped up and ran from the schoolroom in search of Francis. She eventually found him in the gunroom, cleaning a new fowling-piece.

He looked without approval at her flushed cheeks and at the lock of hair escaping untidily from under her cap. 'Oh, Bella! Must you always be running about the place like a hoyden? And can you not leave a fellow in peace for even an hour?'

Parenthetically, she spent a few seconds in denying this injustice. 'It is past midday, and this is the first time I have spoken to you since breakfast-time.' Then she thrust the letter and the necklace at him. 'Look.'

He examined the necklace cursorily. 'Has someone given you this? It is rather pretty, I must own. And very unusual, too. They are some kind of foreign shell, I presume.' He handed it back to her and read the letter, while she watched him impatiently.

As soon as he had finished, she said, 'You see, everything did indeed come right in the end! He is an honest sailor today and all through our doing. Oh! Now I am glad that it all happened! Are not you Francis?'

'I'd not go so far as to say that. But it's not such a bad thing to know that one has been a good influence on someone and helped him to change his way of life and found him an honest trade.' He handed her back the letter. 'Now for heaven's sake go away and stop plaguing me.' His tone of indifference could not hide, even from her, the slightly complacent satisfaction which he felt at this gratifying conclusion to the affair. He turned back to his fowling-piece.

Holding her letter and her necklace, in her mind a picture of a respectable, suntanned and weatherbeaten Seumas embarking and disembarking on a series of slaving voyages from then until old age brought to him an honoured, prosperous and happy retirement in some pleasant little seaside cottage, bought with his honest earnings, saved assiduously throughout the years, she returned to the schoolroom, her mind at last completely at rest regarding Seumas O'Leary and fully believing in her picture of him. For his letter had not mentioned that his first voyage had been also his last, and that the letter itself had been written in Bristol the day before he left there for London. Nor could she know that already, days before it came into her hands, its writer, his debt to the Rimpoles paid, was back among his old friends and associates – Jack Thorne, who kept the diddle-shop where they forgathered, Big Will the Flash-cove, Bridle-lay Charley, Ben the Buzz-napper, and dimber little Sukey – all of them full of merry and profitable projects for the future.

HISTORICAL NOTE

The Duke of Shale is an entirely imaginary character. In 1746, the Lord Lieutenant, in charge of the North York Militia, was, in actual fact, Robert, fourth Earl of Holderness, to whose memory I offer my apologies for depriving him of his office and responsibilities during the spring and summer of that year, for the purposes of this story.

Seumas is the Gaelic form of *James,* found in Ireland and the Scottish Highlands. It is often anglicized as *Shamus,* which – however it may be spelt – is the way it is always pronounced.

In case any reader should, like Bella, misunderstand Seumas's remark on p. 82 it may perhaps be mentioned here that the original cant meaning of *rum* was 'good', not, as in present day slang, 'peculiar' or 'odd'. *Bowman* means 'good' or 'favourable', and a *bowman boy* is a smart, well-dressed thief; a *cheat* is a 'thing' of any kind: for instance, a *lullaby-cheat* is a baby, a *quacking-cheat* is a duck, *crushing-cheats* are teeth; the *nubbing-cheat* is the gallows, from *nub,* 'neck' and *to nub,* 'to hang'. The meaning of any other cant expressions used by Seumas is probably clear from the context, or else the word is still in current use as slang. It may surprise a few readers to know that a great many familiar words and expressions which we tend to think of as modern slang or, perhaps, nineteenth-century schoolboy terms, were originally late seventeenth-century or eighteenth-century thieves' cant. Besides those used in this book, there are many others, familiar to everyone: to *pinch for* 'to steal'; *grub* and *prog* for 'food'; *chum; kid* used for 'child'; *tanner* and *bob; bloke; togs* for 'clothes'; are just a very few of them.

In the eighteenth century a girl, even as young as Bella, would usually have been addressed by acquaintances, even of her own social standing, and by all close friends, as Miss –'; so that Seumas is only being formally polite, according to the usage of the time, and is not displaying any servility, when he says, 'Miss Bella.'

Until about 1755, the Eton halves were quite literally halves, with the two holidays at Christmas and Whitsun.

ACKNOWLEDGEMENTS

While writing the dialogue for the Yorkshire characters in this story, I used, and found helpful in my search for ancient and obsolete dialect words, C. Clough Robinson's *Glossary of Words Pertaining to the Dialect of Mid Yorkshire* (1876) and the *Whitby Glossary* (1855).

And I am indeed grateful to Mr U. R. Mitchell, himself a Yorkshireman, for all his kind advice, and for so patiently and fully answering each one of my queries and reading the MS pages. Without his help I should not have been able to use the words I gleaned from the *Glossaries* to any advantage, and I offer him my most sincere thanks.

B. L. P.

If you have enjoyed this book and would like to know about others which we publish, why not join the Puffin Club? You will receive the club magazine, *Puffin Post*, four times a year and a smart badge and membership book. You will also be able to enter all the competitions. Write for an application form to:

The Puffin Club Secretary
Penguin Books Limited
Bath Road
Harmondsworth
Middlesex